The Vanishing Garden

A CONSERVATION GUIDE
TO GARDEN PLANTS

The Vanishing Garden

A CONSERVATION GUIDE TO GARDEN PLANTS

Christopher Brickell
and Fay Sharman

JOHN MURRAY
IN ASSOCIATION WITH
The Royal Horticultural Society

© Text, Christopher Brickell and Fay Sharman, 1986
© Line illustrations, Christine Grey-Wilson, 1986

First published 1986
by John Murray (Publishers) Ltd
50 Albemarle Street, London W1X 4BD

Typeset by Keyspools Ltd, Golborne, Lancs
Printed in Great Britain
by Jolly & Barber Ltd, Rugby

British Library CIP data
Brickell, Christopher
   The vanishing garden: a conservation guide to
   garden plants.
   1. Plant conservation   2. Garden ecology
   I. Title   II. Sharman, Fay   III. Royal
   Horticultural Society
   635   SB454.3.P5
   ISBN 0-7195-4266-9

Contents

List of Plants

Acknowledgements

Many people have assisted us, in one way or another, during the preparation of this book. We would like to thank the following in particular: Brent Elliott, librarian of the Royal Horticultural Society's Lindley Library, and his assistant Barbara Collecott, for their constant help and guidance as well as their interest; Desmond Clarke and Graham Stuart Thomas, who read the manuscript and offered such constructive criticism and advice; Christine Grey-Wilson, freelance illustrator at the Royal Botanic Gardens, Kew, for her delightful line drawings; and Elspeth Napier, editor of the RHS journal, whose support has been invaluable.

We are also grateful to the director of the RBG, Kew, and his staff; Duncan Donald, curator of the Chelsea Physic Garden, and Kate Donald; Tony Lowe, general secretary of the National Council for the Conservation of Plants and Gardens, and his assistants; Christopher Grey-Wilson, principal scientific officer at the RBG, Kew; James Compton, of the Chelsea Physic Garden; Judith Jepson, librarian at the RHS garden, Wisley; and Vicki Beatson, who edited the book with great care. We wish to express our gratitude to Barry Ambrose, director of RHS Enterprises, for his advice; Klaus Boehm, for his contribution to the project at an early stage; and Daphne Noble, Chris Brickell's secretary, for her patient and practical assistance.

We are indebted to Dick Robinson, who has generously made available the resources of the Harry Smith Photographic Collection, and to his staff. Many of the other photographs have been specially taken for the book by John Garey, and we are extremely grateful to him. Our thanks are also due to Tony Schilling, Roy Elliott, Gillian Beckett, Valerie Finnis, Duncan Donald, Frances Perry, Roy Hay, John White and the late Oleg Polunin for kindly lending us their slides, and to Wilf Halliday for the photographs from the *Botanical Magazine*.

Our publisher, Hallam Murray, has not only shown remarkable tolerance but has been an unfailing source of help and encouragement, for which we thank him.

Sources of plates

C. D. Brickell 1, 3, 6, 19, 22, 23, 26, 28, 29, 34, 35, 37, 41, 42, 45, 56, 58, 65, 67, 70, 72, 75, 78;
J. R. H. Garey 8, 11, 12, 16, 18, 20, 30, 36, 39, 44, 47, 49, 50, 51, 55, 57, 60, 66, 68, 73, 74, 77;
Harry Smith Horticultural Photographic Collection 2, 5, 7, 9, 14, 17, 31, 32, 43, 52, 53, 54, 63,
71, 76, 80; Roy Elliott 10, 25, 79; Tony Schilling 21, 27, 38; Gillian Beckett 13, 33; Valerie
Finnis 40, 69; Duncan Donald 15; Frances Perry 24; Oleg Polunin 4; John White 62; *Botanical
Magazine* 46, 48, 59, 61, 64

Colour plates fall between pp. 118 and 119

Line drawings in text by Christine Grey-Wilson

Introduction

'It is much the rage to obtain new plants and neglect old ones.'
GEORGE GLENNY 1848

The double form of the sweet rocket *Hesperis matronalis*, affectionately known as dame's violet or rogue's gillyflower, was a plant cherished by our ancestors and widely grown in the past. Not so long ago, in the 1930s, it graced the London parks with drifts of fragrant white and purple blossom. This is the last time the double rocket was seen in any quantity. Although it was considered 'one of the handsomest and certainly one of the sweetest of garden flowers', it has since become a much sought-after rarity.

Most of us can remember other old favourites – plants which were once familiar but which for some reason are seldom found these days. Perhaps there were flamed tulips or a scarlet Turk's cap lily in your grandparents' garden, or demure white buttercups with 'bachelor's buttons' for flowers. Maybe the special scent of clove carnations, violets or a creamy musk rose conjures up your childhood. You might recall a grape hyacinth which looked like a purple feather duster, or a crown imperial with variegated leaves, or even a passion flower clothing the roof of the conservatory with dangling crimson parachutes. Where are they now?

The purpose of this book is to draw attention to the serious and immediate threat facing our cultivated plants. It is a threat to their very survival. Just as their relatives in the wild are rapidly diminishing in number, so too the ranks of our finest garden plants are thinning. Many of them are in danger of disappearing from cultivation, many more have already been lost for ever. The problem is worldwide. In Britain, however, it is particularly alarming because such an exceptional range of cultivated plants, both introduced species and 'man-made' varieties, has been accumulated over the centuries. The British acquired a reputation for horticultural excellence at an early stage. As Sir William Temple observed, returning from his embassy in The Hague to the court of Charles II, 'few countries are before us, either in the elegance of our gardens, or in the number of our plants.' Historical and geographical circumstances, combined with a propitious climate, have turned Britain into a showcase for the cultivated plants of the world. It is this valuable heritage which is now at risk.

The tide of foreign introductions, initially from Europe and more distant Mediterranean and Arab lands, can be traced back to the Romans. They are supposed to have brought the pasque flower, the Christmas rose, the sweet chestnut and other plants which have often been regarded as part of the native flora. The Normans continued the process by importing the carnation and the wallflower, which they may have done unwittingly with their building stone. Further contributions came variously from homebound diplomats, crusaders and merchants who had picked up plants on their travels. Later, the Huguenot and Flemish settlers are thought to have introduced not only the auricula and the double sweet rocket but also their own art of floristry.

However, it was not proximity to the Continent but isolation from it that made Britain into a horticultural treasure house. With her emergence as a mercantile and colonising nation from the sixteenth century onwards, 'outlandish' plants began to filter in from every corner of the globe. Missionaries, pirates, adventurers, sea captains, traders, administrators, botanists, plant collectors and explorers all added to the flow of plants from abroad. This reached a peak in the nineteenth and early twentieth centuries. Between the years 1789 and 1814 alone some 7,000 introductions were noted at Kew. The celebrated 'Chinese' Wilson, just one among many plant collectors active in the 1900s, was credited with over a thousand new species. The most remarkable fact was that the majority of these foreign plants could be grown within the confines of the British Isles, whose diverse climate provides suitable conditions for a vast assortment of plants, from the exotics of the Far East and Pacific at one extreme to the alpines of high mountains at the other.

Hand in hand with the introduction of plants went their development by selection and then by hybridisation. The improvement of plants for ornament or economic value was practised by the Turks on the tulip and by the Chinese before them on the peony and chrysanthemum. In Britain it found expression in that peculiar phenomenon, the florist's flower. Floristry in the original sense of the word meant the intensive breeding and meticulous selection of flowers in order to achieve the perfect bloom. It was apparently imported by artisan refugees from Flanders and France and was taken up by cottagers, craftsmen and industrial workers, who vied with each other at local florists' shows in their attempts to meet the rigid standards required. To this end countless varieties of carnation, pink, auricula, polyanthus, anemone, ranunculus, hyacinth and tulip were raised. These were the eight accepted florists' flowers at the beginning of the nineteenth century, soon to be joined by others like the pansy and the dahlia.

In Victoria's reign selection gradually gave way to deliberate hybridisation, although the mechanics of heredity were still not understood. The nurseryman William Lucombe of Exeter was a pioneer with his Lucombe oak in the 1760s, a hybrid which had arisen spontaneously but was one of the first to be commercially successful. The new technique was adopted by amateur specialists and later by professional growers on a large and profitable scale. Few plants escaped the frenzy of hybridisation that overtook the nineteenth century. Its application to tender plants such as the geranium, heliotrope and calceolaria fostered the mania for carpet bedding which the gardening writer

Crocosmia aurea

William Robinson so deplored. In the process, many of the most influential species were overwhelmed by their offspring, as happened with the clear yellow *Crocosmia aurea*, a parent of the common garden montbretias, which has virtually disappeared from cultivation. A glance at the old catalogues reveals the infinite numbers of garden forms produced and, often haphazardly, named in the nineteenth century. In the case of *Dianthus*, where breeders have been at work for over four hundred years, more than 28,000 fancy names have been given to varieties of pink, carnation and sweet william.

Such a proliferation of new varieties and introductions from abroad led inevitably to the demise of many of the older inhabitants of gardens, including the florists' flowers. Joseph Paxton, who was then head gardener at Chatsworth, noted in 1838 how 'plants which are in themselves truly beautiful, and which may be made to answer various ornamental purposes, are either for want of attention (having lost their novelty) wholly annihilated, or are thrown out of large establishments ... and rescued only from total oblivion by the amateur or cottager.' Fashion was a major influence. It has affected horticultural supply and demand since at least the seventeenth century, when the rage for the tulip swept western Europe and erupted in the preposterous Dutch tulipomania. The garden ranunculus was the object of a similar if briefer craze in Georgian England and boasted nearly a thousand varieties at its height. The Parma violet, sported in every corsage and buttonhole, became almost the emblem of Edwardiana before it faded with the age.

Always keen to exploit such swings in public taste, the horticultural trade was well equipped to do so by the nineteenth century, with the constant stream of new plants from overseas and the advent of hybridisation. The rose, for instance, was radically transformed. Older garden varieties were abandoned in favour of new breeds with more formal blooms and a perpetual flowering habit, before these in turn retreated under the onslaught of the modern hybrid teas and floribundas. Happily, the rose is also a prime example of fashion coming full circle. A large number of historic roses might have disappeared completely had they not lingered forgotten in gardens from which they could one day be retrieved. Largely through the recent work of Graham Stuart Thomas, many old-fashioned roses are now restored to popularity and are generally available to gardeners – a salutary lesson in what *can* be achieved with dedication and enthusiasm. Revivals of this kind are unfortunately no longer possible with the more ephemeral plants and the multitudes of anemones, hyacinths, ranunculus and pansies produced over the centuries have gone for ever. Their loss may not be momentous in commercial terms, nor even necessarily to the gardener. But with them has perished a part of our history and culture.

The florists and their flowers were the most obvious victims of the whims of fashion. However, their decline coincided with an unprecedented horticultural boom which in some respects compensated for the losses of the period. This was the heyday of the nurserymen. Leading firms, from Loddiges of Hackney at the start of the nineteenth century to Veitch of Chelsea at its close, had their own collectors in the field and they were responsible for many of the major introductions from abroad. Such enterprise was encouraged and sometimes funded by their affluent customers. The noted lady gardener, Ellen Willmott, was a patron of E. H. Wilson in the early twentieth century, while another wealthy benefactor, J. C. Williams, financed the expeditions of George Forrest and went so far as to offer him a bonus for each new rhododendron species obtained. (This amounted to a grand total of 309 and led to a revision of the whole genus, as well as causing endless confusion over naming.) There was certainly no shortage of sponsors. The Horticultural Society of London, forerunner of the Royal Horticultural Society, employed two of the most outstanding professional collectors – David Douglas in California in the 1820s and Robert Fortune in China in the 1840s. Even head gardeners like Paxton were able to organise trips to secure new trophies.

Nurseries not only introduced but also kept in stock an amazing range of plants. The backbone of their trade consisted of the owners of big private gardens or their head gardeners, who would send in substantial and regular orders. Herbaceous borders, rock gardens, conservatories and stove houses all needed furnishing and formal bedding schemes had to be replenished twice a year. To advertise their wares, which were despatched by rail and post, nurserymen put out lavish and magnificently illustrated descriptive catalogues. *The Floral Guide 1890*, published by Cannell & Sons of Swanley in Kent opened with twenty-four pages of new plants. It contained 469 kinds of dahlia, 846 chrysanthemums, 266 begonias and twelve pages devoted to fuchsias. At that time gardeners visiting the average nursery could have chosen from over twenty sorts of herbaceous potentilla and at least eight forms of the Christmas rose. Some fifteen coloured variants of the wood anemone were generally available before the First World War and Barr & Sons of Covent Garden were still offering about 250 irises and slightly fewer of peony.

It is a far cry from that opulent era to the modern garden centre with its car park and rows of containerised plants. The large estates run by armies of skilled staff have given way to small gardens where reliable, labour-saving and 'instant' plants have priority. The more time-consuming or exacting herbaceous and rock plants have been superseded by flowering shrubs and climbers, ground cover plants and annuals. The tender orchids, passion flowers, tea roses and Malmaison carnations which used to adorn heated conservatories have yielded to standard house plants. There are many explanations for these changes, but much of the blame can be laid on the two world wars and the radical social upheaval which they wrought. Several nurseries were forced to close and numerous plants disappeared as a direct result. Economic pressures and in particular rising transport and heating costs have also played a part. The horticultural trade has had to adopt a supermarket approach, discarding plants that are difficult or slow to propagate, require special care or overwintering, or are simply uncommercial or unfashionable, in order to concentrate on the bestsellers. Famous concerns such as Van Tubergen, the bulb merchants, and Hillier, the tree and shrub nursery, no longer grow all the specialities connected with their names. The huge reservoir of plants, the 'backlist' which was the pride of Victorian nurserymen, has virtually collapsed.

The loss of garden plants is not a new problem, nor one that has gone unheeded. The influential writer and gardener, Gertrude Jekyll, was a vocal champion of the forgotten at the beginning of this century. She recalled the 'garden plants of seventy years ago', the double sweet rockets and wallflowers, the old sweet peas and the hybrid perpetual roses which were 'then in favour' but which had 'passed out of cultivation or can only rarely be heard of'. Her great ally William Robinson was another who promoted their cause and that of hardy plants generally. His book *The English Flower Garden* appeared a little over a hundred years ago and soon became a classic. But to read of the plants he recommends – the 'very numerous' kinds of sweet violet, the 'several varieties' of crown imperial, the 'most popular' carnation 'Souvenir de la Malmaison' – is to realise just how much the English flower garden has altered since then. Even to compare the nursery lists of thirty to forty years ago with those of today shows what a drastic reduction has taken place in the number of plants available. The once weighty Hillier catalogue has shrunk to a thin paperback.

How many firms now stock the beautiful garden varieties of the belladonna lily or indeed the lily itself? Where can one find those elegant forms of the Japanese anemone so popular with the Edwardians; or the gorgeous cultivars of the oriental poppy for which the nurseryman Amos Perry was renowned; or the variations on the graceful *Dierama pulcherrimum*, the wandflower or angel's fishing rod, which were almost a trademark of the Slieve Donard nursery in the 1950s? Who can account for the absence of the great oriental bellflower *Ostrowskia magnifica*, which caused such a stir on its arrival in the late nineteenth century? What has happened to the lovely summer-flowering shrub *Caesalpinia japonica*, with its canary yellow and red blossom, or the unusual scarlet *Clematis texensis* and its even more desirable hybrids? Have the cottage garden favourites, the hepatica, primrose, wallflower and sweet rocket with their double flowers, the carnation and violet with their heavy fragrance, totally eluded us?

One has only to give a few examples to appreciate that each has or had its own intrinsic and irresistible charm. The beauty of garden plants is the most compelling reason for trying to ensure that they remain in cultivation. They are irreplaceable. The hybrid moss roses of today do not compare with the original *Rosa centifolia* 'Muscosa' and the modern double primroses somehow fail to match the quality of the old. Equally undeniable is the historical importance of plants. Collectively they are a testimony to man's achievement in harnessing nature for his own purposes. Individually they often have historical associations in their own right. The tree peony, for instance, was grown in the imperial gardens when China was ruled by the Tang dynasty in the seventh century and it stands as a monument to that ancient civilisation. The anchusa, crocus, gentian, iris, hellebore and countless others were valued by medieval herbalists for their medicinal attributes, whether real or imagined. Many plants are entangled in legend, superstition and religious beliefs. Common names like Our Lady's tears, sops-in-wine, galligaskins, grandfather's whiskers and sowbread tell their own tale and summon up bygone days. Names also commemorate gardeners, nurserymen, plant collectors and personalities from the past. E. A. Bowles is remembered in his crocus, William Lucombe in his oak, George Sherriff in his Himalayan poppy. Plants, and gardens too, belong to our culture in the same way as paintings, pottery, costume, buildings, steam trains or vintage cars. But while these are housed in museums and lovingly preserved for future generations, our horticultural endeavours are barely represented except in literature, illustrations and dried herbarium specimens. There is a massive body of such material but this is not enough. It is essential to maintain our cultivated plants and our gardens in a living state for the record to be complete.

It is obviously impossible to retain all garden plants. In fact it would be pointless to start assembling all the named forms of daffodil or rhododendron or another large plant group. Many of them probably had no lasting value and may have been named purely for profit or personal motives. One could also argue that losses along the way are a concomitant of progress. Does it matter after all if certain garden plants are neglected when new and perhaps superior ones have come in to take their place? If a variegated aspidistra can no longer be found, how much better to have a cyclamen flowering indoors in the winter!

We are apparently blessed with ample plant resources to fulfil our present gardening needs. Presumably we can still manage quite adequately with wild species and their garden offspring and can continue to discard any redundant plants. But who are we to judge? We should not throw away plants simply because they no longer appeal to us or because they seem inferior to their fellows. There are other factors to consider, apart from the individual aesthetic merits or historical significance of garden plants, and we can no longer afford to be complacent.

The conservation of plants in the wild is now an established concept, if a complex one to implement. Each year sees an appalling loss of wild species and it has been estimated that casualties could amount to 40,000 by the middle of the next century. The basic reserve which has so far served our requirements for food, clothing, medicine and decoration is dwindling fast. Plants which are at risk in their natural habitats are therefore prime candidates for being kept in cultivation. A number of plants already owe their existence to cultivation, since they are believed to be extinct in the wild. Among them are the brilliant blue Chilean crocus *Tecophilaea cyanocrocus*, the lovely *Franklinia alatamaha*, an American relative of the camellia, and the maidenhair tree *Ginkgo biloba* from China, the remarkable solitary relic of a prehistoric race. Their rescue was fortuitous and in the case of the ginkgo no one even realised at first that it was a 'living fossil'. Today there is an increasing awareness of the importance of growing and propagating rare and endangered species. *Camellia granthamiana* was discovered in 1955 and distributed to botanic gardens as a precaution should its wild population, a single known tree until very recently, be wiped out. Similarly, stocks have been built up of several cyclamen species in the hope of reducing the pressure of commercial collection on their limited numbers in the wild. Nevertheless, many other endangered species could still slip through

Tecomanthe speciosa

the net, such as *Tecomanthe speciosa* which is rare both in the wild and in cultivation.

Human acquisitiveness is a major hazard to plants. The Victorian vogue for orchids and the rich rewards awaiting collectors sealed the fate of many orchid species throughout the world. In Britain the plundering of the native lady's slipper has gone on for over three hundred years and has left a sole survivor in the north of England. Like all *Cypripedium* species it is very slow to increase and difficult to propagate. Depletion of the natural colonies of these ground orchids will doubtless continue until methods are devised to raise them in sufficient quantity to satisfy gardeners. It is not only orchids that suffer. In 1982 some 370 tons of bulbs were exported from Turkey, most of them garnered from the wild.

Many Mediterranean plants face an additional threat with the advance of tourism, as hotel developments spread like concrete carpets over their natural habitats. The delightful *Daphne jasminea*, known only from several sites in Greece where it clings precariously to the rocks, the flaming orange *Crocus gargaricus*, restricted to two or three mountains in Turkey, and the autumn-flowering *Crocus tournefortii*, confined to a few Aegean islands, may all be destined for extinction in the wild. Fortunately they are fairly easy to grow and increase. As garden plants at least their future is relatively safe, even if as yet they seldom appear in the trade.

Attractive plants, historic plants and plants endangered in the wild manifestly recommend themselves for conservation in gardens. But we should not ignore the rest just because they fail to meet these criteria. Many plants are equally worthy of preservation for different reasons, though sometimes they may be less seductive from the gardener's point of view. Among the plants mankind has evolved, often from species no longer found in the wild, are some with immense genetic potential. Their gene complexes may be able to provide an unrepeatable combination of characters to improve that particular genus, whether by enhancing quality, yield or vigour, by introducing a new colour, or by combating disease and pests. For example, one of our most popular groups of shrubs could soon be transformed in appearance by the arrival of a new species. The fabled yellow camellia so long pursued by plant hunters has been discovered in the guise of *C. chrysantha*, which opens up enormous possibilities in extending the colour range of the genus beyond the normal pink, red and white. Similarly, an old michaelmas daisy called 'Climax' shows marked resistance to mildew, the bane of the larger-flowered modern forms. Expelled from nursery lists by its more showy successors, it has been saved in time and can still be used in future breeding. This underlines the importance of assessing plants critically, rather than dropping them simply because they have lost their charms. 'Nonconformist' plants which flower earlier or later than their fellows may also have great genetic value, however irrelevant or inconvenient they are to the grower. The fact that they do not fit in with the current production line or breeding programme is no excuse for their disposal.

Plants both wild and cultivated have proved their usefulness to man in innumerable ways. They are vital adjuncts to scientific research, not only on account of their genetic importance but because of the insights that can be gained from a study of their chemical and physical make-up. Their healing powers have been appreciated for thousands of years and still are, for many of the plants used by apothecaries of old have a place in modern medicine. Their economic value, as the source of food, drink, clothing, timber, rubber and other materials, is incalculable. In the development of cultivated forms the virtues of the wild species have often been heightened. The saffron crocus *C. sativus*, for instance, is very probably an improved form of the species *C. cartwrightianus*. It has been cultivated since time immemorial for the priceless saffron derived from its long stigmas, which was supposed to cure an incredible number of ailments and was also highly esteemed as a scent, a dye and a spice. It is hard to believe that this plant once formed the main industry of the town of Saffron Walden. It is now very rarely seen in Britain, although it is still grown on a limited commercial scale elsewhere. We should be careful not to take our plants for granted.

The case for the conservation of garden plants is irrefutable and it calls for urgent action. But what can we do and how should we set about it? The first priority is to find out *why* plants are vanishing from gardens and from the horticultural trade, then to pinpoint and locate those types and groups of plants which are vulnerable, and finally to take positive steps to ensure that such plants are grown, increased and distributed.

Plants that are difficult or expensive to propagate are in the front line. They are some of the first to be struck off the nursery lists regardless of their attractions. The magnificent tree peony *P. suffruticosa* 'Rock's Variety' and the golden oak *Quercus robur* 'Concordia' both have a high failure rate with cuttings or grafts and are consequently almost impossible to obtain in the trade. In the same way very few firms have the capital, expertise or time required to graft weeping and special forms of trees. On the other hand, trees that may be easily raised from seed are often slow to mature and reach saleable size, which is also a disincentive to produce them commercially. Many plants are handicapped by this fact that they do not increase fast enough to be worth the nurseryman's time, although they may be comparatively simple to propagate. The tongue-twisting but beautiful yellow *Paeonia mlokosewitschii*, like many herbaceous paeonies, seeds freely but takes several years to flower. It would surely be snapped up by gardeners if only it could be made available, as would plants which are similarly slow to increase, such as the superb *Meconopsis* × *sheldonii*, the hellebore species and the wake robins *Trillium sessile*, *T. ovatum* and, in its double and pink forms, *T. grandiflorum*.

Nurserymen have been compelled by economic circumstances to streamline production. As glasshouse heating costs soar, they are understandably

Trillium ovatum

reluctant to cope with plants of doubtful hardiness involving extra trouble and outlay unless they can be sure of a good market. The ubiquitous chrysanthemum and dahlia now do duty for a whole host of half-hardy and tender plants which used to be equally familiar in the days when overwintering presented no problem. The shrubby salvias so welcome for their late flowering, the alstroemerias and their luxuriant climbing relatives, the bomareas, and many other tender plants no longer feature in catalogues, still less in people's greenhouses. A few half-hardy plants have clung on in sheltered gardens. *Cosmos atrosanguineus*, a relative of the dahlia with deep blackish-red, chocolate-scented flowers borne throughout the summer, has been restored to the lists of some specialist nurseries. So too have a number of old penstemons and several *Osteospermum* (*Dimorphotheca*) species and hybrids, with their summer display of purple, pink or white daisies. But many of the forms of heliotrope, the fragrant cherry pie which was an obligatory ingredient of park bedding schemes, have already gone, their quality unsurpassed by modern seed-raised imposters.

Indeed a large number of garden plants, both tender and otherwise, have become horticultural exiles simply because they have to be propagated by vegetative means (by cuttings, division or grafting) and cannot be raised from seed. These are at a disadvantage today, when 'our lives are so full of rush and hurry' as Gertrude Jekyll put it. Named forms of the poppy anemone, wallflower, polyanthus, ranunculus and pansy have been ousted by breeds selected by seedsmen and by 'mixed collections'. There were also many plants

Daphne genkwa

that relied on personal rather than commercial distribution in the past. It was a matter of routine for cottagers to increase their quaint columbines and bellflowers, double primroses and sweet rockets and exchange them with neighbours. But that tradition has practically ceased and with it some delightful old plants have vanished. Their decline may have been hastened by virus infection, which vegetatively propagated plants, as opposed to seed-raised ones, are more prone to inherit. This has certainly contributed to the disappearance of the double sweet rockets.

There will always be plants to test the skills of gardeners – 'miffs and mimps' like the Asiatic primulas and gentians, the *Dionysia* and *Androsace* species, the tiny campanulas and aquilegias. Ironically, some of the most sensational plants are the most difficult to grow and alpines are not alone in this distinction. The evergreen climber *Mutisia decurrens* with its striking daisy flowers, the delicate rose-pink *Anemone capensis* from South Africa, the Chilean *Tecophilaea cyanocrocus*, the blue amaryllis *Worsleya procera* from Brazil, the distinctive *Daphne genkwa*, and the glorious Oncocyclus irises have all foxed experienced plantsmen. Owners will go to any lengths for their reward, even to the extent of procuring herrings and seaweed for the New Zealand forget-me-not *Myosotidium hortensia*. Such capricious plants are bound to remain outside the province of general gardeners and nurserymen and will have to depend on the skills of specialists for their horticultural existence. Many of them are doubly at risk owing to their rarity in the wild. One can see how precarious their position is by comparing them with species which are similarly endangered or uncommon in nature but which are reasonably secure because they have taken more kindly to cultivation. The vivid scarlet *Tulipa wilsoniana* (or *T. montana* as it is incorrectly known) is apparently threatened by soil erosion and grazing cattle in its native Iran. Thanks to its obliging character it is quite readily obtainable from bulb merchants. The purple *Cyclamen pseudibericum*, found only in a small area of Turkey, is also gradually establishing itself on the horticultural front. Plants like these, both the intractable and the amenable, must be earmarked for conservation in gardens on which their actual survival may hinge. Where troublesome plants are concerned, it is vitally important that they should be grown and circulated among enthusiasts if they are to have a niche in cultivation rather than hover on its brink.

Sometimes an entire genus is afflicted by a reputation for being difficult to grow, not always with justification. Both the stuartias, elegant cousins of the camellia, and the foxtail lilies, the species and hybrids of *Eremurus*, have failed to win widespread recognition from gardeners, although several of them are relatively easy to cultivate. It is curious how many other excellent garden plants do not catch on in gardening circles or quietly slip away as horticultural fashions wax and wane. Lack of promotion is frequently a cause. In the 1920s some lovely forms of *Scabiosa caucasica* were developed by a Bristol nurseryman, but never aroused interest because they were underpublicised and overpriced. Today the pure white variety of *Colchicum speciosum*, one of the finest autumn bulbs with its prolific flowers and freedom of increase, is only occasionally offered and then at a price likely to deter most gardeners. However, the endearing *Viola* 'Jackanapes', which was named by Miss Jekyll after her pet monkey and was similarly scarce a few years ago, is now making a welcome comeback. It shows what can be done if plants are given the necessary boost.

Although the introduction of garden forms and wild species proceeds at a steady pace, very few make the horticultural grade. Nurserymen can be forgiven a conservative approach, since not all plants live up to expectations. However, the bright yellow rose 'Helen Knight' only crept into the catalogues in 1979, ten years after its release to the trade, while the superb *Fremontodendron* (*Fremontia*) 'California Glory' took even longer to enter commerce, despite the accolade of a First Class Certificate in 1967. After this belated start, both are now well established in gardens and nurseries. Many plants introduced from the wild have departed the scene soon after their arrival. Wide distribution at the time is no guarantee of survival, as *Clematis phlebantha* graphically illustrates. A graceful silvery-leaved shrub with white blooms, it was raised at Wisley from seed collected in Nepal in 1952 and then propagated and sent out to other gardens. But when the Wisley plant died a few years ago, attempts to replace it were unsuccessful until a solitary specimen was eventually tracked down. One of George Sherriff's greatest triumphs in his distinguished career as a collector was the pink *Meconopsis sherriffii*. Re-introduced more than once since the 1930s, it has remained a rarity in Britain, although it is admittedly a difficult plant to grow. The same does not apply to Frank Kingdon Ward's discovery, *Lilium mackliniae*, with its rosy-purple lampshade flowers. Yet this, too, is still seldom encountered in gardens or nursery lists. To read the field notes of the plant hunters of the twentieth century is a sad reflection on the impermanence of their achievements.

Plants that are unaccountably neglected, whether through lack of recognition or a slump in their popularity, are perhaps the hardest to identify as targets for conservation and those most likely to be overlooked. It is much easier to regret the losses we already know about, such as *Daphne odora* 'Mazelii', a beautiful variety from Japan. Covered in huge clusters of deliciously scented pink and white blossom throughout the winter, it was far superior to the shrub grown today and was quite common in European gardens in the late nineteenth century. Now it is remembered only in an illustration from that period. There is an obvious need for a system of assessment, both to prevent a repetition of losses like these in the case of older plants and to ensure that new plants are brought to a wider public if they deserve. They should be examined not only on their horticultural merits, which 'Mazelii' plainly possessed, but on grounds such as their historical contribution or their potential for future breeding.

The means to evaluate plants old and new is now emerging with the establishment of national plant collections. Following a conference organised by the Royal Horticultural Society to study the urgent problem of conserving garden plants, the National Council for the Conservation of Plants and Gardens (NCCPG) was set up in 1978 with the specific brief of coordinating and implementing a conservation policy. One of its first objectives has been to form a network of plant reference collections, or national collections as they are called. A national collection is devoted to a single plant genus or group and is designed to contain as many representatives as possible of that genus or group, both species and garden forms. It is a living museum of plants and also a source of material for propagation, breeding and research. The practical value of establishing such a collection is enormous: it will enable a picture to be built up of what is in cultivation and where, and what is not; it will help to identify plants, check that they are correctly named and sort out any discrepancies in nomenclature; it will provide a basis of comparison for assessing old and new garden plants; and it will act as a reserve bank and ensure that plants are maintained for the future. The business of tracking down and assembling plants for a national collection is a daunting one, but so far nearly 250 have come into being – a measure of the success of the scheme – and several more are in the pipeline. They are run by botanical and horticultural bodies, nurseries and specialist societies, local authorities, schools, the National Trust and National Trust for Scotland, and private individuals.

One of the most useful functions of a national collection will be to assist in clearing up confusion over the identity of plants. There are many examples of nurseries offering several distinct garden forms of a plant under the same name, or conversely of applying various different names to what turns out to be the same plant. The nurseryman is not always at fault for he might in good faith have obtained and grown an incorrectly named plant from an apparently impeccable source. At the moment it is often extremely difficult to check with any degree of accuracy that a particular garden variety has been correctly named. However, a national collection will be able to supply the necessary information for identifying plants. In this way their nomenclature can be unravelled and standard named plants established for reference in cases where there is dispute. Perhaps some of the gems from the past may reappear masquerading under another name or languishing anonymously in gardens or nurseries.

Immense numbers of garden varieties of roses, chrysanthemums, dahlias and daffodils have received names and in these cases it may not be practical or even desirable to try to locate or maintain the vast range still in existence. The NCCPG has therefore drawn up guidelines suggesting that the field could if necessary be narrowed to plants in the following categories: historically important in the development of the genus; having genetic potential for future breeding; of aesthetic merit or having distinctive qualities of flower, foliage, scent, etc; valuable to scientific research, medicinally, commercially or in other ways; known to be rare or endangered in the wild. But it would be all too easy to miss or reject a plant that apparently did not fulfil one of these criteria, only to discover later that it did. In the early stages the aim should be to obtain as complete a representation of the genus or group as possible. At the same time it is essential to create duplicate collections as a precaution against some disaster like virus infection, which could lead to the whole stock having to be destroyed.

'The daffodil king', the energetic Peter Barr, wrote over a hundred years ago what could almost be a text for the modern conservation movement:

Narcissus longispathus

The Narcissus is amongst the oldest and most beautiful of the Spring flowering bulbous plants. It has for centuries been one of the highly-prized garden favourites, and has commended in an unusual degree the attention of the scientific botanist. During the epochs when artificial gardening has been in the ascendant, Narcissus, like many other charming flowers, has had to yield to the inexorable goddess of fashion. At such times it has been saved from extinction by the fostering care of our Botanic Gardens, and of those enthusiastic amateurs who love flowers not for what they cost, but for their intrinsic beauty, and who, while they do not ignore new introductions, discard not their old friends, unless the new is an improvement on the old.

The narcissus, however, like many another neglected flower, is now reasserting its position, and claiming its proper place in the general economy of border decoration, and as a cut flower for furnishing vases.

Daffodils, appropriately, are a marvellous example of the success of the national collections. The New University of Ulster garden is a memorial to the outstanding daffodil breeder, Guy Wilson, and started with 160 garden forms of daffodil in 1974. It now consists of some 1,600 distinct daffodils, accumulated through the efforts of a handful of dedicated people. Another national collection, for clematis, includes over 350 species and varieties and is held by the nursery Treasures of Tenbury, who have also inspired the formation of the International Clematis Society. One herbaceous species, C. hexapetala, which grows wild near the Great Wall of China, is being extensively used in Chinese research into cancer cures. It is an apt demonstration of the unexpected properties of plants and underlines the importance of investigating their credentials before dismissing them.

A number of national collections are administered by botanic gardens, horticultural institutions and arboreta, which clearly have a major part to play in their own right since their chief function is the maintenance of plants. Their expertise is crucial to the conservation of species endangered in the wild, plants of scientific or economic value and plants which might otherwise be resistant to cultivation. Their scientific work is also extremely valuable to horticulture and could even revolutionise the nursery trade. Research is now in progress at the Royal Botanic Gardens, Kew, and elsewhere into micropropagation or plant tissue culture, a method of increasing plants from single plant cells or groups of cells, which are taken from small pieces of seeds, tips of shoots, leaves or bulbs and grown under sterile conditions. The development of this technique to a stage where it can be widely applied by nurserymen should make many plants a commercial proposition once more, and notably those that are difficult or slow to increase by conventional means. Meristem culture, in which cells from the growing point are used, could help in another way by preventing the transmission of virus infection in plants which have to be vegetatively propagated. It is reported that micropropagation has been successful with tree peonies in China. Advances have been made at Kew in raising ground orchids from seed and by this means it may eventually be possible to establish good stocks in cultivation in order to safeguard the *Cypripedium* species against further culling in the wild.

Historic gardens, too, have a role in garden plant conservation. Official recognition of their status in the National Heritage Act of 1983, granting powers to register and protect them, is an important step. As the public gradually becomes aware of the need to preserve gardens in the same way as buildings, so will the search for old-fashioned, historic and forgotten plants seem more relevant. 'England's greatest gardener', the National Trust, is responsible for some twenty national collections and has been a pioneer in the restoration and reconstruction of original gardens. Many others are following this lead and thereby creating suitable dwellings for plants from the past. To see the seventeenth-century plants in the Queen's Garden at Kew is a revelation of the treasures from that period and an incentive to acquire and grow them in one's own garden. The wonderful collections of old roses at Mottisfont Abbey in Hampshire and Castle Howard in Yorkshire are the tangible results of the ideals of garden plant conservation and they are there for all to enjoy.

Gardens of every kind, historic and recent, public and private, are the fundamental framework for the maintenance of plants. As they become more accessible and open their gates to visitors, there is greater opportunity to admire and sometimes buy less familiar plants. Small nurseries for their part have responded by admitting the more unusual plants to their lists, often in limited quantities but nevertheless on a regular basis. The charming *Cosmos atrosanguineus* and *Geranium wallichianum* 'Buxton's Variety' have been re-surrected, together with some of the old pinks, violas, primroses and auriculas; a few choice species of iris, lily and tulip can now be obtained from different sources; and maples, until recently stocked by only one nurseryman in any reasonable range, have become available in a remarkable diversity of species and garden forms from several outlets.

Like specialist nurseries, specialist societies play a vital role in the con-servation of garden plants. Members of the Alpine Garden Society and Scottish Rock Garden Club relish the challenge of exhibiting their exquisite but obstinate favourites and any newly introduced alpine species will be men-tioned in their bulletins. The Hardy Plant Society used to publish a directory of herbaceous plants and where they could be bought. It also operates a plant propagation and exchange scheme, as do many similar associations. The recently formed Cyclamen Society is already growing and distributing many of the species. By discouraging further overcollection of cyclamen endangered in their natural habitats, it could be instrumental in the conservation of the genus both in the wild and in cultivation.

In the end it is up to the thousands of ordinary individual gardeners to ensure that they, the chief beneficiaries of Britain's exceptional legacy of garden plants, hand it on intact to future generations. The enlistment of gardeners and the channelling of their support is the principal aim of the NCCPG, which has initiated over 30 groups throughout the country. At this local level members can contribute their own intimate knowledge of gardens, nurseries and plants in the area. They can give active assistance by surveying plant collections, tracing sources of supply, locating and identifying, growing and propagating plants, and helping to protect gardens. They can also if they wish hold a national collection. The NCCPG has kindled a greater interest in and consciousness of rare and threatened plants and has already achieved positive results. A number of the plants included on its first 'wanted' list have been tracked down. Nurserymen too are beginning to appreciate the importance of publicity and marketing if customers are to learn about their uncommon plants. It is a welcome trend that more and more small firms are bringing their wares to Royal Horticultural Society shows and thus to greater notice. But gardeners in their turn must be prepared to purchase these plants, even if they have to pay more than normal, and they should persuade the trade to stock them – rather as the wealthy Victorians clamoured for novelties from their nurserymen, to the mutual benefit of both. Above all, gardeners must grow and continue to grow those plants which would otherwise be lost, or else they will rob their successors of a unique and irreplaceable heritage.

This book is intended as a stimulant, to encourage interest in our garden plants, old and new, and their continued survival in the future. It is not and never could be a *vade mecum* of all cultivated plants in danger, but has been written to draw attention to the grave losses that have already occurred and are

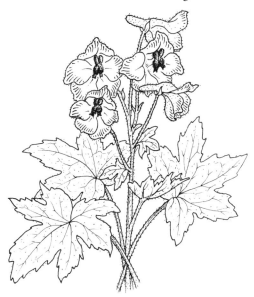

Delphinium brunonianum

still happening now. Reasons for the losses are much easier to find than the missing plants themselves and these are outlined in this introduction. The selection of entries is based on the authors' own knowledge of plants which seem vulnerable and clearly call for conservation measures, although only a few illustrative examples can be given. This is particularly so in the case of vast genera like *Primula*, *Dianthus*, *Campanula* and *Rosa*, where considerable numbers of species and garden forms once in cultivation are no longer grown. However, roses and other groups such as maples and cyclamen also demonstrate that it is possible, despite adversity and neglect, to locate many of the garden-worthy plants in a genus and to propagate and distribute them.

Woody plants (shrubs and trees) are by their very nature long-lived and therefore tend to be better preserved in gardens and less immediately threatened than the more fleeting herbaceous plants, alpines and bulbs. This explains the preponderance of the latter in the book. The fact that annuals, biennials, water plants, ferns, vegetables and fruit are excluded does not mean that they are secure or unworthy of conservation – far from it. Much work is required and has already been done, especially with fruit and vegetables, which will no doubt be written up at a suitable stage. Similarly, several familiar garden plants, for instance chrysanthemum, dahlia, delphinium, daffodil, heather and rhododendron, are omitted, although many of their species and varieties are equally deserving candidates. However, most of the periods in the evolution of these genera are represented in cultivation and without further research it is extremely difficult to decide what should be retained from among the countless forms named over the years and those still available to gardeners.

The entries in this book are arranged by genus in alphabetical order, each one highlighting some endangered members of that genus. Commonly grown species and varieties are also mentioned in order to set the plants in context and some general, historical or mythological background is provided. Quotations are drawn from the early herbalists like Gerard and Parkinson and from later authorities like Reginald Farrer and E. A. Bowles and are included not simply for anecdotal charm, although these writers often have an inimitable style, but to show how much the plants have been appreciated in the past. There are brief comments on cultivation and propagation where appropriate, but readers should consult the many practical books on the market for further details.

The book is not supposed to mystify the ordinary gardener with botanical language, although technical terms such as 'scion' and 'palmate', for which there is no equivalent, are used occasionally in the text. The word 'cultivar', a contraction of 'cultivated variety', occurs throughout except in the introduction, since it is now the accepted usage for 'garden variety' or 'garden form'. At the end of the book are a short biographical section covering some of the major figures referred to, a list of current national collections, a bibliography, and an index of both Latin and common names.

The great question is – where can one get hold of the plants? Unfortunately, or perhaps fortunately, it has been impossible to compile an up-to-date list of suppliers because so many new small nurseries are appearing on the scene, stocking just these kinds of plants. Rather than give an incomplete and quickly obsolete picture, it seemed better to direct readers to the best sources of information, which are noted on p. 242.

The need to conserve cultivated plants is worldwide. This book focuses on the British Isles and is amply justified in doing so because the wealth of plants grown here is probably unrivalled. However, the book is relevant to many other countries where plants form an integral part of the culture. The development and improvement of plants for ornament is an ancient practice in China and Japan and has long been important in Europe, and in the Soviet Union, the United States and Canada, South Africa, Australia and New Zealand. Like Britain other nations are becoming increasingly conscious of the value of old garden plants and are trying to locate and identify them. Schemes are afoot in Canada and Australia to conserve plants which were raised or brought over by the early settlers, who must have taken their favourites with them to remind them of home. It is quite possible that some of the garden varieties now lost in Britain itself will resurface elsewhere. A number of the double Parma violets so dear to the Edwardians have already been traced in Australia and some of the old roses long since extinct in Europe have been found in South Africa, New Zealand and Bermuda. Several of the beautiful nineteenth-century forms of the tree peony may well survive in the USA. It is also highly likely that many of the 'typically English' cottage garden plants still linger in Ireland.

The International Clematis Society and similar organisations with members all over the world have shown just what can be achieved in the conservation of garden plants on a global scale. Greater international cooperation, if only on a horticultural level, will undoubtedly help in the introduction and reintroduction of species from the wild, perhaps from places which were previously closed to outsiders. It is hoped that this book will point the way to a better appreciation of our cultivated plants in general and inspire gardeners to take action to safeguard those in particular whose future is under threat.

Plants by Genus

Abutilon

Abutilon ochsenii

'A plant that caused Collingwood Ingram to leap off the path in his excitement' – that was how one great gardener, E. B. Anderson, reported the reaction of another on his first sight of *Abutilon ochsenii*. This superb species had been described in 1856, but was only introduced to Britain a century later when Anderson was sent seeds by a correspondent in Chile. The parent plant grew in a private garden there and had been collected from the wild in Valdivia province.

The genus *Abutilon* is named from the Arabic word for mallow and contains about 100 species distributed across the tropics and subtropics, particularly in Central and South America. Most of those commonly cultivated are tender in Britain and are often grown in pots in a cool greenhouse and planted out for the summer. Among the best known are *A. megapotamicum*, which is up to 6 feet high with flowers like hanging lanterns in rich red and yellow; several hybrids including *A. × milleri* and others grouped as *A. × hybridum*, in shades of orange, yellow, red or white; and probably the most familiar, *A. vitifolium*. This is a rapid grower generally some 8 to 15 feet in height, with maple-like leaves covered in grey hairs and distinctive hollyhock blooms in pale lavender, purplish blue or white.

Closely related to *A. vitifolium*, *A. ochsenii* (Plate 1) is distinguished by the greener and less hairy leaves and stems, which are also smaller and more slender, and by the colour of its open, saucer-shaped flowers, again smaller. These are bright violet-blue with an intense mauve blotch in the centre, borne singly or in pairs in May. According to the *Botanical Magazine*, it is a shrub of about 6 feet, but W. J. Bean states that it is 'likely to reach a height of at least

12 ft on a wall'. He was proved correct by a plant growing against a wall at Hampton Court in Surrey and free-standing specimens twice the size have been reported from New Zealand. Like *A. vitifolium* it is considered to be one of the hardier species and has performed well outside at Wisley. A plant given by Anderson to Sir Frederick Stern survived in the open without protection at his famous garden of Highdown in Sussex and went on to win an Award of Merit at Chelsea in 1962.

A. ochsenii and *A. vitifolium* are responsible for 'one of the most outstanding hybrids introduced to horticulture in recent years' – *A. × suntense*, which made its début in 1969. It tends to occur spontaneously if the two species are grown together, as happened at Highdown and in other gardens, and was also made as a deliberate cross by Messrs Hiller in 1967. *A. × suntense* is a vigorous, fast-growing shrub up to 15 feet high, with felted, vine-shaped leaves like those of *A. vitifolium*, and produces an abundance of large violet-purple blooms from the end of May.

Its merits were quickly appreciated and like *A. vitifolium* it is now quite regularly available in the trade. But there is no reason why it should have ousted its other equally desirable and floriferous parent. *A. ochsenii* itself is seldom offered by nurseries, although it is just as easy to grow and is readily propagated, in Anderson's experience at least. Fresh seed sown in gentle heat will result in plants of flowering size the following year, while cuttings may be taken in late summer and rooted in mist or in a closed frame. With all its attributes and especially the unusual deep colouring which its rivals lack, *A. ochsenii* surely deserves to be seen more frequently in cultivation.

Acanthus *Bear's breeches*

The derivation of the word *Acanthus* from the Greek *akanthos*, spine, is self-explanatory. Its two common names, brank-ursine and bear's breech or breeches, are more obscure in origin. The first in fact comes from the medieval Latin meaning bear's claw which the plant fairly obviously resembles, but how the bear's claw became his breeches is not clear. The genus consists of some fifty species, ranging from tropical mangrove trees to plants of dry hill and steppe, only a few of which are hardy and grown in gardens. Their chief value lies in the architectural quality of the deciduous leaves, glossy dark green in *Acanthus mollis*, sharply spined and deeply cut in *A. spinosus*, the two best-known species. This handsome foliage is said to have inspired the famous motif on Corinthian columns, though it has not been determined whether the model was *A. mollis*, from southwestern Europe, or *A. spinosus*, with a more easterly distribution including Greece. Both have impressive spires of hooded white or pale pink flowers with purplish bracts, which are produced in late summer.

Acanthus dioscoridis

These are useful for flower arrangements and retain much of their colour when dried, but should be handled cautiously because of the sharp spikes.

A. mollis arrived in Britain in the mid-sixteenth century and was familiar to William Turner, who in his *New Herbal* of 1551 recorded it growing 'plentifully in my Lordes garden at Sion'. Parkinson in his *Paradisus* drew attention to its medical attributes as a 'mollifying herbe' for 'members out of yointe' and for the relief of burns, scalds and gout. Dioscorides, the first-century Greek physician, had extolled its properties for 'ye phthisicall, and ruptures and convulsions' and it was still recommended in the seventeenth century, by John Evelyn, the famous diarist and gardener, as a suitable plant for a physic garden.

In general the *Acanthus* species will grow vigorously in almost any well-drained soil, preferring an open, sunny situation to flower freely. Propagation by root cuttings is all too easy, as anyone who has moved them in the garden discovers the following spring, when a host of young plants arises on the original site spawned from fleshy roots left behind by the parent plant. Plants may also be raised readily from the large dark-brown, bean-like seeds, which should be sown in autumn and usually germinate in the spring.

While *A. mollis* and *A. spinosus* remain the foremost representatives of the genus in gardens, two dwarf species are equally worthy of cultivation, especially where space is limited, yet are seldom seen. Both *A. dioscoridis* (Plate 6), from Turkey, Lebanon, Iran and Iraq, and the closely related *A. hirsutus*, which is restricted to Turkey, possess the same sculptural grace as their larger counterparts. *A. hirsutus* appears to have been introduced from western Turkey about thirty years ago by Dr Peter Davis, the collector and editor of *Flora of Turkey*, and has greyish-green tufts of semi-erect, weakly spiny, cut leaves and 12-inch spikes of creamy-yellow, green-bracted flowers. It has grown well in an open, sunny position at Wisley, where it spreads gently by short suckers without threatening any but the feeblest neighbours. Nevertheless, it is still rare in gardens.

The delightful *A. dioscoridis* is a fine plant for a dry, sunny site, differing from *A. hirsutus* principally in its purplish-red or purplish-pink flowers, in the best forms up to 2 inches long, and in its long suckers. The leaves are often entire and lacking spines, but it is extremely variable in habit and leaf characters. Some forms (var. *brevicaulis*) reach no more than 6 inches in height, others are three times as tall with foliage to match. Although introduced to Kew early this century by the celebrated German collector W. Siehe, *A. dioscoridis* has never become established in cultivation, perhaps because it lacks the ground-covering propensities of the more robust and popular species. A recent collection from southeast Turkey has been grown very successfully in a bulb frame for some years and seems hardy, increasing freely from suckers which appear a foot or so away from the parent. In spite of this slightly alarming feature, *A. dioscoridis*, particularly in its dwarf forms, promises to be a most attractive plant for the rock garden or by a sunny wall, where its narrow spikes of purple-red blooms can be shown off to good effect.

Acer *Maple*

With some 200 species distributed through the north temperate regions of the world and in mountainous areas of the tropics, the genus *Acer* is a prolific source of garden-worthy plants. The majority of maples are deciduous small to medium trees or large shrubs, usually with handsome, opposite, lobed leaves which assume attractive tints of yellow, orange and red before falling at winter's approach. The few evergreen or semi-evergreen species unfortunately survive only in the mildest parts of Britain. Familiar maples include the sycamore *Acer pseudoplatanus*, with salt-resistant foliage which makes it 'very proper to make Plantations near the Sea' in Philip Miller's words, and the beautiful forms of the Japanese maple *A. palmatum*, ranging from the bold, palmate, purple leaves of *atropurpureum* to the delicate filigree tracery of the dwarf weeping 'Dissectum Atropurpureum'. These are staples of the nursery trade, together with several others such as the Norway maple *A. platanoides* and its variegated and coloured-leaved forms; *A. japonicum*, a larger version of the Japanese maple, which is particularly effective in the variants 'Vitifolium', a blaze of autumnal brilliance, and 'Aureum', of quiet, pale gold; and the main cultivars of the so-called box elder *A. negundo*, with compound leaves variegated in yellow or white.

Of easy culture and tolerant of a wide variety of soil types, almost all maples thrive in fairly rich, moist, but well-drained soils, in sunny or slightly shaded sites. However, many do not root readily from cuttings and can only be grafted

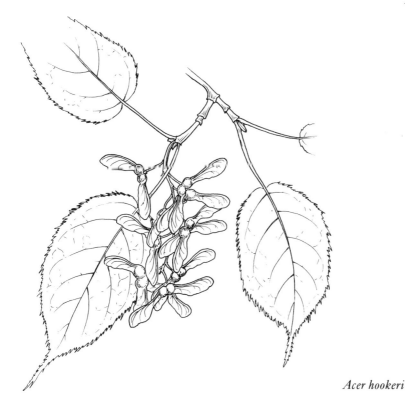

Acer hookeri

successfully on to stocks of the same or a closely related species, which are not always available. The best method of increase is from seed, often freely produced in cultivation, and most maples may be raised without difficulty in this way. But, from the commercial grower's point of view, the economics of doing so are doubtful unless, like the sycamore, they reach saleable size relatively quickly.

As a result of the influx of seed from China earlier this century and a recent awakening of interest in the genus, about eighty species are grown in British gardens, although comparatively few are obtainable in the trade. A welcome development, therefore, is the number of nurserymen specialising in raising maples and other trees from seed or cuttings, who now list many unusual and decorative species as well as the more ordinary ones. Still in short supply, these plants are smaller than those gawky, serried ranks of 5- to 6-foot standards sitting in soldierly fashion in the garden centre or nursery. However, young trees 1 to 2 feet tall are normally easy to establish and will grow away strongly and frequently outstrip their relatives within a few years.

The striking paper-bark maple *A. griseum*, with its peeling bark and scarlet and orange autumn foliage, is one of the finest trees for gardens, flourishing on both chalk and acid soils. Seed is forthcoming but, regrettably, a very low percentage germinates and it is seldom offered in commerce. Similarly scarce are the allied *A. nikoense* (Plate 2) from Japan, *A. henryi*, introduced by E. H. Wilson in 1903 from central China, and *A. cissifolium*, another Japanese species. They belong to a group of maples in which the leaves are composed of three leaflets. With their elegant habit and short stature, generally under 25 feet high, they make ideal specimen trees for the small garden.

Among the least common species in cultivation, *A. giraldii* was discovered in the Chinese province of Shensi by the Italian missionary whose name it bears and introduced from Yunnan by George Forrest. This superb maple, up to 40 feet high, with its three-lobed leaves, dark brown peeling bark and young growth clothed in bluish-grey bloom, was very inadequately represented in Britain until fairly recently. However, young plants have now been raised from seed and it is gradually gaining a firmer hold in gardens.

Another maple introduced by Wilson from China, in 1907, is *A. erianthum*. It has decorative 5- to 7-lobed dark green foliage tufted with white down beneath and abundant pink-winged fruits in the autumn. Somewhat less tolerant of alkaline soils than most maples, it is also very slow-growing and one tree, in the clement conditions of Cornwall, has taken over seventy years to achieve a height of 30 feet. It remains a rarity confined to a few collections.

Much more vigorous and ultimately forming a tree of some 70 feet is *A. velutinum* var. *vanvolxemii*, from the Caucasus. It is remarkable for its large 3- to 5-lobed leaves, often bronze-tinted when unfolding and slightly bloomy on the underside. Like the erect-branched *A.* × *lobelii* (probably a hybrid of *A. cappadocicum*, from Asia Minor, with the Norway maple), it deserves to be more widely planted where space permits.

The majority of maples are grown for the beauty of their foliage and, though pleasant enough, the sprays of yellow, greenish-white or sometimes purple small flowers make little impact. But some species are very lovely in flower, particularly those which produce their blooms on bare branches before the leaves expand. The tall Italian maple *A. opalus*, from southern and central Europe, is wreathed in dense-clustered yellow bunches of flowers during March and April, while *A. rubrum*, from eastern North America, mirrors this spectacle in rich red. Known as the red maple, the latter has the additional bonus of scarlet and yellow tints to the autumn foliage, notable in the clone 'Schlesingeri', which is all too seldom obtainable. An alternative for small gardens is the vine maple *A. circinatum*, from western North America. Admirable as a lawn specimen, this widespreading shrub is bedecked with clusters of small white and crimson-purple flowers in spring, with later colour when the rounded 7- to 9-lobed leaves turn orange and scarlet in autumn. This too appears only occasionally in the trade, despite the fact that it is easily and rapidly grown from seed and readily increased from layers.

The snake-bark maples, so called for the distinctive white striping on the bark of the younger branches and the stems, feature quite regularly in catalogues. A number of gardens possess excellent examples of *A. capillipes*,

A. rufinerve, *A. davidii* and others – with the lamentable exception of *A. pensylvanicum*, the moosewood, from the eastern USA. Once fairly common, this outstanding plant is particularly desirable in the selected clone 'Erythrocladum'. It is distinguished by the bright crimson young shoots, enhancing the attributes of an already highly ornamental small tree, about 20 feet tall, but one that is to be found only after diligent and patient search.

Perhaps the most graceful and certainly one of the most uncommon maples is the 30-foot *A. pentaphyllum*. Rare in its native habitat in Szechwan, China, it is apparently available from a single source in Britain. The bright green leaves, greyish-green underneath, are made up of 4 to 7 (usually 5) narrow leaflets spread like an outstretched hand and borne on crimson stalks. By growing such a delightful tree, one of the gems in this valuable genus, we can not only embellish our gardens but help to secure the future of a species at risk in the wild.

Aconitum *Aconite, Monkshood*

Aconitum hookeri

Legend relates that the monkshood arose from the foaming mouth of Cerberus, Pluto's fearsome three-headed dog and guardian of Hades, as he fought Hercules on the hill of Aconitus. Also known as helmet flower, from the shape of the blooms, it is notorious for its extremely poisonous properties. Yet another of its common names, wolf's bane, refers to the use of the root juices to bait and kill wolves. As Gerard tells us, 'the force and facultie of Wolf's-bane is deadly to man and all kinds of beasts' and 'when the leaves hereof were by certaine ignorant persons served up in sallads, all that did eat thereof were presently taken with the most cruell symptomes, and so died.' The plants should certainly be handled with great care and gardeners are advised to wash their hands thoroughly after cutting flower spikes or dividing tubers. But as the

Victorian botanist Benjamin Maund put it, 'to discard all kinds of aconite would be rather fastidious, inasmuch as the English are not so passionately attached to a vegetable diet as to eat garden herbage indiscriminately.' Out of this vast genus of over 300 species, several are widely cultivated. At least four of them have been grown since the sixteenth century, namely *Aconitum napellus*, *A. variegatum*, *A. vulparia* (*A. lycoctonum*) and *A. anthora*. All native to Europe, they are excellent garden plants and thrive in any reasonable soil.

The stately *A. napellus*, the common monkshood, with its handsome foliage and showy, strongly hooded flowers, may range in hue from the normal indigo-blue to the rare white. The unusual pink 'Carneum' is particularly effective in cooler, moister climates where its colour appears to be heightened. Variation in height, leaf shape and flowering period occurs among the very similar plants of the *A. napellus* complex. Of these, our native *A. anglicum* is distinct for horticultural purposes in its dense, narrow flower spikes of bluish-mauve, its broad leaf segments and its early flowering. A sturdy plant of 3 to 4 feet, it is easily raised from seed but, regrettably, is not often available. The most prevalent of the complex in gardens is the graceful *A. pyramidale*, with a looser cluster of violet blooms and more delicate leaves. Again, it is readily increased from seed and also by division of the swollen carrot-shaped tubers which are typical of most of the genus.

The *A. vulparia* group, however, is distinguished by its thickened fibrous rootstocks. Botanical confusion reigns supreme in the delimitation of this species, the wolf's bane, and its relatives. Names such as *A. lycoctonum*, *A. septentrionale*, *A. lamarckii* and *A. pyrenaicum* are bandied about with various degrees of accuracy. The plants concerned usually match *A. vulparia* itself, which is up to 5 feet in height and characterised by yellow or yellowish-white, narrow-helmeted flowers, carried in 18-inch spires in midsummer above the dark green divided leaves. Slightly sinuous in habit, unlike the stout-stemmed *A. napellus* and its allies, they require staking or supportive neighbours to retain their poise in the border.

The filigree-leaved *A. anthora*, on the other hand, is a stockier European species of 2 to 3 feet, with short racemes of strongly hooded flowers of pale or orange-yellow or, in some forms, bluish-violet. It is a most elegant species and of easy culture, but seems never to have become well known.

The hybrids of *A. napellus* and *A. variegatum* (called *A.* × *bicolor* or *A.* × *cammarum*) and the late-flowering *A. carmichaelii* (sold incorrectly as *A. fischeri*), from central China, are fairly secure in gardens and still appear under different guises in the nursery trade. But they are less familiar now than earlier this century. Even comparative newcomers of the last twenty to thirty years, like the sturdy 'Bressingham Sceptre', violet and white, and the deep purple-blue 'Arendsii', a fine selection of *A. carmichaelii*, are difficult to locate.

Perhaps we should be thankful that *A. ferox* has remained a rarity in cultivation, only occasionally grown in botanic gardens. It is an insignificant-looking but highly toxic species, which in the past was applied to arrow tips for hunting and in its native Nepal was used to poison the water in wells as the British army advanced. It has had considerable medicinal importance in India and its roots are the source of bish, a drug for treating neuralgia and rheumatism.

Not all *Aconitum* species are poisonous. *A. heterophyllum* (Plate 4) is valued for its curative powers under the name *atis* or *atees* throughout northern India and, according to Dr J. F. Royle, a nineteenth-century botanist who worked there, it is 'bitter, astringent, pungent and healing, aiding digestion, useful as a tonic, and aphrodisiac'. It is widely distributed in the western Himalaya from Kumaon to Kashmir, at altitudes of between 8,000 and 13,000 feet, and inhabits moist sites at the edge of woodland or in alpine zones. From 6 inches to 3 feet in height according to altitude, it has blue dark-veined flowers, heavily marked greenish-yellow at the base of the segments – a striking and attractive combination if the plate in the *Botanical Magazine* reproduces the colours truly. It was grown in Europe during the last century but is seldom if ever encountered today.

Similar in tone is the dwarf *A. rotundifolium*, which flowered at Kew in 1912 and was figured in the same magazine two years later. It is recorded from altitudes of up to 17,000 feet in the northwest Himalaya, occurring in subalpine regions, and reaches about 6 to 15 inches in height, with the blooms a curious mix of green and purplish-blue. Some brave soul who consumed a portion of the plant lived to tell the tale: 'the tubers are very small compared with most of its congeners and are of indifferent taste; they produce none of the tingling sensation which distinguishes the poisonous Aconites.'

Most exciting for alpine and rock garden enthusiasts has been the recent introduction of several more dwarf species. Among them is the delightful and diminutive *A. hookeri*, from Kashmir, Nepal, Sikkim and Tibet, with silvery or deep-blue helmets on stems only a few inches high. Found at altitudes of 10,000 to 16,000 feet in short turf or scree conditions, it was collected on the expedition to Nepal in 1954 led by Adam Stainton, W. R. Sykes and John Williams. In fact, it may already have been in cultivation as *A. cordatum*, which was raised from seed received from Kashmir in 1928 and illustrated in 1938 in Thomas Hay's book, *Plants for the Connoisseur*. Unfortunately, stock from both introductions dwindled and *A. hookeri* has now disappeared from gardens.

In Bhutan in 1949 the collectors Frank Ludlow and George Sherriff came across a number of dwarf aconites. These grew in rock crevices of the boulder scree and on steep alpine pastures between 13,500 and 15,000 feet on the Khem La. One, which they dubbed Friar Tuck because of its rotund blooms, proved to be a new species and was named *A. fletcherianum*. Its large flowers, bright violet edged with white, are borne in August and September. Equally beautiful was the widespread *A. pulchellum*, christened Little Tich, with midget violet-purple blooms. Both were sent back as living plants, since seed could not be obtained, and for some years were grown successfully in Scotland and the north of England, flowering well but without setting seed. Both are now lost. So too after only a brief stay in our gardens are the lovely purplish-red or reddish-blue *A. naviculare*, from Nepal and Sikkim, and the intensely blue Chinese miniature, *A. delavayi*. These dwarf aconites are gems among alpines and it is to be hoped that the opportunity to reintroduce them will soon be taken.

Allium *Onion*

Allium macranthum

Onions are not generally noted for their ornamental value. But this large genus, of about 450 species distributed across the northern hemisphere, contains a surprising number of decorative garden plants in addition to the familiar edible ones. The culinary onion, the leek and garlic have been cultivated for so long that their origins are obscure. Garlic was definitely known in Britain before the Norman Conquest and was cherished for its magical power against evil spells, no doubt a reflection of its real antiseptic qualities. All the species have a pronounced oniony smell, particularly when the leaves or bulbs are rubbed. The leaves of our native ramson were also eaten, but only by 'such as are of a strong constitution, and labouring men' according to the seventeenth-century florist, John Rea.

The Elizabethans grew several *Allium* species and referred to them indiscriminately as moly, a name used by Homer. It was later applied to the golden garlic, *Allium moly*, still a popular garden plant, which was highly thought of as an ingredient in charms. But molies soon lost favour, perhaps aided by the herbalist Gerard, who was contemptuous of the superstitions or 'foolish and vaine figments' surrounding them.

The majority grow readily, sometimes too readily, in gardens and many of the most attractive ones, such as *A. christophii* and *A. giganteum*, are easy to obtain commercially. However, several highly desirable species are unjustly neglected, among them *A. macranthum*. This was described by the eminent botanist J. G. Baker in the *Botanical Magazine* of 1884 as 'one of the finest of all the Alliums that have been brought into cultivation'. It was already known to science from a single dried specimen, collected by Sir Joseph Hooker, director of Kew, in the Lachen Valley in Sikkim at an altitude of 13,000 feet. But it was only introduced some thirty years later, when the traveller and naturalist H. J. Elwes gathered living plants in the Himalaya, either in Tibet or Sikkim (not surprisingly, he was uncertain which side of the border he was on) and flowered them in his Cotswolds garden in 1883.

In July and August *A. macranthum* produces its sturdy 1- to 2-foot stems topped with large globes of up to 50 small, bright-purple flowers, which are egg-shaped and ultimately pendulous. Growing in the wild at altitudes of over 10,000 feet, it is perfectly hardy and prefers a cool, well-drained position, where it will increase and flower freely. Established plants are prolific in seed and this is the simplest method of propagation, although the swollen rootstocks may be divided in spring, which is a slower means of increase.

Two other ornamental onions have been offered sporadically in specialist catalogues over the last twenty years, but deserve much wider recognition from gardeners. *A. regelii* has a unique flower head like a candelabra, consisting of up to six whorls of papery flowers, pale pink or lilac with a darker stripe, on stems 3 to 4 foot high. It is still scarce in cultivation and the few existing plants are derived from a collection by Admiral Paul Furse from the Hindu Kush in Afghanistan in 1964. Like many bulbs from Asia it seems quite hardy, although it needs to be kept dry in summer. It is not difficult to grow in a bulb frame, where it increases gently by offsets of the main bulb and sets reasonable quantities of seed.

A. schubertii (Plate 5) is equally remarkable. About $1\frac{1}{2}$ to 2 feet in height, it bears enormous fireworks of starry pink or purplish-pink flowers, which are carried on stems of uneven length in clusters up to 1 foot across, giving it the appearance of a gigantic catherine wheel. It occurs wild in the Middle East, although there is some confusion with a related but shorter species, *A. protensum*, from Soviet central Asia and Afghanistan. Bulbs of *A. schubertii* sent from a Naples nursery to Kew flowered in a sunny border there in June 1897. Sadly it is not very hardy in Britain and normally requires a bulb frame or cold greenhouse, which no doubt explains its rarity in cultivation. It is worth every effort to acquire, both for its magnificence in bloom and for the use of its dried flower heads in arrangements. It also supplies abundant seed for propagation purposes – if one can only obtain the seed.

Alstroemeria *Peruvian lily*

Alstroemeria pelegrina

The genus *Alstroemeria* was named by Linnaeus in honour of Clas Alstroemer, a Swedish baron who is supposed to have discovered in 1753 the first species to be introduced to cultivation. *Alstroemeria pelegrina*, a native of coastal sand dunes in Chile and Peru, had 'found its way into Spain', according to the *Botanical Magazine*, 'from whence by the means of his beloved friend Alstroemer, Linnaeus first received seeds of it; the value he set on the acquisition is evident from the great care he took of the seedling plants, preserving them through the winter in his bed-chamber.'

Linnaeus was quite right to cherish it for, in addition to being slightly tender, *A. pelegrina* is one of the loveliest species. About 1 foot in height, it has the characteristic narrow, upside-down leaves clothing the stem and roughly trumpet-shaped flowers borne singly or in clusters at the top. These appear in early summer and are up to 2 inches long, usually of lilac or pinky lilac marked with purple and flushed yellow in the centre. 'Alba', a variant in creamy white with dark spots and blotches, is known as lily of the Incas and won both an Award of Merit and a First Class Certificate in the 1890s. It is believed to have reached this country in 1877, though there is some suggestion that John Wedgwood, one of the founders of the Horticultural Society, obtained it as early as 1832.

Both *A. pelegrina* itself and its white form were regularly stocked by nurseries at the beginning of this century and by Messrs Van Tubergen, the bulb merchants based in Holland, until the 1960s. But they have never been common in cultivation, mainly, it would seem, because of their lack of hardiness. Most of the fifty or so species of *Alstroemeria*, all of them native to South America, have remained rarities. As the *Botanical Register* remarked in 1839, 'it is not intelligible why those very beautiful flowers should not be more generally cultivated, for surely there is no genus more likely to reward the care of a skilful gardener.'

Another early arrival in Britain was *A. caryophyllea* (Plate 3), which was introduced in 1776 and admired by Philip Miller 'for the largeness of the flowers and for their fragrancy'. These are scarlet or scarlet and white-striped and surmount a leafy stem 8 to 12 inches high. In 1955 it was listed by Van Tubergen as 'the sweet-scented Alstroemeria . . . A very rare plant from Brazil which has been lost to cultivation for more than 150 years', although it was probably then being grown outside in Kenya and other warm countries. It was and has remained extremely scarce in Britain, where it needs greenhouse protection but makes an excellent pot plant.

The only species that has become widespread, too much so in some gardens, is the familiar orange-flowered *A. aurantiaca*, which increases from wandering fleshy roots. This is the plant generally known as Peruvian lily, although it actually hails from Chile. Unfortunately, its yellow form 'Lutea' and the large richly coloured 'Dover Orange' and 'Moerheim Orange' are now seldom seen. The Ligtu hybrids, in a wonderful range of pink, orange, flame and tangerine, have also become very popular. They are derived from *A. ligtu* and *A. haemantha* and owe their origin to 'a friendly passing bee', as the nurseryman Joe Elliott explained. His father Clarence Elliott, who collected for his own Six Hills nursery at Stevenage, reintroduced the two species from Chile in 1927. But both *A. ligtu* 'with glowing pink flowers' and *A. haemantha* 'with fiery orange blooms' are very uncommon in their own right.

Many other hybrids have been raised in the past. 'Walter Fleming', a cross between *A. aurantiaca* and *A. violacea*, received an Award of Merit in 1948 when shown from Borde Hill in Sussex. Its flowers were a striking mix of yellows and maroon. Regrettably, it is no longer available. The Peruvian lily was also responsible, with two other species, for a new race of alstroemerias bred in Holland after the Second World War by J. A. M. Goemans. 'Ballerina' appeared in 1959 and gained an AM two years later. It was followed by 'Parigo's Charm', winner of an AM in 1961, 'Afterglow' and 'Sonata'. In shades of pink, orange and yellow, all are robust plants with large, showy blooms on strong stems and, according to Goemans, are hardy enough to grow outside with winter protection. However, he refused to divulge their pedigree or release plant material to the nursery trade and chose to concentrate on cut-flower production. These beautiful hybrids are therefore denied to gardeners.

Alstroemerias are relatively easy to grow, either in a greenhouse in the case of the tender ones, or outside in fertile, well-drained soil and a sunny, sheltered position. But their fleshy roots are fragile and they dislike disturbance and for this reason may be difficult to establish. In her *Pot-pourri from a Surrey Garden* of 1897, Mrs C. W. Earle maintained that 'they do not mind moving in August after flowering, and they are best increased as Lilies of the Valley are – by digging out square pieces, filling in with good soil and dropping the pieces cut out where they are wanted . . . without disturbing the earth that clings to them.' This does not work for everyone and undoubtedly the simplest method of propagation is by seed. An article by Joe Elliott in the *Journal* of the RHS in 1984 outlines the technique admirably. Named cultivars may be increased by careful division of the clumps in spring or autumn.

Amaryllis *Belladonna lily*

Amaryllis belladonna

The rustic nymph Amaryllis, sung by the classical poets Virgil and Ovid, little realised what controversy would ensue from her name. Some botanists restrict its use to the single South African species, *Amaryllis belladonna*, the belladonna lily; others insist that it should rightfully belong to the South American species normally placed under *Hippeastrum* (and popularly called *Amaryllis*), those spectacular indoor bulbs which have become such familiar Christmas presents. *Hippeastrum* is now officially considered a separate genus, as are the closely related *Brunsvigia*, *Crinum* and *Nerine*, all formerly included under *Amaryllis*. Hybrids have been produced between *Amaryllis* and several of these allied genera, to add to the confusion. Similar bewilderment surrounds the ancestry of the various cultivars of *A. belladonna*, often for the purely practical reason that their growers did not live to see them reach maturity – in one case, some thirty years elapsed between sowing and flowering.

The belladonna lily was apparently introduced from the Cape to Britain at the beginning of the eighteenth century and is still quite generally grown. Its cluster of large trumpet-shaped blooms, sweetly scented and usually of pink turning to rose-red, is carried at the top of a stem up to 2 feet high from late summer into autumn, and is followed by green strap-like leaves. Very variable in flower colour, this beautiful plant has given rise to a number of highly desirable forms which, although well known to gardeners in the past, are not easily obtainable today.

Frequently recommended in gardening books of the last century and particular favourites of E. A. Bowles were 'those sold under the varietal names of rosea perfecta and speciosa purpurea ... flushing a deeper and richer pink every hour of their floral life till they expire in a finish of crimson'. 'Purpurea', marked purple on the segments, was depicted by Jane Loudon, wife of the industrious J. C. Loudon, in *The Ladies' Flower Garden of Ornamental Bulbous Plants* in 1841. It is possibly the same as 'Rubra', which is said to have a reddish tinge to the 3-foot flower stalk and blooms of deep pink and was rechristened 'Rubra Major' by the celebrated Dutch bulb nursery Van Tubergen. This was assumed to have come from New Zealand, but other cultivars were probably imported from South Africa, among them the rose-and-white striped 'Rosea' or 'Rosea Perfecta' already mentioned; the pale rose-pink 'Elata' or 'Pallida', also illustrated by Mrs Loudon, which is of similar height to 'Rubra' and considered equally reliable; 'Spectabilis' or 'Spectabilis Tricolor', its rose-coloured blooms, white within, grouped in substantial umbels and heavily perfumed; and the robust 'Maxima', with many deep pink flowers, which may be identical to 'Rubra'. 'A very handsome variety raised in Australia', 'Hathor' has up to 15 flowers per head, of white touched with ivory or pale gold at the throats. It won an Award of Merit in 1937 and a First Class Certificate in 1949, but is now rare like all these sadly neglected forms of the belladonna lily.

Australia may also have been the source of 'the wonderful form known as the Kew variety, a mysterious creature of whose origin many stories are afloat', in Bowles's words. *A. belladonna* 'Kewensis', as it was known, or × *Brunsdonna parkeri* is stated to be a hybrid between *A. belladonna* and the South African *Brunsvigia josephinae* and bears up to 40 flowers to a stem. These have been described as exceptionally fine and fragrant and 'almost scarlet' or dark pink 'with a flush of apricot orange in the throat'. The original cross seems to have been made in the 1840s in Sydney and then repeated by Lady Parker, wife of the governor of New South Wales, as a result of which the plant called *A. belladonna* 'Parkeri' was given to Kew in 1889 by a friend of the Parkers. A supposed seedling from this gained an AM in 1928, although whether 'Kewensis' is the same as 'Parkeri' or an improved form can only be conjecture. At Kew, unfortunately, it perished when the frame containing the bulbs was filled with soil by mistake. A cultivar with deep rosy-red blooms, sometimes encountered under the name 'Kewensis', is not the true × *Brunsdonna parkeri*, which is doubtfully in cultivation.

One of the few firms to exploit the potential of the belladonna lily was Van Tubergen, who began raising their own cultivars in the 1950s and promoted them as 'very free flowering and great improvements'. 'Jagersfontein', with

large blooms of a rich deep pink and yellowish interior, later the recipient of an
A M, and 'Johannesburg', with numerous white-throated light pink flowers,
were followed by 'Barberton', 'Capetown' (Plate 7) and several more in
different shades of rose. None has achieved the recognition they deserve and,
like the older cultivars, are seldom offered except by a few specialist nurseries.

'This plant is a fickle jade here, and unless the sun has wooed her with
unusual ardour throughout the summer, she grants no favours in buds and
blossoms in the following autumn.' The belladonna lilies undoubtedly require
plenty of sun, as Bowles observed, but are otherwise not too difficult to
accommodate in rich, well-drained soil and a sheltered position where, once
firmly established, they should flower regularly and form dense clumps. These
may be split when the leaves turn yellow in midsummer and replanted
immediately. Seed is freely produced in mild autumns and should be sown as
soon as ripe in a warm greenhouse. The seedlings often take seven to eight
years to reach flowering size and vary slightly in colour. As well as providing
fine flowers for cutting, *A. belladonna* can also be grown successfully in pots.
Given their comparative ease of culture, it seems inexplicable that the
magnificent forms of this beautiful bulb should have become so scarce.

Anchusa *Alkanet*

'The Alkanets floure and flourish in the Summer moneths: the roots doe yeeld
their bloudy juyce in harvest time.' Early writers such as Gerard, here citing
the Greek authority, Dioscorides, valued *Anchusa officinalis* chiefly for its roots.
Also known as bugloss, it and other *Anchusa* species, together with the related
Alkanna tinctoria, had been cultivated since classical times and were much
esteemed by herbalists and apothecaries for their numerous properties both
real and purported. The red dye derived from them was used in cosmetics, to
tint medicines and to dye wood and even at one period to impart a rich ruby
colour to synthetic port wine. The roots had many other virtues besides: they
were supposed to cure melancholy and hypochondria; they could be given 'to
those that have falne from some high place', as Gerard notes, and to 'drive forth
measels and small pox, if it be drunke in the beginning with hot beere'; and,
boiled with 'earth worms purged, in number twenty', they were a remedy for
'deep punctures or wounds made with thrusts'.

A genus of some fifty or so species, *Anchusa* is distributed through Europe
and North Africa to western Asia and provides some fine garden plants. Apart
from *A. officinalis* itself, an attractive violet, blue or occasionally white-
flowered perennial up to 5 feet in height, the most popular is *A. azurea*
(*A. italica*). Grown and described by Philip Miller from the Apothecaries'
Garden at Chelsea in 1768, although known from the sixteenth century in

Anchusa angustissima

gardens, it is native to southern Europe, southern USSR and the Middle East. Its branched spires of pale to deep blue flowers on 5-foot stems are most effective with lupins and irises, flowering together in June. *A. azurea* is easily raised from seed and thrives in ordinary, well-drained border soil, acid or alkaline. The various named clones, like the deep blue 'Loddon Royalist' and the dwarfer 'Little John' which have virtually replaced the older 'Dropmore', may be propagated readily from root cuttings. However, there is a tendency for seed-raised, sometimes variable, plants to be offered incorrectly under these names and the originals will quickly disappear unless steps are taken to maintain vegetatively propagated plants. 'Opal', much used by Gertrude Jekyll and invaluable for its colour of clear pale blue, is already feared to be extinct.

One species that has almost if not completely vanished from gardens is *A. barrelieri*, which bears panicles of blue or blue-violet flowers with yellow or white throats on stems 1 to 2 feet high. Grown at the Apothecaries' Garden in Chelsea before 1822, it occurs wild from Italy to the southern USSR and should not be too difficult to reintroduce from those areas. A report of this species growing in shaded conditions in Greece probably refers to the closely allied *A. serpenticola*, known only from Greece and Yugoslavia. However, there is a strange discrepancy between descriptions of *A. barrelieri*, which is sometimes regarded as perennial and sometimes demoted to annual status. In the past it was certainly considered an attractive border perennial, but its departure from the garden scene may point to its being rather short lived and possibly only biennial.

Such lack of longevity cannot be ascribed to another delightful species, *A. angustissima*, which seems to have shared a similar fate though it was figured as recently as 1963 in the *Botanical Magazine*. It is now held to be synonymous with the Turkish *A. leptophylla* subsp. *incana*, also found in the Balkans and southern USSR. Whatever its taxonomic status, it is (or perhaps was) an excellent garden plant, with numerous upright 12- to 15-inch stems clothed in narrow, bristly leaves and carrying sprays of bright blue flowers from May to late summer. Valuable for its long flowering period, it requires a sunny, sharply drained site. Its absence from nursery lists since the 1950s may be due partly to confusion with *A. caespitosa*, under which name it was frequently sold and received an Award of Merit in 1945 when shown by Messrs Bees of Chester. It has been suggested that *A. angustissima* is merely *A. caespitosa* modified by cultivation. But it quite clearly has nothing to do with this engaging Cretan species and differs not just in habit but in its much less deeply divided calyx and other botanical characteristics.

The superb *A. caespitosa* itself (Plate 9, also spelt *A. cespitosa*) we owe in cultivation to Dr Peter Davis, the taxonomist and specialist in eastern Mediterranean plants. He collected it at 7,000 feet in the White Mountains of Crete, its only definitely known location, although it has been somewhat dubiously recorded from Turkey as well. Davis's account speaks for itself:

> *Anchusa caespitosa* was so overwhelmingly beautiful that it was difficult to appreciate all the other fine plants. Running down all the cracks, flowing in wide blue mats across the scree, even in the bare earth itself, the Anchusa lay like a sapphire carpet. The flowers are as large as a threepenny bit (not of the new twelve-sided variety), and resemble those of *Lithospermum prostratum*, but their incredible blue is accentuated by a snow-white centre. Each bristly rosette, clinging like an emerald starfish to the rocks, bears so many of these wonderful flowers that the plant is completely covered with them.

This superlative alpine was described by the distinguished French botanist and naturalist Lamarck in 1785 yet, curiously enough, did not reach gardens until Davis's introduction in 1937. It gained a Certificate of Preliminary Commendation in March the following year but, owing to the confusion with *A. angustissima*, had to wait until 1960 for the accolade of the Award of Merit.

Still a collector's plant, *A. caespitosa* is now more easily obtainable from specialist nurserymen. Its reputed miffiness in cultivation has prevented it being grown more widely. However, given an open position where its fleshy roots can dive into freely draining soil, it is by no means difficult to grow, particularly with a layer of chippings to keep excess moisture away from the neck of the plant. It has been grown successfully outside in several areas of the British Isles and seems to fail only when it is too coddled, overfed or grown under stagnant air or soil conditions. Propagation is relatively simple, by division of the clumps into single rosettes soon after flowering. The rosettes are best grown in a sand frame in order to establish themselves and will quickly form neat hummocks, displaying their vivid blue flowers in April and May. A useful method of raising additional plants is from root cuttings in December or January. But few gardeners will wish to lift plants at this time of year if rosette cuttings can be taken later in the season. Seed is occasionally set on cultivated plants, though somewhat sparsely, and this is unlikely to become a source for stocks to be established.

Happily the future of *A. caespitosa* appears assured in gardens. Nevertheless, commercial supplies of uncommon plants are always at risk and may dwindle rapidly. It is therefore important for specialist alpine growers to maintain this most beautiful species in cultivation if further depredations on its already limited populations in the wild are to be prevented.

Anemone *Windflower*

Anemone glauciifolia

'This one kind of flower ... is of it selfe alone almost sufficient to furnish a garden.' Parkinson's appraisal of *A. coronaria*, 'so full of variety and so dainty, so pleasant and so delightsome', is an apt comment on the genus as a whole. Numbering about seventy species and concentrated in the northern hemisphere, this versatile race contributes some of our most decorative and useful perennial plants, spanning the seasons from the start of spring to the onset of winter.

The origin of the word anemone is unclear. It is popularly supposed to be derived from the Greek *anemos*, wind, because 'the flower hath the propertie to open but when the wind doth blow', as the Roman naturalist Pliny naively explained. The name was first employed in the fourth century BC by the botanist and philosopher Theophrastus, who also correctly identified three species found in his native Greece. One of these, *Anemone blanda*, had to wait until the present century for horticultural recognition. It is the earliest windflower to bloom and is now a firm favourite. The other two, however, *A. coronaria* and *A. pavonina*, together with the closely related *A. hortensis*, have been cherished in gardens for over three hundred years. In their many cultivated guises they were equally familiar to Parkinson as their descendants are to us today.

Principal parent of the de Caen and St Brigid anemones, *A. coronaria* is distributed throughout the Mediterranean region, its large poppy-shaped flowers ranging from pink, red or violet to white. Like other historic plants, it has a tale to tell: at the time of the Crusades, the bishop of Pisa arrived in the Holy Land 'just too late to be of any use' and returned home with sacred soil for the burial ground of his cathedral, in which the scarlet anemones miraculously sprang up – or so it seemed to the faithful, despite the fact that the plants already grew wild in Italy. In any case, Europeans apparently became aware of *A. coronaria* in a cultivated rather than wild state and it had presumably filtered to the west via Constantinople in the sixteenth century, on the same pattern as the tulip and ranunculus.

'Myselfe have in my garden twelve different sorts', boasted Gerard, 'and yet I do heare of divers more, differing very notably from any of these; every new yeare bringeth with it new and strange kinds.' Already known in numerous forms, the poppy anemones were highly prized on the continent. Another story, set in Holland or France, relates how a local dignitary had to resort to subterfuge to obtain a particularly fine breed which the raiser refused to part with: he donned official robes to visit the garden where the coveted anemones grew and by walking between the flower beds managed to trap the seeds in his furred hem. As well as Holland and France, Italy was a major source of supply in the seventeenth century and was celebrated for double plush anemones with a 'great tuft like Silke or Plush' in the middle. The gentleman gardener Sir Thomas Hanmer lists more than fifty named forms in his *Garden Book* of 1659, remarking that they were 'very much esteemed both here and abroad, and there is good variety of them, and great lovelines in them.' The singles too came in 'almost all colors', sometimes with stripes or other markings.

The cultivation of anemones around Caen and Bayeux in northern France dates from the eighteenth century. In England, as Philip Miller observed, they had been 'so greatly improved by culture as to render them some of the chief ornaments of our gardens'. They soon joined the ranks of the florists' flowers and in this capacity were 'well known' in 1829, according to J. C. Loudon. 'Semidouble flowers are in nearly as much repute as double ones', he maintained, and 'many new varieties have been raised from seed,' although 'they are not named by the florists, as in the case of tulips and pinks.' Perhaps this was a factor in their relatively short existence. Unfortunately, the poppy anemone did not long survive its elevation to the specialists' sphere. Blaming 'the rage for novelty', the *Botanical Magazine* noted its decline as early as 1805 and this was to continue steadily as the century progressed.

A. coronaria is now largely represented by the de Caen and St Brigid anemones. Since the establishment of commercial cultivation in Cornwall in the 1920s, its fortunes have revived as one of our most popular cut flowers. With double or semi-double blooms, the St Brigid race owes its inception in the 1880s to Mrs Lawrenson of Dublin, who wrote gardening articles under the *nom de plume* St Brigid (and also grew the exquisite 'St Brigid' form of *Helleborus niger*). Others carried on her work in Ireland, including the daffodil nurseryman and tulip rescuer, W. B. Hartland of Cork, and William Reamsbottom of Co. Offaly, whose Alderborough breed received an AM in 1902. Little remains of their achievements and, with the disappearance of the old florists' varieties and a sparsity of named cultivars, the gardener's choice is now invariably limited to mixed collections of St Brigids or de Caens. The discriminating E. A. Bowles grew *A. coronaria* in its own right, but he was exceptional and the species itself is seldom seen.

In the same way, its near ally *A. pavonina* has been virtually superseded by the St Bavo race derived from it. The peacock anemone is mainly distinguished from the poppy anemone by less dissected leaves and bracts, the flowers varying in colour from scarlet, purple, pink and whitish, often with a dark centre or pale base. Grown by Gerard and depicted in Dutch paintings of the sixteenth century, it too has been selected for generations. It was much confused with another member of this group, the European *A. hortensis* (or *A. stellata*), a smaller version with starry, narrow-tepalled blooms generally in shades of violet and rose. Hanmer, who refers to them indiscriminately as 'Hard or Great Leav'd Anemones', describes the assortment of single forms, usually with 'a white bottome', in 'Scarletts, Crimsons, Gridelines, Carnations, Pinkes, Whites and Ash colour' and striped, and the 'many fine colour'd Starrs' or doubles.

Several different kinds were still available at the beginning of this century, despite the temporary eclipse of *A. pavonina* reported by William Curtis, founder of the *Botanical Magazine*, in the issue of 1790: this 'most charming spring plant, with which the Gardens abounded in the time of Parkinson, is now a great rarity,' he complained, obviously to good effect because, within a few years, it had apparently returned to favour. Curtis also stated that 'roots of a variety of this plant with scarlet double flowers are imported from Holland . . . and sold at a high price.' Perhaps this was the same as 'Chapeau de Cardinal', admired by both William Robinson and Bowles but, along with other named cultivars, since lost.

The peacock anemone flourishes in full sun and well-drained soil, increasing freely from self-sown seed. But, though considered easier to grow than its highly bred progeny and its relatives, it is little cultivated today. The star anemone, on the other hand, is among the least amenable of the tuberous species and its elusiveness more understandable. Bowles pointed out the incongruity of its epithet *hortensis*, which means 'belonging to gardens'. However, he regarded it as 'one of the most magnificently coloured of all wild plants' and far superior to its garden forms. He was especially fond of the Greek variant, with broader-tepalled flowers of scarlet, pink or white and sometimes white bands in the middle.

A. × *fulgens*, a probable hybrid between *A. hortensis* and *A. pavonina*, luckily inherits the tractable nature of the latter and multiplies rapidly if left undisturbed in a sunny spot. In Robinson's day it carpeted the vineyards of southern France and used to be imported from there annually by the Reverend C. Wolley Dod of Cheshire, an alpine enthusiast, who seems to have had no qualms about its survival in the wild. Its large blooms appear in May and are of brilliant scarlet, with a black boss of stamens usually surrounded by a creamy yellow ring. Occasionally offered in catalogues, it certainly deserves to be more widely cultivated.

'The stocks or kindred of the anemones or windeflowers ... are without number,' declared Gerard. He was acquainted with several species including, not surprisingly, Britain's native wood anemone *A. nemorosa*, which he grew in purple, blush and double white forms. Normally single and white with a pink tinge, its flowers bedeck the woodlands in March and April. However, it is a very variable plant, broadly dispersed as it is across northern Europe to western Siberia, and its countless varieties in the wild have given rise to many garden forms, named and unnamed, over the years.

Some of the oldest have been cultivated since the sixteenth century, among them the double white or 'Alba Plena', probably the one grown by Gerard; 'Bracteata', 'that eccentric Mad Hatter and March Hare in one', as Bowles dubbed it, with loosely double white flowers striped or frilled with green; and the double purple mentioned by the Flemish botanist Clusius in the sixteenth century but now extinct. Their heyday was the late Victorian and Edwardian period, when numerous forms were discovered or developed and ably promoted by Bowles in *My Garden in Spring*. Some came from Ireland – the tall white 'Grandiflora' or 'Alba Major' and the late-blooming 'Blue Bonnet', in addition to the more recent 'Lismore Pink' and 'Lismore Blue'. The lavender blue 'Robinsoniana', located by its namesake in Oxford University Botanic Garden, may also have been Irish. Bowles clearly preferred 'Allenii', 'the largest and loveliest of blue Wood Anemones', and 'Blue Queen', 'the brightest blue of any', which were both raised by James Allen of Shepton Mallet. 'A good soft blue', 'Purpurea', was marketed by the enterprising German nurseryman, Max Leichtlin of Baden-Baden, together with the pure white button double 'Vestal', of uncertain origin. Another of Bowles's treasures was 'Leed's Variety', also called 'Dr Lowe's Variety' and possibly the same as

'Wilks's Giant'. Similar plants may occur from seed in gardens. 'Perfectly shaped and formed like a single Rose . . . its bright green, ample leaves make a fine background for the large flowers . . . nearly two inches in diameter.'

Such diversity is denied to most present-day gardeners, although a few examples of *A. nemorosa* in its various guises may be seen at Cliveden in Buckinghamshire and other great gardens. It is an undemanding plant and quickly naturalises itself in a cool, shady situation and moist, leaf-rich soil. But of the fifteen or so forms portrayed by Bowles, less than half are obtainable and these only from specialist nurseries.

Akin to the wood anemone in appearance and cultural needs is the yellow *A. ranunculoides*. It was also grown by Gerard and known in various forms, among them a double and semi-double, which Bowles thought 'pretty and well worth growing'. Its hybrid with *A. nemorosa, A × seemannii* (*A. × lipsiensis* or *A. × intermedia*), frequently occurs where the parents grow together. A pale sulphur or lemon yellow, it is one of the earliest anemones to bloom, in February. Despite their charms, none of these anemones feature regularly in modern catalogues.

At the other end of the season, the Japanese anemones are among the most valuable of autumn-flowering plants and often last until the frosts. They have been well established in gardens for more than a century, their beauty undimmed by universality. Their wild progenitor, *A. hupehensis*, from western and central China, did not reach Britain until the 1900s. It has always been a horticultural rarity, if a desirable one, with its clear pink flowers of 5 or 6 rounded tepals, crimson on the outside, and its deeply incised leaves. In a semi-double form, however, now known as *A. hupehensis* var. *japonica*, it had long been cultivated by the Chinese and Japanese, traditionally planted in cemeteries. In 1843 it was found by the great collector Robert Fortune on his mission for the Horticultural Society 'in full flower amongst the graves of the natives, which are around the ramparts of Shanghae' and was brought back by him from China the following year. Of similar height to *A. hupehensis*, up to 2 feet, and blooming slightly later in September and October, its carmine-rose flowers are composed of some 20 narrow segments. Although it was re-collected by George Forrest and others, it was believed to be an extremely rare plant in gardens. However it may prove to be much more widely grown than was previously suspected.

A. vitifolia (Plate 8), with lobed, vine-like leaves and white blooms carried on woolly stems, had preceded it in 1829. According to Nathaniel Wallich, director of the Calcutta Botanic Garden, it was 'one of the commonest, as well as the most ornamental of flowering plants in Nepal', but in cultivation it has remained scarce, no doubt because of its reputed tenderness. It was the hybridisation of this species with *A. hupehensis* var. *japonica*, at the Horticultural Society gardens in Chiswick in 1848, that resulted in the common pink Japanese anemone *A. × hybrida*, popularly called *A. japonica*. About ten years later, this produced a white-flowered sport at a French nursery in Verdun, which was named 'Honorine Jobert' after the daughter of the owner. Together these two originals still reign supreme in gardens, impervious to competition from the many forms since created. Their elegant pink or white blooms are borne from August onwards on stately stems up to 5 feet tall above clumps of dark green foliage. Fibrous-rooted, they make excellent garden plants, thriving in ordinary soil and often monopolising it, tolerant of shade and readily propagated from seed, by root cuttings or division.

Some thirty years elapsed before breeders realised the potential of the Japanese anemones. A semi-double white, 'Whirlwind', from the USA, was put into commerce in 1887, followed three years later by 'Lady Ardilaun'. The latter, a superlative form of the white Japanese anemone, was a seedling from 'Honorine Jobert' raised by the head gardener to the Ardilaun family of Co. Galway. It was used by nurserymen on the Continent, notably Messrs Lemoine of Nancy in France, to develop numerous named clones exhibiting 'the greatest diversity of variation in habit, size of flower, doubleness and also in colouring'. Just as easy to grow as the common Japanese anemones, these were warmly welcomed by British gardeners in the early twentieth century.

Only a few stalwarts linger now, such as the American 'Whirlwind', the French 'Mont Rose', and the German 'Queen Charlotte', 'Luise Uhink', 'Lorelei' and 'Prinz Heinrich' (sometimes wrongly listed as 'Profusion'). More modern cultivars, 'Margarete' and 'Bressingham Glow', have also been added. The large white 'Géante des Blanches', which is now known as 'White Queen' and was apparently received unnamed from Holland, may be the same as 'Lady Ardilaun', although there is no proof. However, other classics like 'Beauté Parfaite', 'Coupe d'Argent', 'Collerette' and 'Vase d'Argent' can no longer be traced. Of some thirty forms listed by E. A. Bowles and W. T. Stearn in a 1947 article, none is widely offered today.

Not all anemones are so willingly tamed and some lie tantalisingly beyond the gardener's grasp. 'One of the most beautiful species of the whole genus, the handsome leaves and the delicately rose-coloured, silky flowers exceeding all others in size and gracefulness', is *A. capensis*, which was introduced from South Africa as long ago as 1795. Its pink-tinted blooms, paler within, appear in March and April and are borne singly or in pairs on stems 1 to 2 feet high arising from the stout woody rootstock. It is a greenhouse plant in Britain and has proved resistant to cultivation even in its homeland. According to Marloth's *Flora of South Africa*, it is confined to moist localities in the wild and, unlike the common Japanese anemone, has been a failure in the gardens of the Cape.

Of more recent introduction but equally stubborn in horticultural terms, the tap-rooted *A. glauciifolia* is 'a very beautiful and in every way remarkable species', as the *Botanical Magazine* expressed it in 1925. Native to the Chinese provinces of Yunnan and Szechwan, where it grows in dry alpine pastures at up to 10,000 feet, it was discovered by the French missionary J. M. Delavay and then collected several times by Forrest. From seed sent home by him, it first flowered in 1922 and won the accolade of an FCC the same year. Its flowers of 'deep soft blue' or 'pale soft purplish-blue', in Forrest's words, and up to 4 inches in diameter, are produced in June, singly or in small clusters on stems up to 3 feet high, set off by the silvery leaves. It requires the protection of a cold greenhouse or frame in winter, but has never taken kindly to gardens and, although grown at Kew after its arrival, has apparently slipped from cultivation.

A happier outcome attended *A. biflora*, when tubers were received at Kew in 1936 from a German resident at Tabriz in Persia and flowered in March the following year. This striking anemone, about 10 inches in height, was originally described in 1818 and resembles *A. coronaria*, but differs in the blunter foliage and in having two to three flowers per stem, ranging in colour from bright red or deep crimson to orange or bronzy yellow. An inhabitant of stony hillsides in Iran and neighbouring countries, it adapts well to cultivation in the alpine house, as its successful record at Kew demonstrates. A close relative, *A. petiolulosa*, with brilliant yellow, red-flushed blooms, is found in similar conditions in central Asia and responds to similar cultural treatment. Neither is difficult to grow and both merit greater attention from gardeners to safeguard their position in cultivation.

Aquilegia *Columbine*

The British native columbine *Aquilegia vulgaris* is a classic of cottage gardens and has been grown since at least the fourteenth century. Both the official and the familiar name are suggested by the distinctive shape of the flower, a wide funnel framed with spreading petals which have spurs at the back and resemble birds – either an eagle (*aquila* in Latin) or a dove (*columba*). A more expressive popular name is granny's bonnet. Like other herbaceous aquilegias, it flourishes in almost any situation and seeds itself recklessly, crossing with and usually dominating other species. Division is the only sure method of propagating garden-grown forms and species of *Aquilegia* true to type, but this is not always successful since they are fleshy-rooted and resent disturbance. However, some of the modern seed stocks have been carefully selected and come reasonably true.

Flowering in early summer, the common columbine is very variable and may be 'sometimes blue, at other times of a red or purple, often white or of mixed colours' as Gerard noted. A pure white variant with delicate grey-green leaves, *A. vulgaris* var. *nivea*, was Gertrude Jekyll's favourite and came to be known as 'Munstead White' after her famous Surrey home, Munstead Wood. At the

Aquilegia nivalis

Wisley aquilegia trials in 1914, it was described as 'erect-growing, free-flowering, short-spurred, white; 30 inches'. A nursery list of the 1930s compared it more poetically to 'flights of fan-tailed pigeons'. This beautiful white columbine increases with the usual freedom and will breed fairly true if kept apart from its allies. In the past it seems to have relied mainly on personal rather than commercial distribution for its existence, like the wallflowers, primroses and other quaint plants which neighbours used to exchange among themselves. Today it is conspicuous by its absence from the catalogues, dominated as they are by the modern long-spurred hybrids, and could disappear from gardens too unless efforts are made to retrieve it.

Not all the seventy-odd members of the genus are so robust or amenable. The alpine and sub-alpine species are notoriously temperamental in cultivation and this 'causes them to thrive so well in the north of Scotland while they fail in our ordinary dry garden borders', as William Robinson complained. Some of the most exquisite will no doubt stay within the province of the specialist. *A. nivalis* (Plate 10), for instance, was 'reported a small and special beauty' when Reginald Farrer was writing early this century. Native to Kashmir, it grows sparsely and in a restricted area at an altitude of about 10,500 feet, usually on the slopes of open gullies. The large, solitary, short-spurred flowers, nodding, horizontal or sometimes pointing skywards, are of a dark purple or deep blue with a nearly black centre. According to one observer, the colour 'is of a brilliance that makes it visible from a considerable distance despite its 3- to 6-inch stature'.

Though known for at least a hundred years (and confused with *A. jucunda*) and collected on several occasions, the snow columbine has never secured a firm place in cultivation. A plant was exhibited in 1962, raised from seed obtained by the naturalist, collector and author Oleg Polunin. Another one brought back from the Himalaya was examined by an RHS committee in 1965 but said to have 'only flowered twice in a period of about fifteen years'.

A more promising candidate for the garden is *A. jonesii*, discovered in 1873 by Captain W. A. Jones, leader of an expedition into northwest Wyoming. It inhabits the high limestone ridges and barren slopes of the Rockies, from Wyoming and beyond to the Canadian border and into Alberta, at altitudes up to 10,000 feet. Although restricted to a few sites in the wild, it occurs there 'in the greatest abundance ... as neatly and regularly as though set out by an addict of carpet bedding'. Its huge flowers, of a bold blue or purple with paler centre and short, straight spurs, are carried singly and erect on squat stems and seem out of all proportion to the neat, tufted foliage. According to a New York horticultural journal in 1896, this 'most distinct and beautiful of the American columbines' was 'still untried in gardens'. Some twenty years later Farrer was hoping 'that Mr. Jones will now hasten up there again to procure us his Columbine' and even in 1939 collectors were berated for the fact that it had 'remained so long unobtainable'. Its rarity in cultivation has apparently owed more to negligence than to ignorance. Unfortunately *A. jonesii* is not always free-flowering in nature, still less in cultivation, although it can be grown successfully as a pot plant, in tufa or in scree conditions in full sun. Seldom offered in the trade, it is one of those plants that will probably depend on specialist care for its horticultural survival.

Asclepias *Milkweed*

Called after Aesculapius, the Roman god of medicine, the genus *Asclepias* is relatively unfamiliar in Britain. It numbers at least 120 species, found mostly in North America, and includes some hardy and vigorous plants whose handsome appearance should recommend them to a wider audience. They are perennials, usually with fleshy tuberous roots, and exude a milky sap if the stems are broken, whence the name milkweed. Another name is silkweed, from the silky hairs surrounding the seeds. The floss from the common milkweed, *Asclepias syriaca* or *A. cornuti*, was used as a stuffing for pillows by colonists in New England, whose governor, John Winthrop, sent seeds home in 1670; during the Second World War, it provided a substitute for kapok in the life jackets of the US navy. The flowers of these curious plants are borne in clusters and are distinctive for the hood of folded-back petals and five projecting horns resembling a miniature crown. The central column of fixed stamens and styles which forms the horns is designed to ensure that visiting insects in search of nectar remove the pollen sacs and deposit them at their next port of call.

'One of the finest of the genus', so the *Botanical Magazine* claimed in 1848, is *A. speciosa* (Plate 14), 'a native of the western side of the Rocky Mountains, where it was detected by Douglas'. Also known for a time as *A. douglasii*, after

Asclepias speciosa

the famous Scottish plant collector, it reached Britain in 1846 and first flowered at the nursery of Messrs Lucombe, Pince & Co., Exeter. Its stout, woolly stems, 2 to 3 feet high or more, are clad with large, oval leaves, bright green above and downy beneath, and surmounted by crowded heads of reddish-purple flowers from June to August. It is a fine perennial, spreading gently underground by means of its rootstock, and was grown at Wisley for over forty years.

A. speciosa has several close relatives, among them the common milkweed, *A. syriaca*, which is about 4 feet high with dull purple blooms; the smaller swamp milkweed, *A. incarnata*, with narrower leaves and rose-pink flowers; and, the most sought-after, *A. hallii*. The similarity between them has caused confusion and a more recent account in the *Botanical Magazine*, in 1958, disputes the earlier one of 1848 by suggesting that *A. speciosa* itself was first collected in 1820 by the American botanical explorer Dr Edwin P. James. The name *A. hallii* has also been applied, incorrectly, to cultivated plants of *A. speciosa*.

A. hallii was formerly known as *A. ovalifolia*, and seems to have been collected in about 1863 near Denver, Colorado, by the American surveyor Elihu Hall. It was named in his honour in 1877 by Dr Asa Gray, the distinguished professor of botany at Harvard. Although generally resembling *A. speciosa*, it is smaller – only 8 to 20 inches high, according to one authority – with a rather slender stem, sometimes branched at the base, and leaves covered with a greyish bloom and fine hairs on the underside. The fairly large flowers are carried in groups of about ten and are of pale livid rose or purple. In its natural habitat it occurs on stony slopes and roadsides, distributed from Wyoming and Colorado to Nevada and northern Arizona.

Clearly *A. hallii* was still a rarity when it was illustrated in the *Gardeners' Chronicle* of 1900, from 'a plant obligingly furnished by W. E. Gumbleton, Esq, Belgrove, Queenstown, who obtained it from Herrn Max Leichtlin, of Baden-Baden', the German nursery firm responsible for many introductions of the period. So it has remained, despite the efforts of other plantsmen after Gumbleton. As the same article pointed out, it is perfectly hardy and it is not difficult to grow, given a peaty, moisture-retentive soil and a sunny, sheltered situation. Planting is best carried out in the spring and propagation at the same time of year, by careful division of the roots. It is ironic that its eye-catching but unreliable relative, the bright orange-red butterfly silkweed *A. tuberosa*, should be comparatively better known when *A. hallii* has so much to recommend it as a worthwhile garden plant.

Aspidistra

Aspidistra elatior 'Variegata'

The aspidistra reached this country shortly before gas lighting became widespread in the 1840s. Its ability to withstand fumes soon earned it a place on the what-not in the Victorian drawing room and by the 1930s it had become a cliché among houseplants and the butt of music-hall songs.

Aspidistra elatior (also offered as *A. lurida*, a distinct but seldom grown species) is *the* aspidistra. It was introduced in 1824 by John Damper Parks, a collector for the Horticultural Society who is better known for his acquisition of one of the original tea roses, 'Parks's Yellow China'. The genus contains about eight species native to China, Japan and the eastern Himalaya. It is named from the Greek *aspidiseon*, meaning small round shield, which is probably a reference to the mushroom-shaped stigma of the flowers. These fleshy protuberances, of a dull purple, arise on short stalks directly from the rhizome at soil level. Only occasionally produced, they have the dubious distinction of being pollinated by slugs and are the least significant part of the plant. The foliage has always been the main feature – large, tough, shiny dark green leaves which are broadly sword-shaped and up to 30 inches in length.

No one could call the aspidistra spectacular or rare. But it has a handsome variegated form 'Variegata' (Plate 11), which has unfortunately become very uncommon. The leaves are marked with alternate stripes of creamy white and green, making it altogether a more striking plant. According to *Addisonia*, the journal of the New York Botanic Garden, in 1934, this is the 'most desirable' form, although 'it must be grown in poor soil or the variegation disappears.'

Poor soil is the frequent fate of the long-suffering aspidistra, together with lack of light and water, extremes of temperature and mistreatment which few other plants could survive. As *Addisonia* pointed out (just after the end of Prohibition), 'cases are known of this plant growing in the alcohol-laden air of the old saloon or in more modern speakeasies and beer gardens, receiving its only moisture in the form of discarded beer or dishwater.' It can also be planted outside, where it is almost hardy and provides good evergreen ground cover. Despite its tolerance of general neglect, the aspidistra will obviously respond to proper care and attention – watering and feeding as for any ordinary houseplant and sponging of the foliage to keep it glossy. Propagation is best carried out in spring by careful division of the congested rootstock or by the removal of suckers.

The variegated aspidistra is a prime example of a plant which has been taken so much for granted in the past that it has gradually slipped into oblivion without anyone noticing.

Bomarea

'Bomareas have gone, as so many other good plants have, into limbo.' This was the complaint of a correspondent to *The Garden* in 1920, who could remember when they were grown in quantity at Kew. Judging by William Robinson's entry on these 'curious and handsome plants' in *The English Flower Garden*, they were quite familiar to Victorian gardeners. Today, *Bomarea* seldom rates a mention in the average gardening book.

The genus was named in honour of J. C. V. de Bomare, a French patron of science in the eighteenth century, and contains some 150 species native to South America, the West Indies and Mexico. It is closely related to *Alstroemeria*, the main difference being its normally twining habit. The flowers are similarly trumpet-shaped and are produced from summer to autumn in a gorgeous array of colours, while the leaves are inverted in the same distinctive fashion. Bomareas are generally best grown in the greenhouse, which is

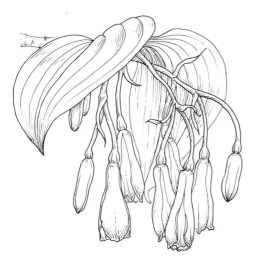

Bomarea carderi

probably one reason why they are so seldom seen today. But they make excellent pot plants and are relatively easy to manage if treated like alstroemerias. Some have even proved successful outside in milder districts and at Kew. According to Robinson, *Bomarea edulis* (so called for its edible tubers) flowered well 'after surviving a temperature of 25° below freezing' in Devon. *B. glaucescens* from Bolivia is another species that has flourished in the West Country and the hybrid *B. × cantabrigiensis* has for many years adorned a sheltered wall at the Cambridge Botanic Garden.

One of the earliest arrivals in Europe, and one of the few non–climbing species, is *B. andimarcana* (Plate 12). Seed was collected by William Lobb, one of the most successful employees of the Exeter nurserymen James Veitch & Son, in the Andamarca mountains of Peru and the resulting plants first flowered in April 1846. Of tall, luxuriant growth, its leafy stem is hung at the top with striking tubular flowers about 2 inches long, composed of three outer petals of orange-red tipped with black, three inner ones of yellow flaked with green, and a tuft of golden anthers in the centre.

The firm of Veitch was also responsible for the introduction of *B. caldasii* in 1863. An inhabitant of Colombia and Ecuador, it was gathered by their collector Richard Pearce in the Andes near Quito and named after F. J. de Caldas, director of the Bogota observatory. This is a twining plant like most of its fellows and bears clusters of up to twenty blooms, orange-yellow edged with green on the outside and spotted crimson within. Another native of Colombia, *B. carderi* reached this country in 1876. It was secured by Mr Carder, of Shuttleworth & Carder, importers of new plants, Clapham, on behalf of William Bull of Chelsea, the orchid specialists. It carries a large head of bell-like flowers, rose with purplish-brown dots inside. At Kew it often grew to 20 feet in height.

B. kalbreyeri was obtained in Colombia by M. W. Kalbreyer, another Veitch recruit. It has magnificent blooms of brick-red and orange-yellow grouped at the end of the stem and apparently made its début in 1883. However, the editor of the French *Revue Horticole* for that year claimed in somewhat aggrieved tones that he had already discovered this and other species and brought them to Europe in 1880. Whatever the case, neither the genus as a whole nor these species in particular enjoy the horticultural recognition they so manifestly deserve.

Brassica *Cabbage*

Brassica balearica

That staple of the British diet, the cabbage, has been cultivated since earliest times. The species from which most of the garden forms derive, *Brassica oleracea*, is a cliff-dweller of the western shores of Britain, France and Spain as well as coastal regions of the northern Mediterranean. Confronted with its broad, spreading, wavy-edged, greyish-green leaves and large panicles of yellow flowers, it is hard to relate this wild plant to the cabbages, kale and brussels sprouts of the greengrocer's shop. But it has been valued in its various guises for well over two thousand years as a food of prime importance.

Colewort, the general name for brassicas in Gerard's day, included 'a certain kinde hereof with the leaves wrapped together into a round head or globe. . . . This is the great ordinary Cabbage knowne everywhere, and as commonly eaten all over this kingdome.' It had many other attributes apart from the edible, among them the alleviation of sunburn and rheumatism, the removal of freckles and, taken raw before meat, the capacity to 'preserve a man from drunkenness' in Gerard's words. The ancients also used this humble vegetable, as a remedy for eye complaints and 'the bitings of venomous beasts', according to the Greek herbalist Dioscorides, and to cure deafness, as the Roman naturalist Pliny suggests.

Sadly, most of the primitive cultivars of cabbage have disappeared and even the more recent selections, which may be of genetic potential if little commercial consequence, can very seldom be found. Out of the vast range of different types described in the 1885 English edition of *The Vegetable Garden* by Vilmorin-Andrieux, only a few are extant. The tree or Jersey kale, for instance, with its straight, woody, 6-foot stems, just survives.

The thirty or so species of *Brassica* recognised by taxonomists include annuals, biennials, perennials and some small shrubs such as *B. rupestris* from Sicily and southern Italy. A number of species native to the islands of the Mediterranean are of very limited population, though not in immediate danger of extinction. *B. macrocarpa*, for instance, a shrub of 1 to 2 feet with yellow heads of flowers, occurs only on maritime rocks in Isole Egadi, Sicily. The similar but slightly smaller *B. balearica*, with leathery, dark-green, oak-like leaves and dense racemes of sweetly scented lemon-yellow flowers, is confined to Mallorca.

It is curious that such attractive plants have not been grown and distributed widely in our gardens. Both have been known to botanists since the early nineteenth century and, while they are restricted in range, their habitats are not inaccessible. *B. balearica* (Plate 15) at least has secured a place in several botanic gardens after recent collections. A delightful spring-flowering small shrub for the cool greenhouse or alpine house, it is easy to maintain and readily propagated from cuttings of young vegetative growth, root suckers or seed. Given a well-drained site in a dry wall akin to the limestone rock fissures of its home, it may well prove hardy in many areas of the British Isles. However, caution would dictate overwintering one or two plants under glass to avoid possible disaster in extreme winters.

It is not enough simply to condemn further collection in the wild of threatened endemics like *B. balearica*. Their propagation and dissemination from cultivated material should be encouraged as an important part of an overall conservation policy. By ensuring that a rare species is available through the nursery trade, its total loss can be prevented should its natural habitat be destroyed; and by making it relatively common in gardens, it becomes less vulnerable to collectors motivated merely by personal kudos or gain.

Caesalpinia

Caesalpinia japonica (Plate 19) belongs to a genus of about forty species of trees and shrubs of the pea family, native to the tropical and sub-tropical regions of the world. The name commemorates A. Caesalpini, a sixteenth-century Italian botanist, philosopher and physician to the Pope. Several Asian and South American species have commercial value as Sappan and Brazil wood, which are

Caesalpinia japonica

a source of dye. Only two or three can be grown in British gardens, and in milder areas at that. The spectacular *C. gilliesii*, sometimes known as bird of paradise, has masses of rich yellow flowers with long scarlet stamens. Introduced from Argentina in 1829, it is too tender to have become widely cultivated, although it will succeed against a hot, sunny wall in very sheltered gardens. *C. japonica* is somewhat hardier, but still appreciates the shelter of a wall or recess. That great authority, W. J. Bean, considered 'there are few shrubs more beautiful in leaf or flower.' It is a loose, straggling bush up to 15 feet high if trained to a support and has dainty deciduous leaves similar to an acacia, of a soft green, and branches armed with formidable thorns. In June and July the flowers appear, grouped in long spires, of a brilliant canary yellow with the upper petals striped red and a conspicuous cluster of red stamens in the centre. Closely akin to *C. japonica* and possibly a variant is *C. sepiaria*. It differs chiefly in having very downy wood and is common throughout India, where it is used for hedging.

   C. japonica was brought to Britain by the famous nurserymen James Veitch & Sons in 1881 and first flowered in their premises at Coombe Wood, Surrey, in 1887, having stood several years undamaged by frost, according to James Veitch. In 1888 it won a First Class Certificate. It seems to have caught on quickly with the gardening public and was soon being recommended in popular publications. William Robinson wrote of it as 'a graceful and distinct summer-leafing shrub or low tree, even at this early date after its introduction proving a picturesque one'. He continued: 'It grows well with me in very poor soil and seems quite happy as a wall or bank bush.' Around the same period, *C. japonica* was planted at Nymans in Sussex, where it was apparently 'perfectly hardy . . . and thrives in an open bed', the foliage being 'improved if pruned hard each spring'. At Kew it has flourished on a west wall and in one of the bays of the Temperate House. At Wisley, on the south-facing wall of the potting shed, it recovered after the severe winter of 1962–3, although it subsequently collapsed and died.

C. japonica has been particularly successful in the warmer parts of Britain. As the *Botanical Magazine* stated in 1908, 'in some Cornish and Irish gardens it is quite at home.' Elsewhere it requires a sunny situation and shelter, but otherwise makes no special demands on the gardener and is often long-lived. Since seed is only occasionally produced in cultivation and cuttings do not root easily, the most reliable method of propagation is by layering of the low basal growths. Among the very few gardens where this lovely shrub can be seen today is Jenkyn Place in Hampshire, Powis Castle in Wales and Trelissick in Cornwall. It should certainly be sought out and grown more widely.

Camellia

Camellia granthamiana

Tea may be the great British beverage, but many of its devotees will be surprised to learn that it is made from camellia leaves. The tea bush, *Camellia sinensis*, has been cultivated since time immemorial by the Chinese and the drink was enjoyed by them long before it reached the West in the seventeenth century. It was still a novelty in Restoration England, when Samuel Pepys recorded in his diary that 'I did send for a cup of tee (a China drink) of which I had never drunk before.' *Ch'a* in Mandarin dialect is the word for both tea and camellia. Other species, notably *C. oleifera*, are valued as a source of vegetable oil, which is extracted from the seeds, and in southern China they are grown in plantations for this purpose.

The genus was named by Linnaeus after the Jesuit G. J. Kamel or Camellus, author of a botanical history of Luzon in the Philippines. It consists of some eighty species of evergreen trees and shrubs, native to Asia and often fairly restricted in their natural habitats. This explains why many have only recently become known. The common camellia, *C. japonica*, was imported to Europe at the beginning of the eighteenth century and is one of our most popular shrubs, with countless cultivars available. Curiously enough, it was treated as a conservatory plant for nearly two hundred years, until its outdoor hardiness in sheltered situations was convincingly demonstrated during some bitter winters of the 1920s. Other species, notably *C. saluenensis*, *C. reticulata* and *C. cuspidata* are firmly established in gardens, together with the familiar *C.* × *williamsii* hybrids. But a number of very fine camellias, some quite newly described, have yet to gain more than a tenuous foothold in cultivation.

One of the most remarkable discoveries occurred in October 1955, when a Chinese forester found a camellia growing wild in the Hong Kong New Territories, a region which had already been thoroughly combed by plant collectors. Though well versed in the local flora, he did not recognise it and it proved to be a new and botanically very distinct species. *C. granthamiana* (Plate 13) is a superb shrub about 7 foot high, with spreading branches and polished dark green leaves, veined on top and warty on the underside. It produces an abundance of large, white, waxen flowers, 5 inches or more in diameter, in late autumn. Named in honour of the governor of the colony, Sir Alexander Grantham, it was quickly introduced to the USA and Britain and may now be seen in a few specialist collections, although no longer at Kew or Wisley where the single plants grown have been lost. In Britain it needs greenhouse protection but is otherwise undemanding and makes a fine pot plant like its relatives, thriving in a well-drained, acid, leafy compost. It is normally grafted on *C. japonica* since cuttings do not root readily.

C. granthamiana may be almost extinct in the wild and until recently was known only from the single tree located by Mr Lau in 1955, which was then probably about seventy years old. Fortunately, the lesson has been learned from another Hong Kong species, *C. crapnelliana*, also white-flowered but with a brick-red bark believed to be unique to the genus. This was reduced to one plant when it was discovered in 1903 and, because it was not propagated then, was subsequently presumed lost. Further examples only came to light some sixty-five years later. *C. granthamiana* itself is now reasonably secure in cultivation. It has already been used for hybridising and attempts have been made to cross it with allied genera such as *Franklinia*. Other plants have since been found in the wild, as happened in the case of *C. crapnelliana*, and some thirty were recorded in 1984. However, it may be on the verge of dying out in nature and it is essential that its future should be safeguarded in cultivation.

In 1843 the plant collector Robert Fortune had been sent out to China with specific instructions from the Horticultural Society to obtain 'camellias with yellow flowers, if such exist'. He did not succeed and this fabled colour eluded all those who sought it. The arrival of *C. chrysantha*, first described in 1965, was therefore greeted with great excitement. In its own right the garden worth of this species may be limited in Britain. It is of doubtful hardiness and has only just flowered outside China. However, it is apparently easy to increase by grafting and, with its blooms of clear golden yellow, it opens up dramatic new possibilities in extending the colour range of the genus beyond the normal pink, red and white.

Campanula *Bellflower*

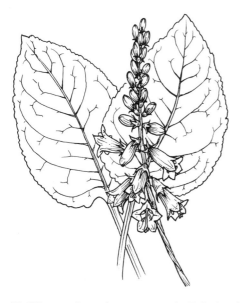

Campanula bononiensis

Bellflowers have been grown in Britain since at least the sixteenth century and their various representatives have acquired some charming names – Canterbury bells, Coventry bells, bats in the belfry, peach-leaved and nettle-leaved bellflower, throatwort, harebell, and in Scotland bluebell. All refer to the characteristic shape of the flowers, as does the generic name from the Latin *campana*, bell. This versatile genus consists of about 300 species, distributed throughout Europe, particularly the Mediterranean region, and beyond. It contains plants suitable for a whole range of situations, from the flower bed to the rock garden to the house. There is also a vegetable, the old-fashioned rampion, and several weeds like the pretty but invasive *Campanula rapunculoides*. The majority of campanulas are hardy perennials or biennials and, with the exception of some alpine species, they are easily grown in any reasonable soil, whether acid or alkaline, in sun or shade. They generally flower from June to August and in most cases can be readily increased from seed or by division or cuttings.

Many members of this ample race have been or have become neglected. The nettle-leaved bellflower or throatwort, *C. trachelium*, is common enough in Britain both in gardens and in the wild, with its numerous broad blue-purple blooms and rampant tendency. But its double and single white forms are less often seen today, while the most desirable of all, the double white 'Alba Plena', is particularly elusive. Another of the tall border perennials, *C. bononiensis*, is of similar stature at about 2 to 3 feet, with long spires of bluish-violet flowers. Introduced from eastern Europe in 1773, it is now rarely offered in the trade. Its beautiful white variant, which E. A. Bowles grew, is even more sought after. Two old garden hybrids of unusual merit, 'Burghaltii' and 'Van Houttei', have 2-foot stems hung with long bells, the first of pale smoky lilac, the second of deep blue. These are probably related to *C. punctata* and were also listed in the past under *C. latifolia*, when they were standard items in catalogues. But they have become equally scarce.

The dwarf *C. cochleariifolia*, 'the most indestructible and amiable of hearty rampers' in Reginald Farrer's words, has long been popular, with its profusion of small bells suspended on 4-inch stems above the leaves. A notable form, but another casualty, was 'Miss Willmott'. It was selected by Clarence Elliott, founder of the Six Hills nursery in Stevenage, Hertfordshire and named after Ellen Willmott, who owned gardens at Warley Place in Essex and on the Continent and supposedly collected it herself near the Rhône glacier. With flowers described as silvery or 'soft luminous lavender blue', it received an Award of Merit in 1915. Farrer, not a fan of Miss Willmott, remarked that the species comes in a range of shades, which are 'only perhaps allowed to stand as "silver" . . . with the names of prominent female enthusiasts to enhance their value'.

'R. B. Loder' is a dainty plant of roughly the same height and no doubt descended from the same species, with distinctive semi-double pale blue flowers. It gained an AM in 1922 and was listed by a few nurseries of the period, usually labelled rare, before it disappeared. However, it may have resurfaced in the shape of a recent arrival, 'Elizabeth Oliver', which is suspiciously similar to the original description of 'R. B. Loder'.

A cultivar of the dwarf *C. garganica* from the Adriatic coast, 'W. H. Paine' was found in an Irish nursery, whose manager it commemorates. It won an AM in 1914 and is tufted and trailing in habit, bearing starry flowers of bright violet-blue with a clear white eye. This 'very delightful addition to our choice campanulas', as Bowles called it, is available today, but only on a limited scale. It would be sad if it were allowed to vanish into obscurity.

'There are so many beautiful Campanulas that to claim that two comparatively new species are well above the rest in beauty is perhaps rather bold,' wrote Graham Stuart Thomas, the distinguished gardener and author, in 1939. One of these, the Caucasian *C. hypopolia*, had been introduced in time for inclusion in Farrer's *The English Rock Garden* of 1919. According to him, it 'suggests rather a frail Cerastium than a Campanula', forming a tangled mat of downy grasslike leaves, about 5 inches high, with thin reddish stems arching above and carrying 'several exquisite bells of cool lilac blue'. Despite a reputation for shy flowering, it is said to be easily grown in light, stony soil and a hot, sunny position and is readily propagated by cuttings. But it has never been common in cultivation and is now very difficult to obtain.

C. betulifolia (*C. finitima*), the other newcomer so admired by Thomas, had been known for some time before it was reintroduced by the collector E. K. Balls in the 1930s. It received an AM in 1937 and is native to Armenia, where it grows in rock crevices at an altitude of about 6,000 feet. The leaves are 'like those of a Birch tree on a small scale', with fragile stems about 6 inches long radiating from the centre, loosely clustered with small white or pinkish-white bells. Although frequently recommended for the alpine house, it is a sound perennial for a sunny crack in the rock garden. But its initial popularity has, inexplicably, never been recaptured.

Unfortunately, some of the loveliest representatives of the genus are not only elusive in the wild but seem destined, in cultivation, to remain within the specialist's sphere. *C. raineri*, which Farrer considered 'the most sensational perhaps of our European Alpine Bells', is confined to limestone precipices in the Bergamo region of the Italian lakes. Growing in cool, shaded crevices and spreading through the cracks by slender runners, it produces in August large china-blue cups 'of serene and unconquerable beauty impossible to express, there in those gaunt places making splashes of blueness up and down the impregnable walls'. There is also a delightful albino and, Farrerian prose apart, *C. raineri* in both blue and white forms belongs unquestionably to the élite of alpines. If the true plant can be acquired, it is by no means difficult to grow and flower well in cool limestone scree and is relatively easy to propagate from runners, cuttings or the occasionally produced seed. Nevertheless, it is still a rarity in cultivation, seen mostly, if at all, as a pot plant gracing the benches at alpine shows.

The same applies to another European, *C. zoysii*, which occurs only in the Karawanken and Julian Alps where it haunts inaccessible crannies of the limestone rockface. From the squat rosettes of tiny, glossy, spoon-shaped leaves arise in late summer perfect pale blue flowers, each like 'a tiny soda water bottle with a ham-frill on the end', in Farrer's phrase. Despite a reputation for being bad-tempered in cultivation and a succulence which tempts marauding slugs, it is fairly simple to maintain in sharply drained limestone scree and with careful watering. Seed is quite freely given, while cuttings of young growths may be successfully rooted early in the year.

The much-prized *C. piperi* (Plate 16) from the northwest United States grows in fissures of granite rock in the Olympic mountains. The open, starry flowers, varying from a rather deep to pale blue with contrasting chestnut-red anthers, appear in late summer on short stems above the neat, dark green, toothed foliage. Again uncommon both in nature and in gardens, it has proved somewhat resistant to attempts to establish it in cultivation. However, all forms of *C. piperi*, including an attractive albino sometimes grown, make superb alpine house plants. Sharp drainage, watering from below and slug protection are the main ingredients of success with this, as with *C. zoysii*.

These campanulas of restricted natural distribution are among the most desirable of alpines. But their horticultural security will almost certainly depend on the specialist grower who has the patience to lavish on them the attention they deserve. The choice garden campanulas of the past rely equally on the ordinary gardener, who has a role to play by growing them and thus preserving them from oblivion. One has merely to compare Clifford Crooks's account of those campanulas in cultivation in 1951, when his classic work was published, with those listed commercially today to realise how fast species and hybrids from a well-known genus can vanish from gardens, unless active measures are taken to ensure their survival.

Cardiocrinum

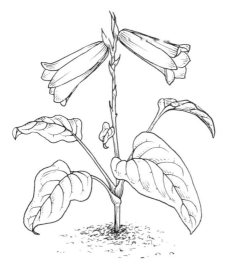

Cardiocrinum cathayanum

'No, I cannot bear to look at them; they are like very beautiful women, utterly ruined by thick ankles.' Few would agree with the fastidious E. A. Bunyard, gourmet, pomologist and author, who so resolutely averted his gaze from a group of giant lilies in the garden at Nymans in Sussex. *Cardiocrinum giganteum* is surely one of the most spectacular garden plants, both in appearance and in the manner of its growth. Gertrude Jekyll described its progress through the year, from March when the bulbs 'thrust their sharply-pointed bottle-green tips out of the earth' and 'soon expand into heart-shaped leaves', to June when 'the flower-stem shoots up straight and tall', to July or August and the appearance of 'the gracefully drooping great white Lily flowers'. Within four months, it grows up to 10 feet in height, with glossy, dark green leaves scattered up the thick stem and the slender, trumpet-like flowers, 6 inches or more in length and as many as twenty at once, hanging from the top. These are tinged faintly green at first, developing to pure white striped with reddish-purple in the throat. Their strong perfume has been compared to honeysuckle or incense.

The 'Prince of Lilies', as it was called by Sir William Hooker, the famous director of Kew, has long been known as *Lilium giganteum*. It now belongs officially to *Cardiocrinum*, a genus of three species distinguished from *Lilium* mainly by the heart-shaped leaves and by the fact that the bulbs die after flowering. The name comes from the Greek *kardia*, heart, and *krinon*, kind of lily. By nature they are woodland plants and thrive in rich deep leafy soil which is moist but well-drained, preferably in part shade. The bulbs should be planted in autumn, a few inches beneath the surface. They are susceptible to late spring frosts as the young shoots emerge and a layer of bracken or leaves over the crowns during winter is a useful precaution. The mature bulbs expend all their energy in producing the vast blooms, after which they die, leaving small offsets at the side of the stem. These can be detached and replanted and will flower in three to four years. Propagation by seed, sown as soon as ripe, is said to result in more vigorous plants, eventually – it can take seven to ten years from sowing to flowering.

C. giganteum towers above its relatives, in both sheer size and beauty. It is native to the Himalaya and was discovered by Nathaniel Wallich, director of the Calcutta Botanic Garden, in 1821. However, it was not introduced until 1848, when the Irish collector, Edward Madden, sent seeds to Dublin, which germinated after two years and first flowered in 1851. Since then, it has been fairly well established in cultivation and can be seen in several great gardens, such as Nymans and Wakehurst Place in Sussex, Crathes Castle near Aberdeen, and the Savill Garden, Windsor, although it is now only occasionally available from specialist nurseries. Even more of a collector's item is the particularly fine var. *yunnanense* (Plate 17) from central China. Slightly smaller, it has a blackish-purple stem and leaves which are pale bronze in the early stages, with creamy white, green-tinted flowers opening from the top downwards.

Predictably, perhaps, the two other species of *Cardiocrinum* have been overshadowed by the giant lily and have remained rare in gardens. *C. cordatum* was mentioned as long ago as 1690 and reached Britain from Japan in the mid-nineteenth century. About 4 to 6 feet high, its leaves are clearly heart-shaped and a distinctive coppery colour when young, forming a rosette at the base and a whorl halfway up the stem. The flowers, usually borne four to six at a time, are white with a yellow blotch and reddish streaks.

The dwarf of the genus, *C. cathayanum*, ranges from 2 to $4\frac{1}{2}$ feet in height and has shiny dark green leaves midway up the smooth stem, surmounted by a spike of three to five flowers of the characteristic funnel shape, which are greenish or creamy white marked with reddish-brown inside. It was described and named in 1925 by E. H. Wilson. using the old name for China, Cathay. Native to the mountains of central and eastern China, it is said to grow abundantly there in dense woodland along the banks of streams. However, following its introduction in 1939, it has never become common in cultivation and the Savill Garden is one of the few places where it has been grown. Like the two other members of this magnificent genus, it certainly deserves a firmer place in horticulture.

Cheiranthus *Wallflower*

Cheiranthus 'Harpur-Crewe'

The wallflower, *Cheiranthus cheiri*, was a very early introduction to Britain from southern Europe which soon became naturalised in this country. According to one theory, it was brought over at the Conquest with the stone used to build the Norman castles and abbeys. True to its name, it clings perennially in walls and stonework in a few sites in Britain.

It was one of the gillyflowers dear to the Elizabethans, along with the carnation and sweet rocket. This old name comes from the French *girofle*, clove, and all were particularly valued in gardens for their scent. From an early stage the wallflower seems to have been familiar in double as well as single forms. In his *Garden Book* of 1659 Sir Thomas Hanmer mentions some of the double kinds: 'wee have the yellow also, very sweet, and the great yellow, markt with blood red spotts or flakes. There is also a double white, but 'tis very scarce and tender.' Other double wallflowers grown were orange, purple, red – the famous 'Bloody Warrior' popular in the north of England in the 1850s – and dark crimson, which was 'almost black and very striking' in William Robinson's words but already, by the late nineteenth century, 'almost extinct'. The double yellow was still the most common and 'a great favourite with cottagers, who propagate it by putting in slips about the time the plants are in flower'. But it had become scarce by the beginning of the twentieth century when Gertrude Jekyll extolled this 'capital plant, now only lingering in cultivation and but rarely seen, that was formerly in almost every garden'.

The old double wallflowers have virtually disappeared and are a rare sight in gardens where they used to be such a universal feature. However, a compact double has survived in the shape of 'Harpur-Crewe' (Plate 20), a neat, bushy plant with greyish leaves and crowded heads of small double flowers, of rich yellow and fragrant. Probably an old Scottish cultivar, it was adopted by the Reverend Harpur-Crewe of Hertfordshire in the late nineteenth century and distributed among his friends, who knew it simply as Harpur-Crewe's wallflower. It received an Award of Merit in 1896 and is still available in commerce, if on a limited scale.

'Pamela Pershouse' is another double yellow of more recent origin, but one which apparently had a brief career in cultivation. It is said to be a hybrid between *C. × allionii*, the Siberian wallflower, and *C. alpinus* (*Erysimum alpinum*) and is a distinct improvement on its parents with its intensely coloured and heavily perfumed blooms. About 9 inches in height, it produces an abundance of large deep-golden flowers over a long period and is equally suitable for the rock garden or the front of a border. It gained an AM in 1919 and was occasionally listed in catalogues of the inter-war years, sometimes under *Erysimum* to which the genus *Cheiranthus* is closely related.

Among the single wallflowers, 'Ellen Willmott' was named for the redoubtable Edwardian lady gardener of Warley Place, Essex. Some 20 inches high, it had bright ruby-red flowers and was highly commended at the Wisley trials in 1924. But, like so many other good garden plants, it never seems to have caught on in the nursery trade and has been very infrequently offered.

Modern wallflowers are generally treated as biennial bedding plants and they thrive in ordinary well-drained soil and a sunny position. The choice old wallflowers were less accommodating and 'reputed to be rather tender', according to Miss Jekyll, although our ancestors had no trouble in growing and increasing them for generations. However, since they do not produce seed and can only be propagated by cuttings, it is probable that they became gradually debilitated by virus infection. This may well have contributed to their demise. 'Harpur-Crewe' has remained resilient, but it should be replaced every few years from cuttings. Obligingly, several short young growths appear around the flowering stems after blooming, which should be rooted either as softwood cuttings under mist or in a closed case, or later in the summer as semi-ripe cuttings in a cold frame.

Clematis

Clematis phlebantha

'Trust not the Clematis which climbs slyly up the walls and shows her little head at the edge of the window, where young maidens go at evening to talk. The artful Clematis gets possession of their secrets.' Heedless of Grandville's warning in *Les Fleurs Animés*, a nineteenth-century collection of fanciful tales and illustrations of flowers, gardeners have long valued the clematis for its elegant if unruly habit and abundant blooms. The genus is the source of some of our most popular garden plants.

The name *Clematis* is derived from the Greek *klema*, vine shoot. On the same basis, our native clematis (whose epithet *vitalba* means literally white vine) was originally christened *Vitis sylvestris*, wood vine. It is a familiar hedgerow plant, particularly on chalk soils in southern Britain, and is widespread in Europe. Its fragrant, creamy-white blossom is succeeded in autumn and winter by the silvery Struwelpeter seed-heads which give rise to such common names as old man's beard, grandfather's whiskers and old man's woozard. Gerard dubbed it travellers' joy 'because of its decking and adorning waies and hedges where people travel'. Country folk, who used to smoke the woody stems like cigarettes, called it gypsies' bacca, shepherd's delight or smoking cane. A rapid and effective cover for unsightly buildings, *Clematis vitalba* is generally too rampant to allow into gardens. In beauty and horticultural merit it is surpassed by many of its Asian and European relatives and their numerous garden descendants.

Earliest and among the most important of these foreigners was the purple *C. viticella* from southern Europe, which flowers from July to September. It was grown before 1569 by Hugh Morgan, the queen's apothecary – whence, if J. C. Loudon is correct, the common name virgin's bower, as a compliment to Elizabeth I. By the end of the sixteenth century at least two variants, red and blue, were known. Parkinson in 1629 also tells of a double 'of a dull or sad blewish purple colour', which was probably one of those referred to earlier by Gerard.

The introduction from Japan of various garden forms of the Chinese *C. florida* in the late eighteenth century was followed by the closely allied white-flowered *C. patens*, also a Chinaman by way of Japan, and in 1850 by the large-flowered azure *C. lanuginosa*, one of the many trophies obtained in China by the collector Robert Fortune. These led to a flurry of hybridisation. In the forefront stood the Woking nursery firm of George Jackman & Son, who were to become famous for clematis and several of whose hybrids are still available. These include the vivid violet-purple *C. × jackmanii*, which is perhaps the most widely grown of all and claims *C. lanuginosa* and a red form of *C. viticella* in its parentage. But where, today can we find the lovely and influential *C. lanuginosa* and *C. patens* themselves? Both species, blooming from mid- to late summer, fully deserve a place in gardens in their own right, but have passed out of commerce and are probably no longer grown. However, it is to be hoped that they will soon become obtainable through the efforts of the recently formed International Clematis Society. Contacts have been established with Chinese botanists and seedlings of *C. patens* are being raised from seed sent by the Beijing (Peking) Botanic Garden, with a view to eventual distribution.

C. chrysocoma suffered a similar fate. It was discovered in the Chinese province of Yunnan by the French missionary and botanist J. M. Delavay and introduced to Kew in 1910. However, it was then superseded by its offspring *C. × vedrariensis*, a cross between *C. chrysocoma* and the ubiquitous *C. montana*. This hybrid is a vigorous climber which quickly reaches 20 feet with appropriate support. *C. chrysocoma* itself is much more sedate, seldom exceeding 6 to 8 feet and more shrubby in habit, with a covering of shaggy down. Its 2-inch white or pink-flushed blooms in May and June are set off by a central boss of rosy-purple pistils within a collar of bright yellow-anthered stamens. Fortunately, this charming species has now been reintroduced in both the pink- and white-flowered forms following the Sino-British expedition in 1981.

One of the most delightful of Reginald Farrer's 1914–15 introductions from the Chinese province of Kansu was *C. nannophylla*. In typical Farrerian style he portrays it as 'the lovely little parsley-leaved Clematis of the hot gravelly banks in these parts, that mounds itself into stiff-stemmed, massive bushes of two feet high and four across, bedizened all over with multitudes of bright golden little half-pendulous Maltese crosses with a dark eye'. Flowering in midsummer, it was at one time represented at the Royal Botanic Garden, Edinburgh, and Wisley, but is no longer grown in either. Planted in a cool house at Wisley, no doubt in deference to Farrer's suggestion that it was tender, it died in the mid-1960s and has not been located elsewhere.

C. phlebantha was described as a new species only in 1968. Its horticultural career is a salutary warning of how a recently introduced plant, which has apparently been secured in cultivation, can quickly come to the brink of disappearance. A native of the Dhaulagiri massif in western Nepal, it is a silvery-leaved shrub with long trailing stems and white, gracefully veined, two-inch blooms from May to July. It was raised at Wisley from seed collected on the 1952 expedition by Oleg Polunin, W. R. Sykes and John Williams and, proving amenable to propagation by cuttings of half-ripe shoots, was widely distributed. However, the Wisley stock was lost one winter in the early 1980s when a large plant in the cool section of the greenhouses succumbed to the constant but unnoticed attentions of a dripping tap. Attempts to replace it were unsuccessful, until a plant was found to be still growing at Wakehurst Place in Sussex. Thanks to the generosity of Kew, which administers the garden, *C. phlebantha* is now reinstated at Wisley. The lessons of this case are clear. It is essential not only to propagate and circulate a new and uncommon plant, but also to maintain more than one representative of it in a particular collection and to keep an eye on its status in cultivation.

Unique in colour among cultivated species is *C. texensis* (Plate 18), with hanging, urn-shaped flowers of rich scarlet (purple and pink forms are also recorded) and greyish-green divided leaves. It occurs wild in Texas, as the name implies, and was imported to Europe in 1868. Though said by the *Botanical Magazine* to be 'perfectly hardy against a wall', it requires some winter protection in most areas of Britain. It has remained a rarity in gardens and, like many clematis species, has been overtaken by its more garden-worthy hybrids.

These hybrids, pruned almost to ground level each year, produce their blooms on the new growth in late summer and make admirable companions for earlier-flowering roses. They were very popular at the beginning of this century, but by the 1940s had dwindled in number. Some, such as 'Grace Darling', 'Duchess of York' and 'Admiration', seem to have disappeared. Another, 'Sir Trevor Lawrence', was a near casualty 'rescued from oblivion' by Christopher Lloyd, the noted gardener, journalist and author of a well-known book on clematis. He found a single plant at Sissinghurst Place in Kent (not the better-known Sissinghurst Castle), as a result of which further plants have been distributed. Its blooms resemble those of an open lily-flowered tulip and are bright crimson, carried almost upright on the sinuous stems. The pink

'Duchess of Albany' is of similar habit and flower character. The more demure 'Etoile Rose', with nodding flowers in deep cherry, silvery-pink at the margins, was restored to the nursery trade soon after the Second World War, having been traced to Abbotswood in Gloucestershire through the work of Graham Stuart Thomas, the writer and gardens consultant to the National Trust.

One more of this delightful group of Clematis which has yet to return to the fold is 'Countess of Onslow'. It was described by A. G. Jackman of the celebrated nursery as having flowers of 'bright violet purple with a broad band of scarlet down the centre of each sepal'. The recent discovery of a plant at the countess's home of Clandon Park in Surrey augured well, for it seemed highly likely that she would have had her namesake growing in her garden. But sadly it has turned out to be an imposter and the search continues.

Other treasures from the past have still to be retrieved. One example is the double form of the herbaceous *C. recta*, producing in July and August 'pure white flowers which differ from those of the type in being fully double, like the silvery button-like blossoms of *Ranunculus aconitifolius plenus*'. But on the credit side, many of the fine early introductions have stayed with us. Notable among them are *C. florida* 'Sieboldii', a mélange of green, white and purple, and the double greenish-white 'Plena'; and the large-flowered *lanuginosa* hybrids 'Lawsoniana', in rosy-lavender, and 'Henryi', white with brown anthers.

Clethra

The genus *Clethra* consists of some seventy deciduous or evergreen shrubs and small trees, native to North America, the Far East and the Canary Islands. The name comes from the Greek for alder, a reference to the similarity of the leaves, but it is for their long clusters of fragrant white flowers that the clethras are prized. The sweet pepper bush *Clethra alnifolia* is probably the commonest in cultivation. It is a hardy deciduous shrub from the eastern USA and is valuable for its late-summer flowering. The exquisite evergreen *C. arborea*, known as the lily of the valley tree, grows wild in Madeira, but is unfortunately too tender to survive outside except in the warmest areas of Britain. Somewhere between them in hardiness stands *C. delavayi* (Plate 21), which is generally considered the finest species for the garden, yet seldom – too seldom – grown.

It was discovered in 1884 by J. M. Delavay, the French missionary and plant collector in China, and eventually brought to this country in 1913 by George Forrest. The *Botanical Magazine* described it in 1922 as 'one of the most charming introductions from Yunnan', while W. J. Bean was 'much impressed by its beauty' when he first saw it in flower. It won a First Class Certificate in 1927. A deciduous shrub or tree up to 40 feet high, it has slender, tapering leaves of rich green which are downy underneath. The flower spikes are about 6

Clethra delavayi

inches long, held sometimes almost horizontally, and crowded with small, scented cup-shaped blooms of white tinged with yellow. The whole plant is covered with blossom in July and August to spectacular effect, all the more remarkable if it lasts until autumn when the leaves turn red and gold.

C. *delavayi* has had a variable record in British gardens, which may account for its rarity. Messrs Hillier of Winchester, who offered it until quite recently, claimed that it was 'injured only by exceptionally severe frost'. It has been known to thrive outside in such diverse counties as Northumberland, Argyll, Dorset and particularly Sussex, where examples may be seen at Wakehurst Place, Nymans and Borde Hill. However, at Kew it had to be confined to the cool greenhouse after repeated trials in the open. Slightly tender when young, C. *delavayi* should be protected for the first winter or two in all but the milder parts of the country. Like other members of the genus it needs a lime-free, leaf-rich, well-drained soil and a sunny or lightly shaded position. Propagation is relatively easy, by softwood or greenwood cuttings taken in summer and rooted in mist or a closed frame in gentle heat. Flowering in late summer when the garden is often at an in-between stage, this delightful shrub surely merits greater attention from nurserymen and gardeners.

Colchicum   *Autumn crocus, Meadow saffron*

'As I came along I saw one of the prettiest sights in the flowering that ever I saw in my life. It was a little orchard; the grass in it had just taken a start and was beautifully fresh; and very thickly growing among the grass, was the purple flowered Colchicum in full bloom.' The plant which William Cobbett, the radical politician and journalist, so admired on one of his *Rural Rides* was

Colchicum autumnale. In the past it was variously known as upstart, naked ladies, naked nannies and star-naked boys, all referring to the emergence of flowers without leaves which is characteristic of many of the autumn-flowering species. Another name in Parkinson's time was 'Filius ante Patrem', 'the Sonne before the Father, because (as they think) it giveth seed before flower'. Parkinson, unlike some of his contemporaries, obviously realised that the spring-produced seed pods resulted from the autumn blooms. Autumn crocus and meadow saffron, the familiar names today, are misleading too. The genus is a member of the lily family, not the iris family to which the crocus belongs, and saffron is derived from a species of crocus. Colchicums have six stamens, not the three of crocuses, and swollen, corm-like storage organs, usually upright but in a few species running horizontally through the soil.

C. autumnale is very widespread in Europe, often as a meadow plant, and is extremely easy to grow, either naturalised in grass or in the border. Its cup-shaped blooms of deep rosy-purple, occasionally slightly chequered, appear during September or October. Pure white forms are not uncommon, but the double white 'Alboplenum' and 'Pleniforum', with double rosy-purple flowers, are seldom found in bulb merchants' lists. The single-flowered, pink-and-white striped 'Striatum' is more curious than lovely, but it too seems to have disappeared totally from commerce (although single and double forms of *C. autumnale* may sometimes adopt a pied aspect in cold spells).

At Colchis in Asia Minor, the determined traveller Jason found the object of his quest and carried off not only the Golden Fleece but the king's daughter, Medea, in marriage. The region, from which *Colchicum* takes its name, probably lay between the Black and Caspian Seas and was said to be rich in poisonous plants. *C. speciosum*, which is poisonous like all colchicums, occurs here and could well have been the basis for the potion brewed by Medea to rejuvenate Jason's father, Aeson.

While the ancients were certainly aware of the poisonous properties of colchicum, opinions differed in the Middle Ages as to its value in medicine. It would seem that several eastern species, known collectively as Hermodactyl, were considered beneficial, whereas others, grouped as meadow saffron and including *C. autumnale*, were deemed harmful. Rembert Dodoens or Dodonaeus, the Flemish physician from whom Gerard borrowed his herbal, recommended the former for 'gowte, sciatica and all paynes of the joyntes' and dismissed the latter as 'corrupt and venemous, therefore not used in medicine'. Gerard himself, not surprisingly, was careful to distinguish between the true Hermodactyl and the 'Meadowe or Mede Saffron'. However, like the Arabians and Egyptians before him he recognised the efficacy of colchicum against gout. For this purpose, mixed with a 'powder of unburied skulls', it was prescribed for King James I by his physician. Colchicine, the active ingredient extracted from the corms, is still employed as a drug and to exterminate vermin (in France the juice was supposed to subdue fleas) and also today in chromosome

Colchicum macrophyllum

manipulation. Slugs, unfortunately, attack the corms with impunity, but it is to be hoped that the cumulative effects of the poison apply to them as well as to humans.

Curiously enough, the well-known *C. speciosum*, from the Caucasus, Turkey and Iran, is not often available now, except occasionally in the form sold erroneously as *bornmuelleri*. Its flowers are white as they emerge from the soil in September, turning to rosy-lilac with a white throat, and they have yellow anthers as opposed to the purple ones of the true *C. bornmuelleri*, a close relative. Forms of the large-flowered *C. speciosum* range in colour from a very deep rich purple to pure white and all are excellent garden plants, also lasting for several days in the house when cut. The pure white *album*, raised by Messrs Backhouse of York, is outstandingly beautiful, with abundant tulip-shaped blooms of fine substance borne on sturdy greenish-white stems during late September and early October. Although it proliferates freely, it has always been in short supply and expensive. At the opposite end of the spectrum, the selected clone 'Atrorubens' is a rich, glowing deep purple, a shade unequalled by any other colchicum. Again, it is not readily obtainable, though by no means slow to increase. In the same way, many of the named forms of *C. speciosum* such as 'Huxley' and 'Darwin' and a number of its hybrids with *C. bivonae*, including 'Danton', 'Conquest', 'President Coolidge' and others once offered in the Dutch bulb trade, are now confined to collectors and one or two specialist nurseries. They can be thoroughly recommended for their mass colour effect in shrub borders, where they thrive with little attention and each autumn provide a handsome return for their allotted space in the garden.

C. bivonae, sometimes grown as *C. bowlesianum*, is distributed naturally from western Turkey through Greece to Sicily. Its large hooded flowers are attractively chequered with purple and sweetly scented, a trait which is very noticeable when they are cut and brought into a warm room. The true plant, however, as opposed to its hybrid offspring, is seldom offered in commerce. *C. macrophyllum*, from Crete, Rhodes and western Turkey, is allied to *C. bivonae*. It is also autumn-flowering and similarly tessellated, but with spreading funnel-shaped blooms and greenish-grey, not yellow, pollen. As the name suggests, its broad, pleated leaves are very large, up to 1 foot in length. Both species grow well in the open garden and have proved hardy in the south of England over many years.

Less amenable is *C. variegatum*, a denizen of the Aegean islands, Greece and the western Turkish coast. In the shape and appearance of its purple, chequered flowers it resembles *C. macrophyllum*, except that these are smaller, as are the greyish-green undulate leaves which spread level with the ground. Usually regarded as an alpine house or frame plant, it may succeed out of doors in very hot, dry, sunny conditions.

C. boissieri, from the mountains of southern Greece and western Turkey, is distinctive in its slender horizontal corms or soboles from which, in autumn, arise one or two neat purple cups about an inch long, followed in spring by two or three narrow leaves. Quite hardy in this country and increasing gently by means of its corms, it is a delightful species for a well-drained position in the rock garden. But it is not easy to locate through the nursery trade. A near relation, *C. baytopiorum*, has been only recently described from three or four sites in western Turkey. It has similar horizontal corms and flower shape, but larger blooms which are accompanied by the young leaves as they open in October.

One of the most tantalising of colchicums both to acquire and to grow successfully is *C. atropurpureum* (Plate 22), a diminutive, autumn-flowering species with blooms of rich, glowing red-purple. Apparently introduced by the famous Dutch bulb firm Van Tubergen, from the Meuse valley in France this century, it was almost certainly known and grown 300 years before. It is highly unlikely that such a striking plant could have been overlooked as a native of northern France and it may well have been cultivated locally. It is difficult to flower regularly, but is more than worthy of a sunny, well-drained situation in the rock garden.

C. callicymbium is a black-anthered species whose leaves begin to show as the purple-throated lilac flowers fade in autumn. Its origins are obscure. Although it was described from garden-grown specimens said to have been gathered in southwest Bulgaria, the exact locality is uncertain and it has not been collected in the wild for many years. Long grown at the University Botanic Garden, Cambridge, it is now lost to cultivation.

Small lilac-purple or occasionally white flowers are the normal pattern for the European and Turkish spring-flowering species, among them *C. hungaricum*, *C. triphyllum* and *C. szovitsii*, which produce leaves and blooms together. Further east, Turkestan, Afghanistan and Kashmir are the source of two colchicums with unusual colouring for the genus. *C. kesselringii* has narrowly trumpet-shaped flowers an inch or so long, white with violet stripes down each segment, while *C. luteum* is the only known species with yellow flowers. Both have been cultivated spasmodically for many years, since they are fairly common in the wild and have quite often been brought back by collectors. Given open well-drained conditions, they are not too demanding and in Britain bloom in January or February. But neither has secured a permanent place in our gardens nor, perhaps because of their early flowering habit, gained popularity. Nurserymen understandably do not bother to retain plants if there is no demand for them and, without sufficient publicity, these and other desirable candidates for gardens seem doomed to a short stay in cultivation.

Convallaria *Lily of the valley*

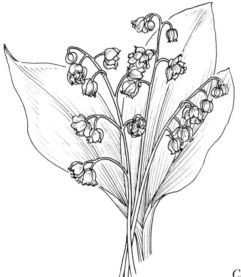

Convallaria majalis 'Prolificans'

'The Wood Lillie or Lillie of the Valley is a flower mervallous sweete, flourishing especially in the springtime and growing properly in woods.' So remarked Thomas Hyll of London, one of the earliest practical gardening writers, in the mid-sixteenth century, adding that it 'of late years is brought and planted in gardens'.

Convallaria majalis (from the Latin *convallis*, valley), was known by various common names including May lily, lily constancy and Our Lady's tears. The latter alludes to a German legend that it grew where Mary shed her tears by the Cross. Wherever it was found, it has become entangled in local folklore. In England it supposedly originated in St Leonard's forest, Sussex, springing from blood shed by the saint in his battles with the local dragons. It had a special association with Whitsuntide and both in Britain and on the Continent expeditions to gather the flowers on Whit Monday provided an excuse for dancing and other festivities. According to Syme's *English Botany* in 1869, 'at one time it grew in profusion on Hampstead Heath, but to our sorrow has now disappeared from that locality'. It is today very rare in the wild in Britain.

In the Middle Ages the lily of the valley was prized as the source of *aqua aurea* or golden water, which was held to be a sovereign remedy for many ailments. Gerard, inevitably, gives a recipe for this elixir: 'The flowers of the May Lillies put into a glass, and set in a hill of ants close stopped for the space of a moneth, and then taken out, therein you shall find a liquor, that appeaseth the paine and griefe of the goute, being outwardly applied.' He also suggests that a distillation of the flowers in wine restores speech to those with 'the dum palsie', alleviates apoplexy and cures heart complaints. This last application seems to have been extended to that of a love potion, while further uses, from the unlikely pen of Robert Louis Stevenson in *Kidnapped*, included the treatment of colic and sprains.

C. majalis is a member of the family *Liliaceae* and closely related to another cottage garden favourite, Solomon's seal. Once established, lilies of the valley are apt to become invasive and are best grown among trees and shrubs, where the vigorous, wandering rhizomes will spread freely through the leafmould to make an effective groundcover of leaves in spring and summer, enhanced by the sprays of fragrant, nodding, small white bells in May. *C. majalis* is considered by many botanists to be the only species in its genus, although names have been bestowed on geographical variants such as *C. keiskei* from the Far East. If regarded as a single species, it is widely distributed throughout the north temperate areas of the world and not surprisingly has given rise to a number of horticultural forms. Of these, the large-flowered lusty plants selected under names like 'Major' and 'Fortin's Giant' and used in the cut-flower trade are the most frequently seen today. But others which were well known in the past have become very uncommon in gardens.

Pink forms, grouped as var. *rosea* and varying slightly in the depth and clarity of shade, have been grown since the late sixteenth century, although the 'blush colour' was 'very scarce' even in 1659 when Sir Thomas Hanmer completed his *Garden Book*. They are now reduced to the one or two clones occasionally offered. The red form mentioned by Gerard and Parkinson, which was stated to be more sweetly scented than the white, has disappeared. Perhaps this was merely the var. *rubra* reported in recent horticultural literature and evidently held in low esteem, with blooms depicted as a dull or dirty rose-mauve. The Reverend William Hanbury, in *A Complete Body of Planting and Gardening* published in 1770, refers to a red-striped, a double white and a double variegated kind 'delightfully striped with purple and white'. Parkinson had also recorded a variety with double variegated flowers, received from

Holland, which is probably the same plant. Sadly this is no longer to be found, if indeed it ever existed.

Even in 1931, seven forms of the lily of the valley were apparently in cultivation, as briefly described in Parey's *Blumengärtnerei*. Of these, the double rose-red 'Rosea Plena' and the sturdy 'Robusta' cannot be traced. Still extant are 'Albimarginata', with white-edged leaves; the curious 'Prolificans' (Plate 24), which bears branched clusters of bloom, sometimes malformed, instead of the normally simple elegant flower head; the double white; the single pink; and 'Albistriata' (also called 'Variegata'), with attractively gold-striped foliage. But these linger only in the gardens of collectors who cherish the unusual.

It would be idle to pretend that the loss of some of these variants is of great horticultural moment. Nevertheless, 'Rosea Plena' in particular would be valuable both to gardeners and to commercial florists if it could be retrieved and others like 'Albimarginata' would certainly be welcomed by a wider audience. Propagation of all these forms is easily effected, by division of the rhizomes in early spring just before active growth begins. It is difficult to understand why they should have virtually departed from the garden scene.

Cosmos

Cosmos atrosanguineus (Plate 26) was introduced to Britain in 1835 when William Thompson of Ipswich (forerunner of Thompson & Morgan, the seed merchants) received seeds from Mexico. It belongs to a genus of annuals and perennials which is closely related to *Dahlia* and mostly native to Central America. The name comes from the Greek *kosmos*, beautiful. As the epithet *atrosanguineus* implies – literally, black or very dark, and blood red – the outstanding feature of this perennial species is the intense colouring of its flowers. E. A. Bowles called it 'as dark a maroon as can exist without being black as your boot, which no one would desire', and the *Botanical Magazine* referred to it as 'a deep purple blood-colour'. The velvety, daisy-like blooms are more than 2 inches across and deliciously chocolate-scented. They appear from the end of June and continue into November and will also last well in water as cut flowers.

With its finely dissected foliage and tuberous roots, *C. atrosanguineus* resembles a miniature 2-foot dahlia. It should be treated in the same way, doing best in deep, rich, moisture-retentive soil in a sunny position. Although plants may survive a mild winter with the help of a protective mulch over the crown, it is wiser to lift them in the autumn after the leaves have become blackened by frost. The roots should be stored for the winter in peat or a similar medium in a dry, frost-proof place, before potting them up in early spring and planting out once the danger of frosts has passed. Like the dahlia, it

Cosmos atrosanguineus

is easily increased in spring by severing newly formed shoots from the rootstock and rooting them individually as softwood cuttings. Division of the old tubers is also possible but less satisfactory.

C. atrosanguineus represents a triumph in the cause of horticultural conservation. Despite the bestowal of an Award of Merit in 1938, this unusual and lovely plant had seemed in danger of disappearing from cultivation. It has only recently been relocated in several gardens and, as a result, has been propagated and is now offered by a number of specialist nurseries.

Crocus

As Ovid recounts, the beautiful youth Crocus was enamoured of the nymph Smilax and metamorphosed for his impatience into the flower that bears his name. The Latin word comes from the Greek *krokos*, which in turn has roots in some ancient Semitic tongues and may be related to the Hebrew *karkom*, saffron. To our ancestors, one species was of paramount importance – *Crocus sativus*, valued by Greeks, Romans, Mongols, Arabs and many other races as the source of saffron. This seemingly insignificant, if very pretty, plant has been cultivated for so long that its origins are lost in time and even the derivation of its name, probably an anglicised version of the Arabic *za-feran*, is disputed.

Credited in the past with an immense range of properties, saffron is composed of the styles and stigmas of the flowers. Gerard describes these as

Crocus robertianus

'thicke fat chives of a fierie colour, somewhat reddish, of a strong smell when they be dried, which doth stuffe and trouble the head'. His warning of the dangers of an excessive dose is supported by the seventeenth-century French botanist J. P. de Tournefort, who tells how a lady of Trent was 'almost shaken to pieces with laughing immoderately for a space of three Hours, which was occasioned by her taking too much Saffron'. It was the supreme cure-all of the age. Hertodt, in his *Crocologia* of 1670, devotes 300 pages to the virtues of saffron and it was apparently prescribed to treat every disease known to man, sometimes mixed with oddities such as fat of the mountain mouse or dragon's blood. No doubt the fact that it is rich in vitamin B2 partly justifies this fantastic reputation.

Saffron was also prized as a scent, a disinfectant, an unguent, a dye for cloth, often with special symbolism, and as a flavouring for food – including those violently coloured buns so beloved in Cornwall, now alas tinted by other means. Such recourse to cheaper substitutes once carried fearsome penalties and in 1444, as E. A. Bowles records, a culprit was burned at the stake in Nuremberg with his adulterated saffron. It was, and is, an expensive commodity, requiring well over 4,000 flowers to make one ounce. In a fascinating account of the industry at Saffron Walden, Philip Miller mentions a price of 30 shillings a pound, a huge sum for those days. Saffron was probably introduced to Britain by the Romans, despite the appealing story by the Elizabethan chronicler Richard Hakluyt of how a pilgrim 'brought the root into the realme, with venture of his life'. No longer grown commercially in this country, it is manufactured on a fairly small scale in Kashmir, Turkey and Spain, whose climate is more conducive to flowering.

C. sativus displays its large, attractively veined, red-purple blooms during October, the long, bright orange-red styles and stamens protruding like lolling dogs' tongues. The flowers remain open in dull weather unlike most crocuses, but are only sparingly produced. However, its near ally *C. cartwrightianus*, a

Greek species from which the saffron crocus was almost certainly developed, is much more free-flowering and also variable in colour, with white as well as pale to deep purple forms. It was named after a British consul at Constantinople by William Herbert, dean of Manchester, the great early Victorian authority on bulbous plants, who wrote a *History of the Species of Crocus*. Both *C. sativus* and *C. cartwrightianus* increase readily, enticing voles and mice with their fat corms, but are rarely seen today in gardens or nursery catalogues.

A horticultural newcomer is the closely related *C. oreocreticus* (Plate 23), with more slender, beautifully veined flowers plentifully borne in October and November. It is known only from a few mountains in Crete, where it grows in abundance at altitudes above 5,000 feet. However, since the corms proliferate willingly and it is easily raised from seed, it should soon be available to gardeners.

A number of autumn-flowering crocuses (not to be confused with the *Colchicum* species inexactly referred to as autumn crocuses) such as *C. niveus*, *C. goulimyi* and *C. hadriaticus* have become reasonably established in gardens, though commercially scarce. But the charming *C. banaticus* (also called *C. iridiflorus* and *C. byzantinus*), from damp meadows and woodlands in Romania, Yugoslavia and the Ukraine, still fails to grace the bulb merchants' lists. This is surprising considering its ease of cultivation and speed of increase from seed and offsets, but may be connected with its need for a moist, leaf-rich soil, unlike the sun-drenched positions preferred by the majority of crocuses. It is also unusual in the genus for having the inner segments of the flower considerably shorter than the outer ones and for its feathery style branches of light purple, rather than orange-red or yellow. It varies slightly in colour from deep to pale purple. Pure white forms also occur, if seldom in the wild, and may be seen occasionally in the gardens of collectors. The named clones 'Rosamund', 'President' and 'Ruby' were raised earlier this century by the discerning enthusiast, James Allen, of Shepton Mallet. But they should not be mourned too greatly, since patient selection of seedlings would undoubtedly provide plants of comparable worth. As a woodland plant, naturalised in moist grassland or any garden site where it is not subject to summer baking, *C. banaticus* will make itself at home, showing its elegant pointed blooms to good effect during October and November.

One of the most reliable and attractive of the autumnal group is the sweetly scented *C. longiflorus*, with a fragrance so strong that a few flowers will perfume a room. Native to southern Italy, Sicily and Malta, it withstands with equanimity the British climate and produces pale to deep lilac blooms, sometimes deeper striped, with flaming orange-red styles, as the leaves emerge in October and November. It used to feature regularly in bulb catalogues, but is now curiously neglected. From further east in the Pindus mountains of Greece, another autumn-flowering species, *C. robertianus*, has been known only since 1968. It is already rated highly for its substantial rich lilac blooms, with large frilly orange stigmata reminiscent of the familiar spring-flowering *C. sieberi*, to which it is closely related. In a well-drained, partially shaded situation in the open garden it will increase gently, but it is still uncommon and unlikely to be obtainable for some years.

Similarly rare in cultivation is the true *C. karduchorum*, from the area around Lake Van in Turkey, as opposed to the imposters generally offered under this name, which often turn out to be *C. kotschyanus* var. *leucopharynx*. Like *C. banaticus*, the species does not tolerate a summer baking and requires cool growing conditions to flower in early autumn, its lilac-blue blooms having feathery white style branches. Also collectors' items are *C. scharojanii* (*C. lazicus*), the only known orange-coloured autumn-flowering species, and the white *C. vallicola*. Both grow wild in the southern USSR and adjacent north-east Turkey, and frequently together, although the latter favours rich meadows or alpine grassland whereas the former is a plant of wetter turf at the edge of streamlets. Neither has adapted eagerly to British gardens and, despite several introductions, they do no more than exist in the care of the dedicated.

Most striking and possibly the most sought-after of the autumn species is *C. autranii*, with pointed, goblet-shaped flowers of deep rich violet and a distinct white zone at the base. In the wild it is confined to one small area of Transcaucasia, in conditions akin to *C. vallicola*. Those lucky enough to trace an odd corm to grow would be wise to give it a well-drained, peaty, leafy soil, away from the summer sun and dry heat it clearly abhors.

Gardeners tend to be better acquainted with the spring-flowering species and cultivars than with their autumnal relatives, in particular the widely grown *C. vernus* and its numerous offspring, the so-called Dutch crocuses, *C. chrysanthus* and *C. flavus* (*C. aureus*). This last, immortalised by Sophocles in *Oedipus Coloneus*, is very probably the crocus depicted by Gerard with 'flowers of a most perfect shining yellow colour, seeming afar off to be an hot glowing cole of fire'. *C. flavus* is an excellent and prolific garden plant in its own right, its fiery orange-yellow goblets appearing during March or April in this country, as in its native habitat of the Balkans and Turkey. However, it has virtually been ousted in cultivation by its lush hybrid, the larger-flowered 'Golden Yellow' or 'Dutch Yellow', which suffers from the mischievous depredations of sparrows. In the *Botanical Magazine* of 1787 William Curtis, its founder and editor, advised 'placing near the object to be preserved, the skin of a cat, properly stuffed', which was presumably an effective alternative to today's black cotton.

C. chrysanthus, from the same region, has waisted flowers ranging in colour from orange-yellow to pale yellow and an occasional creamy white, sometimes marked purple or brown. A near ally is the extraordinarily variable *C. biflorus*, whose flower colour extends from purple-blue to white, variously striped or feathered and with black or yellow anthers. The two species have intermingled in gardens, as they can do in the wild, giving rise to the popular cultivars grouped under *C. chrysanthus* in catalogues, such as the widely available 'Cream Beauty', 'Ladykiller' and 'E. A. Bowles'. Bowles himself, that most remarkable of botanist-gardeners whose *Handbook of Crocus and Colchicum* has been a standard work on the genera for sixty years, selected a number of seedlings and called many of them after birds. Sadly, only 'Snow Bunting', a white with blue feathering, remains with us. Apparently lost for ever, unless they still cling to cultivation in the gardens of enthusiasts, are 'Yellow Hammer' and 'Golden Pheasant', both with yellow, strongly purple-brown feathered blooms; 'Bullfinch' in creamy yellow, richly feathered crimson-purple outside; 'Blue Throat' and 'Blue Rock' in purple and blue; and others, like the sulphur, purple-banded 'John Hoog', the yellow-striped 'Bumble Bee', 'Siskin' in bright yellow freckled with grey, and 'White Egret'.

All the more encouraging, therefore, that another of Bowles's crocuses has recently been recovered. It was sent to Wisley by a correspondent in Latvia who had maintained a stock for many years. The species from which it is derived, *C. korolkowii*, occurs in the southern USSR and neighbouring Afghanistan and northern Pakistan. Dubbed the celandine crocus by Bowles, it varies from plain yellow to yellow with rich purple or brown external markings. One especially delightful seedling with blackish-brown outer segments margined yellow reminded him of the water beetle *Dytiscus*, after which he named it. Like the species itself, 'Dytiscus' grows vigorously in any well-drained soil, increasing steadily from offsets and flowering regularly in February and March.

Bowles recounts that in 1923, 'after thirty years of hopeful expectation', he raised two white-flowered seedlings of the normally purple- or lilac-flowered *C. sieberi*, the better of which he christened 'Bowles' White' and distributed. According to Bowles, it increased freely, but is seldom if ever encountered in the trade today. A variant known as *tricolor* (now botanically placed under *C. sieberi* subsp. *sublimis*), from the mountains of the northern Peloponnese, has striking blooms of lilac-purple on the upper portion, separated from the golden throat by a band of white. Although it is by no means difficult to grow or propagate, its place in cultivation is equally insecure.

The same applies to *C. scardicus*, a lovely species with orange-yellow, purple-based flowers. It is doubly at risk because of its very limited distribution in nature on a few mountains of southern Yugoslavia and Albania, where it blooms as the snows melt in May and June. Found in the same areas and also in northern Greece, *C. cvijicii* follows a similar flowering pattern. In Britain, unhindered by snow, its blooms of deep yellow to lemon or creamy white appear in late February or March. Bowles suggested imitating a sneeze to pronounce the name of the eminent scientist, Professor Cvijić, whom it commemorates.

C. gargaricus, again a mountain plant, is known only from three localities in northwest Turkey, where it carpets the high meadows during April and May.

These dense populations result from its stoloniferous habit, with a mass of cormlets developing around the parent corm. Its small, neat flowers are rather globular and usually bright orange, though paler forms arise sporadically. The secret of success with these three mountain species is not to give them the dry dormant period which is often regarded, mistakenly, as obligatory for crocuses. If a summer baking can be avoided, they will spread happily in the rock garden. Unfortunately, all three are uncommon in cultivation and rarely offered by nurseries.

Intensive botanical investigation of the Turkish flora recently has led to the discovery of several new species, including the enchanting *C. baytopiorum*. Described only in 1974 and restricted to a few mountain areas of southwest Turkey, it is unique to the genus in colour – a pale, clear, opal-touched blue with slightly darker veining, reminiscent of delicate china. It is to be hoped that this exquisite plant will become more generally available once the very small stocks collected have been established.

None of these crocuses can be dismissed as difficult to grow and yet, despite their undoubted garden merit, they remain in horticultural obscurity. Unless some patient and enterprising nurseryman acquires and builds up stocks for distribution, their already tenuous hold on cultivation will slip still further and perhaps be extinguished completely.

Cyclamen

Cyclamen is a genus of some seventeen species, dispersed in southern Europe and countries bordering the Mediterranean, through Turkey and the southern USSR to Iran. Most occur in deciduous or light coniferous woodland or in shaded sites on rocky hillsides, with a general altitude range from 1,000 to 7,000 feet, although some grow near sea level. The origin of the name, from the Greek *cyclos*, circle or whorl, has been variously explained. It may have been suggested by the rounded shape of the tuber or whorled appearance of the flowers or, alternatively, by the spirally twisting stalk of the seed pod. As Parkinson noted, 'the heade or seede-vessel shrinketh downe, winding his footestalke, and coyling it selfe like a cable.'

William Turner, the 'father of English botany', had not seen cyclamen in Britain when, in his *New Herbal* of 1551, he proposed the common name sowesbread, 'lest it should be nameless, if ether it should be brought into England, or be found in anye place in England'. According to Philip Miller, 'it is call'd Sowbread, because the Root is like a loaf, and the Sows eat it.' Known as *pain de porceau* in France, it is said to have provided food for wild boars in parts of southern Europe and Turkey. Mrs Beeton, the famous Victorian cookery writer, claimed that the pigs' diet of cyclamen bulbs imparted special

Cyclamen pseudibericum

flavour to the pork products of the Périgord.

Cyclamen were valued by apothecaries long before they were cultivated. The Roman Apuleius, author of *The Golden Ass*, recommends 'in case that a man's hair fall off, take this same wort, and put it into the nostrils,' while the ancient Greek botanist Theophrastus gives numerous uses, among them the treatment of suppurating boils and the dressing of wounds. The plant inspired much respect for its powers of inducing childbirth, causing Gerard to fence in his cyclamen 'less any good matron accidentally stepping over should have a miscarriage'. He also reported it 'to be good amorous medicine to make one in love if it be inwardly taken', although Parkinson scorned such beliefs, declaring 'but for any amorous effects, I hold it meere fabulous.'

Curiously, in view of their reputed medicinal properties, cyclamen were not known in Britain until the late sixteenth century, when Gerard had in his garden two of the common species cultivated today, *Cyclamen hederifolium* (*C. neapolitanum*) and *C. coum*. Parkinson records ten species and varieties, including a 'Double flowrd, Sowebread of Antioch', apparently autumn-flowering and sometimes with two or three blooms on a stem. He mentions similar spring-flowering plants as well, which were possibly forerunners of the modern greenhouse cyclamen.

These derive from *C. persicum*, which was certainly grown in Britain by the early eighteenth century, probably from stocks introduced from Cyprus. It is native to the eastern Mediterranean region and occurs naturally in rocky outcrops or in shady spots among low scrub and under pines, producing its display of elegant, sweetly scented, purple, pink or white blooms in late winter and early spring. Its variation in leaf markings, which may be patterned or zoned with silver and grey-green or almost plain, has been utilised by breeders to create numerous selections with attractively patterned foliage. With a considerable range of flower colour as well and a flowering season which has been extended from August to April, the tender florists' cyclamen is now a major horticultural crop. Even the perfume, which was virtually lost in the achievement of larger blooms during the nineteenth century, has been recaptured in many of the new small-flowered cultivars. These 'mini cyclamen' are bred by back crosses with the wild species and are extremely popular today as house and greenhouse plants.

Among gardeners, particularly rock garden and alpine enthusiasts, there has been a great demand for *Cyclamen* species in recent years. Bulb merchants have not been slow to exploit the market and have obtained huge quantities of corms from the wild, especially from Turkey, which has led to wholesale destruction of populations. This is not only reprehensible but, if continued, could bring certain species to the brink of extinction in their natural habitats. The case of *C. mirabile*, a little-known autumn-flowering species from Turkey with pink blooms and pink-flushed leaves, highlighted the danger. It was imported on a vast scale during the 1970s and was sold in chain stores as the familiar *C. hederifolium*, arousing a justifiable storm of protest from conservationists and resulting in much-needed legislation to control importation of *Cyclamen* species. Further colonies of *C. mirabile* have since been located in southwest Anatolia but, had looting of the sites carried on unchecked, this charming species – which is readily raised from seed in cultivation – might have disappeared from the wild.

Such a fate could still befall the superb *C. rohlfsianum*, which is restricted to a small area of Libya between Benghazi and Derna and grows in damp, shaded crevices of limestone rocks in the foothills. Its blooms of pale to deep pink, with crimson patches at the base of each petal, appear in autumn at the same time as the angular glossy foliage, dark green and silver-patterned above in the best forms, beetroot-red beneath. It is not hardy in Britain, but makes an admirable plant for the cool greenhouse, often filling the air with its lily of the valley fragrance.

The distinctive, propeller-like pink or white flowers of *C. trochopteranthum* (from *trochos*, wheel, and *pteranthus*, winged flower) are borne in late winter and early spring. Also known as *C. alpinum*, it was introduced in 1956 by the collectors Dr Peter Davis and Oleg Polunin from Anatolia, where it inhabits limestone outcrops at the edge of the pine and cedar forests. Apart from the flower shape, it differs from the related and unscented *C. coum* in its heather-smelling blooms and in the absence of a pale eye at the mouth of the flower. Happily, this beautiful cyclamen is now being distributed reasonably widely, mainly through the Cyclamen Society, whose members are propagating from cultivated stocks most of the threatened species as well as the more usual ones. The horticultural availability of such species will reduce pressure on their wild populations, which is essential if they are to be prevented from dying out in nature.

Another rarity in the *C. coum* alliance is the spring-flowering *C. parviflorum*.

It is a diminutive species from northeast Turkey, found in moist mountain pastures and concentrated around the Zigana pass. With its neat, orbicular, dark-green leaves, less than one inch across, and small, stubby, pale lavender-pink flowers, it should prove a challenge to specialists since it is by no means easy to maintain in cultivation.

Much more amenable and horticulturally desirable is *C. pseudibericum* (Plate 25), yet another Turkish endemic known only from the Amanus mountains and Cilicia. Though described at the beginning of this century, it was scarcely grown before 1957, when stocks were replenished by Davis and Polunin. The buds are produced in late autumn in cultivation, remaining quiescent until February or March when the flowers open 'with leveret ears laid back', as the writer Vita Sackville-West aptly described the cyclamen bloom. They are bright purplish-red marked deep purplish-brown and white at the base.

Sharing a similar pattern of growth, *C. libanoticum* is confined to a small locality in the mountains northeast of Beirut at altitudes of 2,500 to 4,500 feet, 'growing in shady situations under rocks and roots of trees ... where fresh snow made further investigations unprofitable'. This delightful species, with its striking, clear rose-pink flowers, rimmed white and crimson at the mouth, may be grown outside in some districts, but is safer in the alpine house where its large blooms can be enjoyed without damage from the elements in early spring.

Several other species – the strongly fragrant *C. cyprium*, blooming in autumn and winter, the spring-flowering *C. balearicum*, in white and pale pink, and the graceful white *C. creticum*, appearing in April – are very limited in their habitats, although fairly abundant where they grow naturally. Stocks of all these species are now in cultivation in Britain and should become available as they are propagated, thereby assisting the aims of the International Union for Conservation of Nature (IUCN) to curb indiscriminate and highly damaging collecting for the horticultural trade.

Propagation by division of the tubers, formed in cyclamen from the swollen hypocotyl, the tissue between root and shoot, is occasionally successful. However, the species are best raised from seed which, with few exceptions, is freely produced and will germinate readily if sown fresh, as will old seed soaked in water for a day or so. The young seedlings should be encouraged to continue growing as long as possible and not dried off. Even after the leaves have died down, the tubers should be kept slightly moist to avoid shrivelling. Apart from the *C. purpurascens* (*C. europaeum*) group which are evergreen, though often experiencing enforced dormancy under snow in the wild, all the species require a rest period. Using a gritty, free-draining, leafy compost, with an annual top dressing as they come into growth each season, they will thrive in containers for several years.

While measures to stop overcollecting of cyclamen in the wild must not be relaxed, the maintenance, increase and distribution of almost all the species from material already in cultivation represents a success story. It is vital that this conservation model should be followed for other endangered plants in the future.

Cypripedium *Lady's slipper*

Cypripedium japonicum

'Touching the faculties of our Ladies' Shoo we have nothing to write, it not being sufficiently known to the old writers, nor to the new.' While Gerard may have thus dismissed the native *Cypripedium calceolus*, his contemporaries were already aware of its potential in gardens. As a result of collection by man over hundreds of years, it has been brought to the brink of extinction in the wild in Britain. At the beginning of this century Reginald Farrer recorded how it lingered 'in the woods where Mrs. Thomasin Tunstall ... quarried it so pitilessly to send to Parkinson'. Today it is reduced to a sole survivor in the north of England, which is protected by law.

    C. calceolus is not the only species to be threatened with such a fate. In order to meet commercial demand ground orchids are regularly obtained from the wild and consequently their natural populations are dwindling fast. Such devastation is particularly alarming given the fact that only a tiny proportion of the plants manage to survive in gardens, since they are often uprooted when in full growth and are difficult to establish. Unfortunately, like many ground orchids, the *Cypripedium* species have so far resisted attempts to raise them from seed in cultivation. Until methods of propagation can be devised, their existence in the wild will no doubt become increasingly precarious.

The name *Cypripedium* is derived from the Greek Kypris, Venus, and *pedilon*, slipper, whence the English equivalent lady's slipper and the French *sabot de Venus* or *de la Vierge*. The genus contains some fifty species, widely distributed throughout Europe, North America and the Far East. The group known as slipper orchids, popular as cut flowers and for the greenhouse, was formerly included but has now been extracted to form a separate genus, *Paphiopedilum*. The flowers generally appear from late spring to early summer and are composed of four outer petals framing a prominent lower lip or swollen pouch like a slipper, with folded, often hairy leaves surrounding the stems. Though none is commonplace in gardens, one of the best known is *C. reginae* from the USA, bearing large white blooms with a rich rose pouch.

C. japonicum (Plate 28) has always been scarce in cultivation owing to the difficulties of importation and culture. It is native to Japan, where at one time it grew abundantly around Tokyo, and to parts of China, where it is called the devil's umbrella. Although it was described as early as 1784, nearly a century elapsed before its introduction to this country through Dr Alexander Wallace, agent for Kramer's nurseries of Yokohama, who offered it in their 1873 catalogue. Farrer portrayed it in his inimitable way as 'a curious species from the mountain woods, with stems of some 8 inches or more, and big solitary slippers of apple green with rosy lip, carried high above a single pair of corrugated leaves that are cut across their ends in a straight line (like 'Arriet's toes, as square as a nangkerchief)'. It received an Award of Merit in 1931.

C. × ventricosum probably reached Britain in 1828, when a member of the Russian embassy sent roots to Sir George Staunton of Leigh Park in Hampshire. It is a natural hybrid between *C. macranthon* and *C. calceolus* and was said to flower plentifully in the woods of western Siberia. It is distinctive for its long, narrow, twisted petals and globular slipper, usually yellow, veined and tinged with purple, or sometimes greenish-white. This did not prevent it from being confused with a Japanese species in the past and, despite the award of a First Class Certificate in 1908, it has remained 'a very rare and handsome plant'.

C. tibeticum was discovered in 1879 but not introduced until 1892, when 'Chinese' Wilson brought home plants for James Veitch & Sons, the great Chelsea nursery responsible for so many introductions of the period. These flowered in June 1906 and won an FCC the following year. Farrer considered it 'a small squat thing, rather like a malignant Tibetan toad in appearance (no less than in character) when it produces its single stumpy stolid flower of immense size, on a stem of some 3 or 4 inches'. The bloom is a greenish-yellow marked with reddish-purple and has an inflated pouch of very dark purple. It occurs in 'reckless profusion . . . in the rough grassy slopes, among countless other plants in the high open ridges of Tibet'. It has also been found in other Himalayan states and was collected again in Bhutan in 1949 by the celebrated plant hunters Frank Ludlow and George Sherriff. One of these plants was grown successfully at Keillour Castle in Perthshire, but like many of its fellows this species has never gained more than a foothold in cultivation.

Cypripedium species frequently occur in regions of extreme cold and all are apparently hardy in Britain. However, in the uncertain climate they are liable to produce premature growth which may be damaged by frost. For this reason they are often best grown in a cold greenhouse or frame. Otherwise they require a loose, leaf-rich, well-drained soil and a cool, shady, north-facing position outside where early growth is less likely to occur. Planting may be carried out in autumn or early spring. The thin, wiry rootstocks are spread out in a layer of leafmould and covered so that the plump growth buds are just below the surface. Established clumps may be increased in March or April by carefully teasing out the crown buds with their attendant roots and replanting.

These exotic and unusual plants pose a dilemma for the conservationist. At the moment, each one that is brought into gardens, and then not always successfully, represents a loss to the wild colony. Only when the means has been found to propagate ground orchids on a commercial scale will it be possible to arrest the decline of their natural populations and to build up and distribute stocks in cultivation. Once this has been achieved, gardeners will be able to grow them with an easy conscience and also make a positive contribution to safeguarding the future of the genus both in the wild and in cultivation.

Daphne

In Greek mythology the elusive nymph Daphne was translated from the animal to the plant kingdom to escape the unwelcome attentions of Apollo. The genus which has taken her name is widespread throughout Europe and Asia and contains some seventy species of evergreen or deciduous shrubs, many of them very beautiful and particularly suitable for small gardens. In spite of a reputation to the contrary, most are easy to grow and may be propagated without difficulty from seed or cuttings or sometimes by grafting or layering. In nature they often occur on alkaline soils but in gardens, given good drainage and moisture-retentive soil, they will thrive in both acid and alkaline conditions which are not too extreme.

Sadly, the number of species and hybrids offered by nurseries is now extremely limited. It is understandable that several of the dwarf species like the delightful *Daphne arbuscula*, *D. petraea* and *D. jasminea* should be in short supply, since they are slow-growing and not quickly increased. But many others without these disadvantages are equally hard to trace and some may have disappeared altogether from cultivation.

One of the finest forms of the well-known evergreen *D. odora* was introduced to France from Japan in about 1866 by E.-A. Mazel of Montsauve.

Daphne × hybrida

'Mazelii' soon became quite common in Continental and British gardens and was far superior to the cultivars normally grown today and to the species itself. It was about 4 to 6 feet high with clusters of intensely fragrant blooms, purplish-pink with white centres, borne not only at the tips of the branches but along them. These appeared in November and lasted through the winter, unlike many forms which only start flowering in late February. It was also considered hardier than *D. odora* itself, although W. J. Bean recommended winter protection near London. An Irish nursery which provided the plant figured in *The Garden* in 1878 claimed that 'Mazelii' succeeded against a wall or in the open or 'in a full south aspect'. Almost a century later, according to the eighth edition of Bean's classic work, this superb shrub was 'very rare' and it is feared that it has since been lost from gardens in Britain.

A hybrid of *D. odora* and the compact evergreen *D. collina* is *D. × hybrida*. The original cross is believed to have been made in France in about 1820 by a certain Monsieur Fion, a gardener whose history, like that of his garden offspring, is ill-recorded. The great merit of this attractive shrub is its ability to produce sweet-scented clusters of purplish-red flowers virtually throughout the year, with only a slight pause in summer. It is still to be seen in a few gardens, but is all too seldom offered in the trade.

The origin of *D. × houtteana* is similarly obscure, although it is very probably a hybrid of the deciduous *D. mezereum* and the evergreen spurge laurel *D. laureola* – an unusual combination which has resulted in a charming plant. It was supposed to have come from a Belgian nurseryman and was illustrated in *Flore des Serres* in 1850 by another Belgian nurseryman, the celebrated Louis van Houtte, after whom it was named. It forms a stiffly branched shrub, eventually reaching 3 feet or so in height but often smaller and dome-shaped, and carries bunches of lilac-purple bloom in March and April.

It is especially valuable for its evergreen or semi-evergreen foliage, with the glossy dark purple leaves contrasting well with brighter plants in the border. A few examples of *D. × houtteana* have recently been located and are being propagated and it is to be hoped that it will soon regain its rightful place in catalogues.

D. mezereum itself is a superb early-flowering species, 3 to 5 feet high, and an old favourite. It is generally held to be native to Britain and Philip Miller in 1759 mentioned 'a Discovery made of its growing in some Woods near Andover, from whence a great number of plants have been taken in late Years'. The mezereon was highly esteemed by apothecaries for the treatment of a whole range of afflictions from toothache to ulcers. According to Gerard, the leaves 'do purge downward, flegme, choler and waterish humours with great violence', while 'if a drunkard doe eat one graine or berry of this plant, hee cannot be allured to drinke any drinke at that time.' Its poisonous properties were also respected, rightly so, and Linnaeus warned that six berries were sufficient to kill a wolf.

With its masses of heavily perfumed purplish-red blossom in early spring and tiny red fruits in summer, the mezereon is a familiar sight. However, the lovely 'Alba Plena', a cultivar with double white blooms, seems to be another casualty. Although frequently referred to in horticultural literature of the nineteenth century, it has not been found in cultivation in Britain.

The genus includes many species that would be excellent garden plants if only they were propagated and released to gardeners. Several yellow-flowered species from China and Japan have made a fleeting appearance in cultivation and are still grown in a few gardens. Among them is *D. aurantiaca*, an evergreen up to 5 feet high with bright yellow fragrant flowers, from northwest Yunnan and Szechuan. It was introduced in 1906 by George Forrest, but this introduction was apparently slightly tender. It won a FCC in 1927 and is easily propagated from cuttings. Another yellow-flowered Chinese species, *D. giraldii*, is also easy to increase, in this case from seed, and is hardy, although 'difficult to cultivate successfully' in Bean's words. It was discovered by the Italian missionary Guiseppe Giraldi in 1894 and introduced from Kansu in 1911 by William Purdom, on an expedition jointly sponsored by Messrs Veitch and the Arnold Arboretum in the USA. A small deciduous shrub, it is 'especially to be prized for its yellow flowers' and in the autumn is frequently covered with bright red fruits. The Japanese *D. jezoensis*, on the other hand, has shown its tolerance of a wide range of situations in gardens and has been grown in slightly alkaline soils in the open border, on peat banks and as a pot plant. Up to 2 feet in height, it flowers in winter and early spring and becomes dormant during the summer, before making fresh growth in the autumn. This means that it sheds its leaves in late spring, which can be alarming to the unwary owner. Despite their attributes, none of these delightful daphnes is regularly listed by nurserymen.

Unique to the genus is *D. genkwa* (Plate 29), about 3 feet high and bearing soft lilac flowers on upright twiggy branches in April and May. Its blooms resemble the lilac's in shape as well as colour and 'these long, slender wands of blossom, the comparatively long-stalked clusters, and especially the opposite leaves, make this daphne very distinct' as Bean remarks. It was introduced from near Shanghai in 1844 by the Horticultural Society's illustrious collector, Robert Fortune, and first flowered in Britain two years later. There have been several further introductions since then, which vary considerably in the size of flower and leaf and also possibly in hardiness. Much has been written about the foibles of this species in cultivation, although it is more readily increased than one is led to believe. Seedlings from South Korea have been grown outside at Wisley for some years now, where they flower freely and have been propagated from soft cuttings. While *D. genkwa* may not be the easiest species to obtain or grow, it is certainly one of the pearls in this beautiful genus and worth every effort to acquire.

Decumaria

Decumaria sinensis

Decumaria is a genus of only two known species, one native to the southeastern USA, the other to central China. The name comes from the Latin *decimus*, tenth, and alludes to the fact that the petals, stamens and other parts of the flower are grouped in tens or multiples of ten. They are climbing shrubs which cling by aerial roots in the same way as ivy and are closely related to *Hydrangea*, except that the flowers are fertile, not partially sterile. Although neither is common in cultivation, the American species is more familiar, perhaps because of its relatively early introduction in 1785. *Decumaria barbara* is deciduous and grows to about 30 feet high. It has slightly hairy stems and young leaves and bears clusters of small, white, scented flowers in June and July, followed by tiny, white, ridged berries. The discerning E. B. Anderson planted it in his West Country garden for its fragrance. It thrives in warmer areas of the British Isles such as the southwest and Ireland, but needs to be grown against a sheltered wall elsewhere.

Its Chinese relative *D. sinensis* (Plate 27), is a vigorous evergreen shrub which reaches a more manageable height of 10 to 15 feet. It forms a thick mat of leaves, roughly oval in shape and shiny smooth, although the new shoots and buds are covered in down. The yellowish-white flowers appear in late May and June in dense clusters about 3 inches long and across. They have a faint perfume variously described as 'deliciously honey-scented' and unpleasant. *D. sinensis* was discovered in 1887 by Dr Augustine Henry, an Irishman who was then based in Ichang by the gorges of the Yangtze river where he started studying the local flora in his spare time. He came across it as a 'creeper hanging down from the walls of the cliffs with beautiful clusters of fragrant white flowers'. E. H. Wilson, who finally introduced it in 1908, said that it was often found growing over rocks.

This 'beautiful hardy species', as William Robinson called it, is easily grown in Britain. Like the climbing hydrangea it is happy in sun or shade and may be trained against a wall or up a tree. However, propagation is difficult which is probably the reason why it has never been adopted by the nursery trade. Cuttings of ripe growth, taken in late summer or early autumn, treated with hormone rooting powder and placed in a cold frame, have been successful and softwood cuttings earlier in the season are also worth trying. Layering is another possibility, but extremely slow. *D. sinensis* has flourished on a south wall at Kew and in a few other gardens but its value as an attractive evergreen climber has yet to be widely recognised.

Dianthus *Carnation, Pink*

Few of our garden plants have lasted so well as the carnation, florists' flower *par excellence* from the seventeenth to nineteenth centuries and again today in the modern sense of the term. Its wild progenitor *Dianthus caryophyllus*, a native of central and southern Europe, was known to the ancients and was mentioned in the fourth century BC by the Greek botanist and philosopher Theophrastus. He was also indirectly responsible for the generic name, which he gave as *diosanthos*, from *dios*, divine, and *anthos*, flower, and which Linnaeus shortened to *Dianthus*. In Britain the history of the carnation stretches back to the Norman Conquest, when it is supposed to have been brought over by the monks, either deliberately or, like the wallflower, accidentally in the Caen stone imported for building abbeys. It was used to flavour ale and wine, whence the

Dianthus fragrans

name sops-in-wine, and was of course endowed with vague but always comforting medicinal properties. Above all it was cherished for its beauty and fragrance, charmingly expressed by Parkinson: 'But what shall I say to the Queene of delight and of flowers, Carnations and Gilloflowers, whose bravery, variety and sweete smell joined together, tyeth every one's affection with great earnestnesse, both to like and to have them?'

In his *Paradisus* of 1629 Parkinson devotes a whole chapter to them, an honour accorded to few other plants, and lists fifty-two kinds. Gerard, some thirty years earlier, lacked space 'to write of every one ... considering how infinite they are'. The reign of Elizabeth had seen numerous additions to their range, with singles and doubles in various colours and – a great novelty and forerunner of the flakes – white with red stripes. There was still a distinction between the clove gilloflower and the carnation. The former, Gerard observed, 'endureth better the cold, and therefore is planted in gardens', while the latter was normally grown in pots, a practice followed by the later florists. It seems to have been introduced from the Continent and had larger 'very faire flowers of an excellent sweete smell and pleasant carnation colour; whereof it took his name'. This flesh colour may have been one explanation of the word, but others derived carnation from coronation, since the blooms were made into garlands or, alternatively, resembled a coronet.

Although many of the original gilloflowers disappeared during the Civil War, supplies were quickly replenished, mainly from Holland. In 1676 the gentleman gardener and author John Rea could muster 360 sorts, singling out for praise those 'which are well striped, flaked or powdered upon white or blush with darker or paler red, crimson or carnation, sadder or brighter purple, deeper or paler scarlet'. Improvement of the carnation in order to achieve a smoother outline and more regular markings was already in hand and by the mid-eighteenth century the division between flakes, bizarres and picotees began to emerge. Edged with a band of colour on a white or sometimes yellow background, the picotee was a special favourite of royalty and nobility. Thomas Hogg of Paddington Green, in the 1823 edition of his *Treatise* on florists' flowers, catalogues thirty-six named forms of this class alone.

The carnation was then approaching the peak of perfection as a florists' flower. Confined to the greenhouse, its culture became a specialised art and its display was governed by meticulous rules. 'Admiral Curzon' was a supreme example of the show type, a bizarre with scarlet and maroon flakes on a pure white base, which was raised in 1844 and last exhibited in about 1901. With this robust exception, the florists' carnations of the last century were generally of delicate constitution and it is hardly surprising that so few are left.

Given its lengthy evolution, it is inevitable that most of the older cultivars of the carnation should also have perished. In 1839 Hogg noted that 'the Clove Gilliflower, or the true Old Clove ... is now lost to the country. One flower, they will tell you, would scent the whole garden.' However, the 'Old Crimson Clove' of the Elizabethan lingers on, even if it is no longer 'too well known to need description' as one catalogue put it in the 1920s. Its dark crimson flowers are semi-double and heavily fragrant. From the same period the 'Painted Lady' is also extant, possibly because it had remained a garden rather than a florists' flower. Its white petals are painted pink or red on the upper or under side and it has a pronounced clove scent. Some forty versions were recorded in the past. One of them was 'Lord Chatham', from the eighteenth century, which was rediscovered and renamed 'Raby Castle' in 1850. It is also known as the 'Salmon Clove' and is a glowing dark salmon deepening in the centre and perfumed.

Their persistence is certainly remarkable, but these old carnations are by no means common and probably less so than in the 1930s or even 1950s. One of their leading champions was the Reverend C. Oscar Moreton, who in 1955 published details of twenty-six 'old survivals' recovered by himself and K. W. Sanderson of Leeds. Among them are 'Granado', illustrated by Parkinson; the 'Fenbow Nutmeg Clove', found in the garden of Colonel Fenbow where his ancestor planted it in 1652; 'Old Flame', a striking fire red, also known as 'Old Man's Head'; 'Lucy Glendill', named by an eighteenth-century squire after his sweetheart; and 'Peter Pan', a relic of the florists' flakes which was produced by the Victorian enthusiast, C. H. Herbert of Birmingham. It is doubtful whether any are readily obtainable, if at all, today.

Outside the purists' province to which it retreated in the nineteenth century, the carnation was being transformed along different lines. The tree carnation, which could be trained as a large bush or to the roof of a conservatory, was a French creation but its appeal was somewhat limited. It was more important for its role in the evolution of the perpetual flowering carnation, which caused a sensation at the beginning of the twentieth century and is now one of our most popular commercial cut flowers. Finally in the 1920s the carnation returned triumphant to the garden in the shape of the modern hybrid pink bred by the Sussex firm of Montague Allwood. Grouped under *D.* × *allwoodii*, this race of hardy plants with their long flowering season has continued to be a valuable feature of our borders.

One of the most interesting developments of the carnation was the Malmaison, all the more fascinating in view of its rapid descent from high fashion to obscurity. The original 'Souvenir de la Malmaison' apparently occurred in France in 1857 as a seedling of the tree carnation. It was called after the rose 'Souvenir de la Malmaison' from a fancied likeness and also came to be known as 'Old Blush'. Of imposing presence, tall and broad-leaved, its huge 3- to 4-inch blooms were fully double and blush-coloured and exuded a strong clove fragrance. Its attraction for the Victorians is understandable and by the 1870s it was widely grown in Britain. During the decade 'Souvenir de la Malmaison' produced pink and crimson sports and new forms were added from the 1890s onwards, chiefly by Martin Smith of Kent. These were in shades of rose, crimson, salmon and scarlet, as well as the white 'Nell Gwynne' and the pink striped 'Sir Evelyn Wood'.

All the Malmaison carnations needed greenhouse protection and could only be increased by layers or cuttings. Some such as 'Lady Middleton', a deep blush striped with rosy red, were notoriously erratic. But the plants would live for several years and reward the skilful gardener with a succession of bloom in spring and summer. Despite their demanding nature and the rival claims of the perpetual flowering carnation, the vogue was sustained well into the twentieth century. According to George M. Taylor, looking back in the 1940s, 'many of the great gardens of the country had at least one, and sometimes more, structures entirely devoted to their cultivation.' The subsequent demise of the Malmaison is due more perhaps to changing taste than to difficulty of culture and there seems no reason why it, like the Parma violet of the same period, should not be revived as a pot plant. Several cultivars have in fact been located and are now being grown at Wisley and distributed from there.

The pink had much humbler and rather later beginnings than the carnation, though it too was to achieve ultimate excellence as a florists' flower. Familiarity with native species of *Dianthus* – the maiden pink, *D. deltoides*, the Cheddar pink, *D. gratianopolitanus*, and the annual Deptford pink, *D. armeria* – may partly account for its lowly status as a useful but ordinary garden plant. Henry Lyte in *The New Herbal or History of Plants* in 1578 spoke dismissively of 'the Pynkes and small feathered Gillofers' which 'are like to the double or Cloave Gillofers, saving they be single and a great deale smaller'. Gerard merely glanced at them in his *Herball*, but he did take credit for naming *D. plumarius* or the feathered pink, in allusion to its ragged petals. This species had by then arrived from eastern Europe (exactly when is not clear) and was to be the principal parent of the future.

Several named forms of pink belong to the sixteenth and seventeenth centuries, but in contrast to the carnation no great advance was made. In 1676 Rea considered pinks 'of little esteem. . . . Most of them are single and there are some double sorts, the best, those which are called "feathered Pinks".' A hundred years later, the Reverend William Hanbury in *A Complete Body of Planting and Gardening* referred to 'Old Man's Head', 'Pheasant's Eye' and others by name and commented 'they are all well-known plants, and besides their spicy fragrance, look well anyhow.'

This indulgent tone soon changed with the advent of the laced pink. It seems first to have arisen as a seedling in about 1770 in the care of James Major, gardener to the duchess of Lancaster, who named it 'Lady Stoverdale'. With its distinct outer margin of colour to the petals, repeating that of the centre, in this case red on a white ground, it ushered in a new class of florists' flowers and became for a time the foremost expression of that art. During the first half of the nineteenth century the laced pink was adopted and embellished in countless ways, especially by the weavers of Lancashire, the miners of Durham and Northumberland and, most famously, the muslin workers of Paisley in Scotland (although recently some doubt has been cast on the story of the Paisley pinks and whether their reputation was deserved). Standards were as exacting as for the carnation. According to the nurseryman and writer James Maddock of Walworth in 1810, 'the petals should have very fine fringed or serrated edges', although it would be 'a very desirable object to obtain them perfectly rose-leaved, i.e., without any fringe at all'. The smooth petal had become the norm in 1863, when the properties of the pink were defined by George Glenny, who was well known for his pronouncements on florists' flowers.

Unlike the more fragile carnation, the florists' pink was hardy and easily grown outside. It was essentially a working man's plant, a fact reflected in such names as 'Kentish Yeoman' and 'Reformer' ('Beauty of Ugliness' must have been a last resort in the rush of new kinds). Consequently, its legacy has been greater. A number of pinks have been handed on to us and others no doubt still haunt cottage gardens undisclosed. Moreton's list of 'old survivals', twice as long as that for carnations, includes the Stuart 'Pheasant's Eye' and 'Queen of Sheba', both with deeply fringed petals; 'Bat's Double Red' (Plate 30), from Thomas Bat, an early eighteenth-century grower near London, which was also known as 'Double Ruby Pink' and had long featured in the Oxford University Botanic Garden; 'Musgrave's Pink' or 'Green Eyes', called by other names as well, of about 1730, which was tracked down this century by George Allwood, a member of the family connected with the modern development of *Dianthus*; the Scottish 'Cockenzie Pink' or 'Montrose Pink', of similar date; the pale rose 'Inchmery', always a rarity; and 'Paddington', from Hogg of Paddington Green.

The salmon pink 'Emile Paré' and crimson 'Napoleon III' were bred by André Paré of Orléans in about 1840. Their clustered flowers show the probable influence of the sweet william, *D. barbatus*, and they tend to be short-lived in the same way. The most celebrated pink of all was 'Mrs Sinkins', a scented blowsy full white. Produced by the master of the Slough workhouse, who called it after his wife, it was marketed by the local nursery of Charles Turner. It won a First Class Certificate in 1880 and in 1938 was immortalised in the coat of arms of the borough. 'Sam Barlow', white with a dark purple centre and free flowering, was another favourite of cottagers.

All these garden pinks are in commerce today, if only in limited quantities. Despite a relatively short season of bloom, they are well worth acquiring, not just for their historical associations but for their beauty and unmistakable clove scent. The laced and Paisley pinks, on the other hand, were more ephemeral, although efforts have been made to retrieve them with some success. 'William Brownhill' from about 1780, white laced with dark maroon, is a recent example. Another is 'Dad's Favourite', located by A. J. Macself (and sometimes called after him), editor of *Amateur Gardening*, in a northern garden whose aged owner had forgotten its real name. With dark purple lacings and eye, it is presumed to date from the late eighteenth century and is very close to 'Paisley Gem', found by George M. Taylor.

There have naturally been some regrettable casualties among the pinks. Products of the seventeenth century were 'Painted Lady', white on the upper surface of the petals and pink beneath and, of the same type, 'Nonsuch' and 'Unique'. The slightly later 'Old Man's Head', curiously spotted and splashed with purple and cream, was lost, then rediscovered in Yorkshire, but now seems untraceable. 'Beverley Pink', dark red flaked with white or yellow; the deliciously perfumed 'Lincolnshire Lass' or 'Lothian Lass'; the double rose 'Fettes Mount'; 'Black Prince', double white with an almost black centre; the violet laced 'John Ball' from Turner's Slough nursery; the Victorian 'Ruth Fischer', with small, very double white flowers – these represent but a sample of the many that are still sought.

Distributed in Europe, Asia and Africa, the genus *Dianthus* consists of some 300 species of annuals and perennials. Comparatively few have been granted garden room, overshadowed as they are by the carnations, pinks, sweet williams and their ilk. However, the species can boast several indispensable rock plants, among them *D. fragrans*, a native of the Caucasus. It makes an untidy mat of numerous sprawling stems about 12 inches long and in July bears small white or pink-flushed flowers with finely toothed petals. It is seldom seen today and its delightful double form is even rarer. The latter has the merit of being 'more compact than the type, and its white flowers are perfect little rosettes.' It was obviously uncommon at the beginning of this century when it was said to have been 'noticed one summer in the nursery of Mr Charles Turner of Slough'.

A regular item in catalogues of that period was *D. pavonius*, which was usually offered under the incorrect name of *D. neglectus* and had been introduced from Europe in 1869. It forms dense tufts about 6 inches high, with thin grey-green leaves and blooms of pale or deep pink, buff on the reverse of the petals. Its hybrid 'Roysii' is a particularly choice plant, having much larger flowers of rich rose red, with wide overlapping petals also buff-coloured on the outside. Messrs Ingwersen of East Grinstead, Sussex, sometimes had 'a few to spare' in the 1930s but it is difficult to increase and has always been lamentably scarce in cultivation. It is now probably extinct.

Dicentra *Bleeding Heart*

Dicentra chrysantha

Bleeding heart, lady's locket, Dutchman's or Chinaman's breeches, lady in the bath, Our Lady in a boat – the string of affectionate names bestowed on *Dicentra spectabilis* suggests that it is an old and cherished inhabitant of gardens. A native of Siberia and Japan, it was in fact introduced at the beginning of the nineteenth century and was soon taken up by gardeners and even by designers of wallpaper patterns. Today its tall, arching sprays of rose-red blooms are less often seen and it has been generally superseded by smaller species like *D. eximia* and *D. formosa* and by their cultivars. However, a pure white form of *D. spectabilis*, which breeds true, has recently been made available and has quickly become popular.

Gracefully hanging heart-shaped flowers in pink or yellow and delicate fern-like leaves are characteristic of members of this genus. Some were known in the past under the generic name *Dielytra*, but *Dicentra* is now the accepted usage. It is derived from the Greek *dis*, double, and *kentron*, spur, and refers to the twin spurs of the flowers. The genus contains some twenty species in all, several of them just as lovely as *D. spectabilis* but unaccountably scarce.

D. chrysantha was discovered in California by the celebrated Scottish collector David Douglas and introduced in 1852 by the Cornishman William Lobb on behalf of Messrs Veitch of Exeter. Unlike many of the introductions for which these men were responsible, this one unfortunately never became common in British gardens. It was exhibited about forty years later by Sir Frederick Moore, curator of the Irish National Botanic Gardens, Glasnevin, but had to wait until 1929 for the accolade of an Award of Merit, when it was described as 'a distinct species, rare in cultivation'.

D. chrysantha differs from its fellows in several respects – its greater height, 3 to 5 feet, its later flowering time, and its stiffly held rather than pendulous clusters of bloom. The golden yellow flowers appear in August and September, complemented by finely cut greyish foliage. 'The contrast between the gray dull leaves and gay glittering flowers is particularly agreeable,' as *Paxton's Flower Garden* observed. It is also unusual in preferring a sunny position in dry soil. But it is by no means an easy plant to maintain in cultivation, still less to obtain, though seed is occasionally offered by botanic gardens in the USA.

Like most members of the genus, *D. oregana* (Plate 32) needs a cool, shady situation in moist but well-drained soil. Some authorities now consider it a subspecies of *D. formosa*. Grown for some time in its native USA, it is a relative newcomer to Britain and at the end of the 1930s was described in one catalogue as 'new to cultivation, a valuable addition'. It forms a compact hummock about 6 inches high, with silvery, deeply divided leaves, and in May and June produces flowers like dangling lockets of creamy yellow tipped pink inside.

Another rarity in this undeservedly neglected genus, and also rare in its native habitat, is *D. macrantha*. It was found in central China by Dr Augustine Henry, who was responsible for many discoveries in that region which were subsequently introduced by E. H. Wilson. According to James Veitch, Henry 'detected the herb in a wood in Hupeh, and only obtained one plant'. Through Wilson, who later collected seeds, it reached Britain in 1889. It has dissected, greyish leaves, jagged at the edges, and bears drooping clusters of pale yellow, elongated flowers in spring. It is nearer *D. spectabilis* in scale at about 18 inches high and no more difficult to grow. It seeds reasonably well and, once established, can also be increased by careful division of the rather fleshy rootstock. Good examples of this beautiful species can be seen at Wisley and Wakehurst Place, Sussex, and plants may now be bought from one or two specialist nurseries.

Dierama *Wandflower*

Dierama pulcherrimum

'In late summer, tall, thin, but toughly wiry stems of 4 feet or so, wavering and swaying this way and that beneath a long dropping shower of chaffy-cupped rose-purple bells on pedicels so fine that they hardly seem to be attached at all'. *Dierama pulcherrimum*, the subject of Reginald Farrer's description, and the smaller but similar *D. pumilum* are the chief representatives in Britain of this South African genus. Previously included under *Sparaxis*, it consists of about twenty-five species and takes the name *Dierama* from the Greek word for funnel, referring to the narrow, trumpet-shaped flowers. The gracefully arching, slender stems explain the delightful common names – wandflower and Venus's or angel's fishing rod.

The charms of *D. pulcherrimum* have never been fully appreciated. As the nurseryman and collector Clarence Elliott observed in the 1950s, 'it is the rarest thing to find it in gardens.' Mr W. Slinger and his son Leslie, of the Slieve Donard nursery in Northern Ireland, had already attempted to remedy the situation by hybridising and selecting from *D. pulcherrimum*. One of their earliest successes was 'Windhover', with flowers of deep lilac-rose borne on stems up to 9 feet high. It won an Award of Merit in 1920, as did the white 'Album' in 1921. These were followed over the years by about twenty named forms in various shades of pink and purple, mostly called after birds and all about 5 to 6 feet in height. 'Heron', 'Kingfisher', 'Skylark' and 'Falcon' received Awards of Merit in the 1920s and 1930s, as did 'Plover', one of the last, in 1956 and again in 1975 after a Wisley trial. But by then only 'Albatross' and 'Blackbird' (Plate 33) were left in the Slieve Donard catalogue.

Meanwhile, so the story goes, a South African lady presented the nursery in 1939 with two unidentified dwarf dieramas, one rose-coloured, the other yellow. The latter died, but not before it had been used for hybridising, and crosses between these and *D. pulcherrimum* yielded a new race of hybrids. There were about twelve altogether, in colours of pink and violet and usually with Shakespearian names such as 'Ariel' and 'Oberon'. Less drooping and about $2\frac{1}{2}$ to 3 feet high, they are more practical for a small garden.

Dieramas need a rich, moist but well-drained soil and a sunny, sheltered position. The large corms are best planted in spring, about 6 inches deep, and the plants should be protected from frost in winter with bracken or similar material. Transplanting may also be carried out in spring, an operation which, as Leslie Slinger warned, causes them to lose their foliage. In both cases, they take a year to establish themselves before flowering, but will eventually create clumps and seed freely. Named forms may be propagated by separating and replanting the small offsets.

'It is a fair question to ask why these lovely plants are not seen more often if they grow with such freedom with me,' wrote Slinger in 1957. They have never earned the recognition they deserve and with his death in 1974, followed by the sad closure of the Slieve Donard nursery, they lost their principal advocate. Most of the named hybrids have disappeared from commerce and from gardens, where they have been overwhelmed by their wilful seedlings. However, efforts are now being made in Ireland to track down and rescue any survivors.

Eremurus   *Foxtail lily*

The genus *Eremurus* has been strangely neglected by both gardeners and plant collectors. As presently known, it consists of about forty-five species native to western and central Asia and chiefly concentrated in the southern Soviet Union. Of these, very few are in general cultivation and even then are not widely grown or readily available in commerce. The number of new species brought in by recent expeditions suggests that there are more still to be discovered and introduced.

The generic name *Eremurus* comes from the Greek *eremos*, solitary, and *oura*, tail, and like the common name, foxtail lily, refers to the most outstanding feature of these majestic plants – the enormous spires of tightly packed flowers with protruding stamens, each one like a miniature lily. The genus belongs to the family *Liliaceae* and its members are all very similar in appearance. The

Eremurus spectabilis

large, strap-shaped, folded leaves emerge in spring and die away in summer, forming a loose clump at the base of the tall, straight, bare stem, topped with its huge cone of blossom. In the wild the foxtail lilies grow in abundance on dry, stony hillsides and mountain slopes, where they enjoy a copious rainfall in spring followed by baking summer heat and snow in winter. These unusual conditions are not easy to emulate in cultivation. The *Eremurus* species and hybrids need a rich, thoroughly drained, sandy soil and a sheltered position in full sun and, although generally hardy, the precocious rosettes should be protected against frost with dry leaves or bracken. Propagation from seed is slow and they can take up to six years to reach flowering size. However, the crowns may be lifted when the foliage has withered and carefully separated into piece without damaging the long, fleshy, brittle roots. After replanting, they should be left undisturbed for two or three years.

Partly, no doubt, because of their cultural demands and partly because of their sheer magnificence, the foxtail lilies are poorly represented in gardens. 'Their whole aspect is so surprising and the height of the giant flower stem so great that they are out of scale with ordinary garden plants,' commented Gertrude Jekyll. There is also a practical problem in accommodating them. '*E. robustus* has large roots that radiate horizontally, much like a cart-wheel without the tyre, so that each plant requires an uninvaded root space of five feet diameter.'

Together with *Eremurus elwesii* (*E. aitchisonii*), *E. himalaicus*, *E. olgae* and *E. stenophyllus* (*E. bungei* of gardens), *E. robustus* remains one of the best-known species. Introduced from Turkestan in 1874, this 'doyen of the genus' produces in June a mass of deep salmon-pink bloom covering half the 8-foot stem, above broad, bluish-green leaves. A more vigorous, taller and later flowering form was grown in the past, notably by the great plantsman Sir Frederick Stern of Highdown in Sussex. It was named *E. robustus tardiflorus* by H. J. Elwes, the distinguished gardener, botanist and author, but now unfortunately seems to have disappeared.

Another of the more familiar and amenable species is *E. stenophyllus*, long known as *E. bungei*. Distributed in Iran, Afghanistan, Pakistan and the neighbouring USSR, it is up to 5 feet tall and bears orange-yellow flowers in June and July. The subspecies *aurantiacus* is distinguished by its downy stem and sharply ridged and channelled leaves, which are dull green and numerous. Its lemon-yellow flowers faintly tinged with green are crowded into a cylinder up to 1 foot long. 'This fine Asphodel' was first described from specimens gathered in Afghanistan in 1840. Ian Hedge and Per Wendelbo, writing in 1963 of their expedition to Afghanistan, observed that it was the commonest of all species there and grew in most mountainous parts of the country, as well as being planted in graveyards. Glue is apparently made from the roots and, according to William Robinson, the leaves are cooked as a vegetable 'upon which the inhabitants depend for at least two months of the year'. Prolific in its native land, this striking plant is now very seldom seen in gardens.

The most widespread species in the genus, which is found from Lebanon to Soviet central Asia and Afghanistan, is one of the rarest in cultivation. *E. spectabilis* was an early introduction and may have been grown at the Apothecaries' Garden, Chelsea, in 1827. The *Botanical Magazine* of 1855 called it 'a really handsome, hardy, Asphodelaceous plant', although it is very variable in the dimensions of its greyish-green leaves and in flower colour, which Hedge and Wendelbo considered 'not very attractive' when they saw it in the wild. From 2 to 5 feet in height, its blooms at their best are of sulphur-yellow slightly tinted orange and with bright red anthers, closely clustered in a tapering spike. It flowers in June before many of its fellows.

In contrast to the broad-ranging *E. spectabilis*, *E. afghanicus* has been recorded only from a small area of Afghanistan near Kabul. It was described as recently as 1954. Above the spongy, felted foliage its stem rises to about 6 feet and is surmounted by a large head of small, pure white flowers. Hedge and Wendelbo thought that it might be 'a worthwhile plant and probably no more difficult of cultivation than *E. robustus*'. They were also impressed with *E. kaufmannii*, a dwarfer species up to 3 feet high with downy leaves and a narrowing raceme thickly set with white, yellow-centred flowers. Neither of these highly desirable plants has yet secured a place in gardens.

In Afghanistan Hedge and Wendelbo came across a number of beautiful natural hybrids. These occur frequently in the wild and have also been raised in cultivation. The Shelford hybrids, in shades of orange, pink, yellow and white, are the most usually grown today and are said to have been derived from *E. bungei* and *E. olgae*. They were developed by Sir Michael Foster, professor of physiology at Cambridge and a noted iris specialist, in his garden at Great Shelford.

Two other great plantsmen associated with the improvement of the genus were H. J. Elwes and Sir Frederick Stern. The former is commemorated in

E. elwesii, one of the most beautiful of the foxtail lilies with its blooms of clear pink or white and thankfully quite well established in gardens. From several hybrids given him by Elwes in 1920, Stern went on to produce his own Highdown hybrids. Vigorous and flowering in mid- or late June, there were 'many coloured forms from deep pink, light pink, lemon, apricot and pure white' as Stern recounted. One particularly fine plant had much larger individual flowers than normal, of pale pink and borne in a $2\frac{1}{2}$-foot spire on a stem of about $3\frac{1}{2}$ feet high. It won an Award of Merit in 1962 as 'Highdown Dwarf' (Plate 31). Sadly, this exquisite hybrid and the rest of the Highdown stable are no longer obtainable from the trade and, unless they still linger in a few gardens, have probably faded from cultivation.

Franklinia

Franklinia alatamaha

It is pleasant to record a success story in the conservation of a plant no longer known in the wild. *Franklinia alatamaha*, also spelt *altamaha* (Plate 34), was discovered by John Bartram in 1765, the year of his appointment as botaniser royal for America, on one of his journeys through the southern part of the country. On the coastal plain of Georgia by the Altamaha river and near Fort Barrington, he found it growing in moist, sandy, acid soil within a small area of about two to three acres. His son William, who accompanied his father on this occasion, subsequently returned in 1773 and again in 1778 to collect seeds and seedlings. These became established in the Bartrams' garden in Philadelphia (now famous as the first American botanic garden) – which was just as well because, by 1790, the original wild population had apparently ceased to exist. All the plants now in cultivation derive from plants or seed introduced by the Bartrams and by Moses Marshall, the botanist who described the species in 1785. At Bartram's behest, he named it after 'their distinguished friend and neighbour Benjamin Franklin', the American statesman, scientist and philosopher.

Franklinia took well to garden cultivation. Writing to J. C. Loudon's *Gardener's Magazine* in 1831, William Wynne mentions a tree some 50 feet high flowering in the Bartrams' garden and one of their plants is said to have lived into the twentieth century. The Bartrams were generous in distributing stock and *Franklinia* reached this country in 1774. Sadly it arrived too late to be seen by their wealthy patron and fellow Quaker, Peter Collinson of Mill Hill, who had been responsible for the introduction of so many North American plants before his death in 1768. At the end of the nineteenth century C. S. Sargent, in his monumental *The Silva of North America*, reported it as 'flourishing in England and central Europe'.

William Bartram considered *F. alatamaha* 'of the first order for beauty and fragrance of blossoms'. It is a most attractive deciduous tree of neat, symmetrical growth, usually 20 to 25 feet in height, with lightly toothed leaves 5 or 6 inches long which are arranged alternately on their short stalks and turn a warm scarlet before they fall. The large 3-inch cupped blooms resemble those of a single camellia, to which it is allied, and are freely borne towards the ends of the branches from late summer into autumn until the frosts intervene. Delightfully scented, each consists of 5 snow-white petals, frilled at the margins and complemented by the bright yellow central boss of stamens, and together 'make a gay appearance', as Bartram put it. Seed capsules are frequently set on mature plants, opening by a curious zig-zag splitting of the hard coat to release the woody seeds. This is one character differentiating it from *Gordonia*, a closely related genus in which it is sometimes placed.

F. alatamaha is firmly established in botanic and private gardens in the United States, although much less common in Europe. It may be propagated without difficulty from seed or by half-ripe cuttings or layering, but requires long, hot summers to produce regular and abundant bloom. Unfortunately, in the uncertain climate of Britain, it flowers only intermittently. However, it is a charming small tree for our gardens, with the added bonus of its fine autumn foliage, and deserves to be much more widely grown in its own right. *Franklinia* is almost certainly extinct in the wild, whether through human agency or from natural causes, and is also the only known representative of its genus, which makes it all the more important to maintain good stocks in cultivation.

Fritillaria *Fritillary*

Fritillaria alburyana

The genus *Fritillaria* is a large and fascinating one, particularly so since several of its members have been only recently discovered. Related to *Lilium* and *Tulipa*, it numbers at least eighty species distributed across the northern hemisphere. Britain's native snakeshead, *Fritillaria meleagris*, with its bell-shaped flower hanging from the top of the stem, is now unfortunately restricted to a few meadows in southern and eastern England. Like its close European allies, it has the chequered petals which inspired the generic name, from the Latin *fritillus*, dice box. Fritillaries are spring-flowering and generally hardy, though not all are amenable to cultivation. Apart from *F. meleagris*, which can be naturalised successfully in grass, some of the easiest to grow are *F. acmopetala*, *F. camschatcensis*, *F. pallidiflora* and *F. pyrenaica*, all of which will thrive in any well-drained but fairly moisture-retentive soil.

The crown imperial, *F. imperialis*, has long been grown in gardens. Native to the western Himalaya, southern USSR, Iran and Turkey, it was first cultivated by the Turks and seems to have been introduced to Vienna in 1576 by the pioneering Flemish botanist, Clusius. The Persian lily, as it was called, reached England soon afterwards. As Gerard records, 'this plant hath been brought from Constantinople, amongst other bulbous roots, and made denizons in our London gardens, whereof I have great plenty.' It was known originally as *Corona imperialis*, perhaps from its association with the Hapsburg court, or in allusion to the ruff of pointed leaves crowning the cluster of large, pendent, bell-like blooms. These surmount a sturdy stem of 3 feet or more, the lower half clad in whorls of glossy green foliage. The bulbs give off a strong, foxy odour which has led to another name, stink lily.

Such a distinctive plant has conjured up various legends. It was apparently too proud to bow with the other flowers as Christ entered the Garden of

Gethsemane; when reproved, it hung its head and flushed red with shame and ever since has had tears in its eyes – the drops of nectar in the petals. Today the red form is relatively uncommon, yellow or orange being more usual, but these are a poor relic of the many variants grown in the past. Parkinson, who admired the crown imperial 'for his stately beautifulnesse', mentions several different kinds in 1629, 'whereof some are white, others blush, some purple ... some spotted'. An eighteenth-century nursery catalogue offered over twenty named forms, without actually stating the names, including double and variegated ones.

The crown imperial seems to have suffered an eclipse in Victoria's reign and was often listed by nurserymen merely as 'common sorts'. But the eight cultivars mentioned by Philip Miller in 1759 were still available in the early twentieth century. It is only since then that the double and, more regrettably, the variegated forms have become so rare. E. A. Bowles was particularly 'fond of the two variegated forms, both the golden and the silver; the mingling of burnt sienna, green and cream colour in a young shoot, is very beautiful.' He grew them in his garden at Myddelton House on the outskirts of London, where they are said to have survived into the 1960s.

Like the Madonna lily, the crown imperial used to flourish in cottage gardens where it was left to its own devices. It requires a rich, heavy soil, preferably in full sun. The dormant bulbs should be planted in July, about 5 inches deep, and not disturbed. Once established they sometimes spread by seeding themselves, but more often increase by offsets from the main bulb. When clumps become congested, they should be lifted and replanted after dying down in the summer. They may also be propagated by carefully breaking off the thick bulb scales, which will form small bulbs if grown on in a sand frame.

In contrast to the historic crown imperial, one of the newest species dates from the 1960s. It was encountered coincidentally on three separate occasions by different people and it was subsequently named in honour of S. D. Albury, a member of the expedition which first discovered it in June 1966, who died on a later plant-collecting trip to Nepal. *F. alburyana* was a spectacular find, not only because its existence was unsuspected but because it is botanically unique to the genus. Its appearance is certainly striking. Up to 4 inches high with green, pointed leaves, it produces one or two large, open flowers, almost saucer-shaped and usually held horizontally. These are pale rose to purplish-pink, faintly chequered a darker pink and with a cluster of brown and yellow anthers protruding from the centre.

F. alburyana is native to the province of Erzurum in northeast Turkey, where it grows in peaty soil and scree by patches of late snow, at an altitude of 6,500 to 10,000 feet, and blooms from May to July. It is of limited distribution in the wild and in cultivation has proved very difficult to flower. As Albury wrote in 1970, 'it has not yet settled down'. Of the few plants collected and distributed to specialists, only one could be induced to bloom, grown in scree conditions protected by a plastic roof at Birmingham.

Like this outstanding fritillary, many other species are uncommon or very localised in their natural habitats. The yellow *F. conica* and dark purple *F. davisii*, both confined to southern Greece, the pale green, darkly chequered *F. involucrata* from southern France and northwest Italy, the yellow *F. sibthorpiana* from southwest Turkey, and the curious *F. michailovskyi* (Plate 35), yellow with a reddish-brown base, from northern Turkey, are some that fall into this category. Fortunately, they are fairly easy to grow in a bulb frame or alpine house. The pale cream and green *F. liliacea* is now virtually extinct in its native California owing to the pressures of urban development and agriculture, although again it is not too difficult to grow. But several other species are doubly at risk, in the same way as *F. alburyana*, because of their capriciousness in cultivation. Among these may be mentioned *F. purdyi*, another Californian, and the pale lemon *F. forbesii* and diminutive *F. minima*, both from Turkey. It is obviously important that all these rare fritillaries, however intractable, should be maintained in cultivation and increased, as a precaution and a preventive measure against further threats to their populations in the wild.

Galanthus *Snowdrop*

The word snowdrop, from the German *schneetropfen*, came into general usage in the seventeenth century. Older English names for this well-loved plant, such as fair maids of February, Candlemas bells and white ladies, arise from its association with the Feast of the Purification of the Virgin or Candlemas Day on 2 February, when it was the custom to scatter snowdrops on the altar and bring them into the house. It was regarded as an emblem of purity and also, according to St Francis, as a symbol of hope. After Adam and Eve were expelled from the Garden of Eden, goes the legend, an angel transformed falling snowflakes into flowers to announce that spring would not be long delayed. The early herbalists including Gerard and Parkinson considered the snowdrop to be a 'bulbous violet'. They apparently owed this belief to Aristotle's disciple, the Greek botanist Theophrastus, who in the fourth century BC had applied the word *Leucoion*, literally white violet, to bulbous plants with white flowers, as well as to stocks and wallflowers. Only in 1735 was it allocated by Linnaeus its own genus, *Galanthus*, from the Greek *gala*, milk, and *anthos*, flower.

Whether the common snowdrop *Galanthus nivalis* is native to Britain is a matter of debate. It is found wild in many parts of the country but almost always, it has been suggested, in the vicinity of ancient monasteries where it would have

Galanthus reginae-olgae

been grown for its religious significance. It is certainly widespread throughout Europe, from northern France to the USSR and southwards to the Balkans and Greece, as a woodland plant proliferating happily in the leafmould. Produced from February to April depending on locality and altitude, its elegant, drooping white blooms with their green-tipped inner segments have the additional bonus of a honey fragrance if placed in a warm room. As might be expected of such a broadly dispersed species, variations are not uncommon.

Such was the enthusiasm for the genus in the late nineteenth century that a snowdrop symposium was held by the RHS in 1891. Three distinguished horticulturists, James Allen, D. Melville and F. W. Burbidge, contributed detailed papers and mentioned the many selections that had been named. Although few of these have survived, 'Atkinsii', said to have been procured 'from somewhere in the Kingdom of Naples' and offered as long ago as 1875 by Messrs Barr & Sons of Covent Garden, remains very popular today. The curious form known as *scharlokii* or the donkey's ear snowdrop, with the separate flower spathes elongated into a pair of 'ears' above the flower, is also still available, if somewhat more difficult to please. It is recorded as occurring wild in the valley of the Nahe, a tributary of the Rhine and, apart from its ears, differs from the common snowdrop in having green lines at the top of the outer segments and green patches on the inner ones. A very late-flowering form, in which the outer segments are pale green shading to white at the edge and the inner segments entirely green, is called 'Virescens'. Strangely attractive but not easy to grow or maintain, this is now extremely hard to trace except in one or two specialist collections.

A number of variants with yellow markings on the inner segments and a yellow ovary have been found in the wild in Britain and are referred to as either *lutescens* (Plate 37) or *flavescens*. The latter, occasionally dubbed 'Howick Yellow', supposedly indicates a more robust plant. Both were located in gardens in Northumberland in the late nineteenth century, but there is some doubt as to which is now in cultivation. James Allen claimed that *flavescens* was the more rewarding. One stock passed around by modern 'galanthophiles' increases rapidly and grows happily in a leaf-rich, well-drained, slightly shady position. It is a most worthwhile plant under whatever name, providing a warm glow of gold to complement the cooler green and white garb of its fellows during February. Equally delightful though perhaps less amenable is the double yellow 'Lady Elphinstone'. According to E. A. Bowles, it was found in a garden near Crewe around the turn of the century. He describes it as a 'loosely formed graceful double, with the usual markings of the inner segments of a good bright yellow, and a very charming thing when looked full in the face'. Some reversion to pale green is normal after transplanting but, once settled, it returns to its characteristic colouring and, as Bowles put it, repays 'patience with pure gold'.

Gardeners are often unaware of the existence of other species of *Galanthus* beside the common snowdrop and its double form, and only the large greyish-leaved *G. elwesii* features regularly in catalogues. Nevertheless, the majority of the ten to fifteen species recognised are in cultivation and a few of them are listed in limited quantities each year by specialist nurserymen. *G. reginae-olgae*, named after Queen Olga of Greece in 1876, is native to Greece, Corfu, Yugoslavia and Sicily and has recently been discovered in western Turkey. It grows in light woodland or more open rocky sites and is allied to *G. nivalis*, but distinguished from it by the recurved green leaves with a marked grey central stripe and also by the flowering period. This varies from September to December, while forms from the northern part of the range, which have been classed as subspecies *vernalis*, bloom in January or February. *G. reginae-olgae* has not proved particularly difficult to grow and increases fairly quickly by seed and daughter bulbs. There is no reason why it should not become more readily obtainable, to join the autumn crocuses, colchicums and sternbergias which are so appreciated by gardeners as the year fades into winter.

G. cilicicus is now ranked as merely a tall, slender form of *G. nivalis* and has intensely grey-green leaves which are well developed at flowering time. It is an outlier of the common species, occurring in a few areas of the Cilician Taurus in western Turkey and Lebanon, and is valuable for its December or January blooming. However, lack of availability and a certain distaste for the northern European climate mean that it is only very rarely seen. More biddable but again in short supply are several of the bright green-leaved snowdrops, including *G. rizehensis* from the Black Sea coast and *G. ikariae* from some of the Greek islands, together with its subspecies *latifolius* from the Caucasus and northeastern Turkey. None asks more than an open, well-drained situation in reasonably fertile soil to thrive and seed freely. The almond-scented *G. allenii* appeared among a consignment of bulbs of *G. ikariae* ssp. *latifolius*, which

Allen had purchased in 1883 through an Austrian nurseryman. Its large, dark green, slightly bloomy leaves set it apart from the *G. ikariae* variants we know in gardens, but it may be simply a further variation on that theme. As a garden plant, it increases easily except in very acid soils and presents no problems, apart from attacks by the narcissus fly and the 'snowdrop disease', *Botrytis galanthina*, to which all snowdrops are prone. But it is still confined to specialist collections and has not made any impact on the trade.

From a commercial point of view, most snowdrops are slow to increase. However, it is possible that the micropropagation techniques currently used in the daffodil industry might be applied in due course to snowdrops. As members of the same family, the *Amaryllidaceae*, and with a comparable bulb structure, they should respond without too much additional research. Unfortunately such an advance would come too late to enable us to retrieve some of the outstanding cultivars raised since the last century. 'Allen's Perfection', 'Anne of Geierstein', 'Cupid' and 'Jenny Wren', 'Rebecca', 'Romeo', 'Tomtit', 'Valentine' and 'White Swan' have apparently perished for ever. On the other hand, there are many excellent hybrids which are eagerly sought but seldom offered. 'Merlin', for instance, has substantial blooms borne on long stems and displaying the clean outer segments in contrast to the deep green solid mark on the inner ones. Such desirable plants could be subjected to intensive propagation methods with great benefit to gardeners.

Gentiana *Gentian*

Gentiana farreri

With its brilliant blue trumpets, *Gentiana acaulis* is universally familiar from chocolate boxes and travel posters – if not from our gardens where it often declines to bloom. In the popular imagination it stands as a worthy representative of this diverse and beautiful race. But another less spectacular gentian, the tall, yellow-flowered *G. lutea*, far outstrips it in historical importance. Valued by the ancients for utility rather than ornament, gentians have been associated with man for over four thousand years and are recorded on papyrus in a tomb at Thebes among the plants prescribed in medicine. However, according to Pliny in his *Naturalis Historia*, the first to learn of their tonic properties was Gentius, king of Illyria in the second century BC, whose name was officially adopted for the genus by Linnaeus.

The root of the gentian, known to Gerard and his contemporaries as felwort or bitterwort, was applied in the treatment of stings and bites, as an antiseptic and to reduce fever. The sixteenth-century herbalist William Turner tells us that it not only counteracts poisoning, but 'helps biting of mad dogs and venemous beasts, opens the liver and procures an appetite. Wine where in the herb hath been steept, being drunk, refreshes such as are over-wearied by travel or are lame in the joynts by cold or bad lodgings.' Even in the nineteenth century it remained 'the principal European bitter used in medicine', as J. C. Loudon observes. It was employed in brewing before the advent of hops and still imparts its bitter flavour to the French aperitif 'Suze' and other alcoholic drinks.

Occupying 'extensive tracts of ground untouched by any cattle', *G. lutea* abounds in the alpine pastures of Europe. Reginald Farrer compared this stately plant, 4 to 5 feet high, to a 'stalwart torch crowded with radiating sparks of sunlight in successive tiers'. Like many of its fellows, unfortunately, it does not take kindly to lowland gardens. As Parkinson gloomily remarks, some species 'will abide no culture and manuring'. Britain's delightful spring gentian, *G. verna*, now very rare in the wild and protected by law, he considered will 'encrease reasonable well if it finde a fit place and ground to grow, or else will not be nursed up, with all the care and diligence that can be used'.

With some 400 species recognised, gentians are widely distributed through-out the world, except for the African continent. The funnel-shaped bloom is fairly typical, but they vary immensely in flower colour, habit and size. The vast majority are plants of high mountain regions subject to heavy rainfall, where the air is saturated and the soil drainage is very sharp. Blanketed by snow in winter, they enjoy fairly constant conditions, protected from extreme damp which would rot the crowns, while the melting snow in spring provides a continuous water supply at the roots as they surge into growth. Farrer called them 'children of pure mountain air and moisture' and it is scarcely surprising that they dislike the changeable climate of most parts of Britain, apart from Scotland. At the beginning of winter, he suggests, such gems as *G. verna* and *G. bavarica* should be covered with panes of glass to keep excess moisture from their resting rosettes. 'The sufficiently enthusiastic', he continues, 'have been known to subsist entirely through the summer on glass-potted tongues and shrimps in order that the receptacles of those delicacies should afford a sufficient number of roofs to shelter all their Gentians in winter.'

Several species thrive happily in our gardens, including the woodland willow gentian, *G. asclepiadea* from Europe and western Asia, with arching wands of blue or white, and *G. septemfida* from the Caucasus and Asia Minor, with its deep blue flower clusters in late summer. The superb autumn-flowering *G. sino-ornata* from the Himalaya usually presents no problem in acid soils and the famous trumpet gentian of the Alps and its close relatives can be grown by most people, if not always flowered. However, many gentians are much more demanding and notably the high alpine species. But they are so lovely as to merit almost any effort from the gardener to achieve the reward of their blooms.

Eastern Asia is the source of several exquisite gentians, secured by Wilson, Kingdon Ward, Farrer, Forrest, Ludlow and Sherriff and other celebrated collectors. As a result species like the magnificent deep blue *G. veitchiorum* from western China and *G. ornata* have become established in cultivation, though still uncommon even in botanic gardens. Originally collected over 150 years ago, *G. ornata* (Plate 38) has provoked great controversy and twice been wrongly figured in the *Botanical Magazine* as a different species. It is a charming, compact alpine with tubby, bell-shaped flowers of clear pale blue, borne in August and September and staying open even in dull, wet weather. It is by no means easy to maintain in cultivation, but may be propagated by careful division of the basal rosettes as growth begins. Seed is an alternative method, although this tends to produce hybrid offspring if *F. ornata* is grown near others of its race.

The same hazard besets *G. farreri* and no doubt explains its disappearance from gardens. It was introduced in 1914 by Farrer and his companion William Purdom from the high alpine area of the Da-Tung (Tatung) mountains in northern Kansu and hailed as one of the finest of all gentians. Farrer's enthusiasm was unbounded. He describes how it could be seen a quarter of a mile away growing in the turf, the flowers 'an indescribably fierce luminous Cambridge blue within, with a clear white throat, while, without, long vandykes of periwinkle-purple alternate with swelling panels of nankeen, outlined in violet and with a violet median line'. It was excellently illustrated in the *Botanical Magazine* of 1938, where it was stated to be 'a feature of many gardens, particularly rock gardens, since its robustness of habit and freedom of flowering make it especially desirable'. Sadly, this is no longer the case. *G. farreri* is occasionally offered, but the plants are apparently hybrids from marriages with allied species such as *G. hexaphylla* and *G. sino-ornata*. Despite their attractions, these do not compare with the original introduction, which has probably slipped from cultivation.

A similar fate has befallen *G. kurroo*. It is found at altitudes between 5,000 and 11,000 feet in the western Himalaya and is related to our native bog gentian, the more demure *G. pneumonanthe*. Again, Farrer's portrayal of this superlative plant cannot be bettered.

G. kurroo forms a single and unmultiplying tuft of a very few long, very narrow, grooved and glossy leaves of dark-green. From this in late summer, proceed one or two smooth mahogany stems, set here and there with a pair of leaves, and once or twice (or yet again) emitting a separate flower-stalk. Those dark and shining stems, although so solid, do not stand erect, but lie along the ground for 4 or 5 inches and then rise up with the grace of a swan's neck, to show off at respectful distances from each other those three or four magnificent great flowers, widely gaping cups of pure rich blue, with folded lobes, and flecked with interior pallors and altogether lovely.

Farrerian eulogies aside, it ranks unquestionably among the most superb alpines. However, the plants now available as *G. kurroo* have been incorrectly named and less worthy gentians have usurped its position. It is to be hoped that, following recent expeditions to Kashmir, the authentic plant will soon be restored to our gardens in all its glory.

Geranium   *Cranesbill*

Geranium wallichianum
'*Buxton's Variety*'

The genus *Geranium* (not *Pelargonium* of bedding and pot-plant fame) is the source of some of our most valuable hardy perennials – vigorous, free-flowering, adaptable and willingly increased. This fact was recognised by English gardeners of old when they tamed the native wild cranesbills and early adopted other species from abroad. The European *Geranium macrorrhizum*, for instance, arrived in 1576, while the dark-flowered *G. phaeum*, known as mourning widow, was grown by the herbalist Gerard and is one of several that have become naturalised in Britain.

Cranesbill is an oddly direct translation of the official name, from the Greek *geranos*, crane, and alludes to the long beak of the seed vessel, which often opens explosively to release the ripe seed. The flowers are characteristically saucer-shaped with five petals and the normally five-lobed leaves, deeply incised and jagged, range from fresh green to greyish, sometimes richly tinted in autumn. This large genus numbers some 400 species, of cosmopolitan distribution, perhaps thirty of which are generally available to gardeners, not including cultivars and hybrids.

One of the commonest is the meadow cranesbill *G. pratense*, a native of northern Europe, including Britain, and Asia. Clump-forming and about 2 feet high, it has long-stalked, deeply divided leaves and flowers usually of violet-blue. White, pink, white-streaked and double forms are also relatively familiar. However, a particularly choice cultivar, 'Mrs Kendall Clark', seems to have become rare. The flower colour, according to a catalogue in 1946, is 'not easy to describe. The nearest we can get to it is pearl-grey flushed with softest rose.' Although a plant was submitted to the Wisley trials under this name, it lacked the unusual colouring and was probably not the true 'Mrs Kendall Clark', whose survival is now in doubt.

'It has always been a matter of astonishment to me that such splendid subjects as the hardier geraniums are so rarely grown in the average garden' wrote A. T. Johnson. If any one person is associated with the genus, it is he. Plantsman, fisherman, journalist and author, he gardened in north Wales, not far from Bodnant, until his death in 1956. The well-known *Geranium* 'Johnson's Blue', probably a hybrid between *G. himalayense* and *G. pratense*, originated from seed of *G. pratense* sent by Johnson to a Dutch nursery and was put on the market in 1950. He also selected *G. endressii* 'A. T. Johnson', with silvery pink blooms, and, on a visit to southwest Scotland in the 1930s, he found 'Glenluce', a clear pink form of the native *G. sanguineum* or bloody cranesbill.

Johnson exchanged many plants with his neighbour and friend, E. C. Buxton, who is commemorated most notably in *G. wallichianum* 'Buxton's Variety' (Plate 36) or 'Buxton's Blue' as it is often called. *G. wallichianum* itself was discovered in the Himalaya by collectors for Nathaniel Wallich, the Danish naturalist and surgeon in charge of the Calcutta Botanic Garden, and was introduced in 1820. 'A showy species', in the words of the *Botanical Magazine*, it is of trailing habit, 6 to 9 inches high, and has toothed leaves and stems covered in soft hairs. The purple flowers are dark-veined with a pale centre and provide a continuous display from the end of June into the autumn. Its merits were evidently appreciated in the last century and in a survey of gardeners and nurserymen in 1891 it was voted one of the best hardy summer perennials.

However, the form raised by Buxton in his garden at Bettws-y-Coed 'totally eclipsed' the species itself, in Johnson's opinion. 'The $1\frac{1}{2}$-inch, bowl-shaped flowers of Buxton's Geranium are such a lovely nemophila blue, accentuated by the bold eye, that those of the average G. Wallichianum seem a muddy lilac by comparison', while 'the fresh green, prettily lobed downy leaves often assume an emerald tint with purple cloudings, and the stems a ruddy hue.' Johnson first saw 'Buxton's Variety' in a very unpromising situation, 'a bed mostly composed of slaty rock on the north side of a damp wall, and considerably overhung by Laurel branches'. He recommended that it should be grown in shade, although it is equally happy in full sun, in any good, well-drained soil, and is suitable for a rock garden or the front of a border. Like most members of this amenable genus, it can be planted from autumn to spring and is easily propagated by division at the same time of year or by seed sown when ripe or in spring. There may be some variation in colour over the years, but it comes 'tolerably true' from seed.

In 1929 'Buxton's Variety' won an Award of Garden Merit, which is bestowed on plants of outstanding garden value. Johnson believed it was 'destined to endure', but even at the time it was 'very scarce' according to one catalogue. Although it has remained surprisingly unfamiliar to gardeners, it is now beginning to appear in the lists of a number of specialist nurseries and is well worth seeking out.

Another geranium connected with Buxton is a miniature pure white form with green stems of *G. robertianum*, the common wild herb robert, which is normally pink-flowered and brown-stemmed. Sometimes known as 'Celtic White', it had been given to Buxton by a friend but is only occasionally to be found in gardens today.

Ginkgo *Maidenhair tree*

The maidenhair tree is a not uncommon sight in the parks, gardens and streets of Europe and America. The famous tree at Kew was planted in 1762 and is one of the largest in the British Isles, over 70 feet tall. First described in 1712 by the German physician and traveller, Engelbrecht Kaempfer, *Ginkgo biloba* (Plate 39) was brought from Japan to the West, probably first to Holland, around 1730 and to Britain in 1754. James Gordon of Mile End, regarded as one of the most knowledgeable and skilful nurserymen of his day, was at that time reported to have a tree and he remained for several years the sole source of supply. Whether he could have been the unfortunate in J. C. Loudon's tale of how the ginkgo got to France is not specified. One Pétigny, on a visit from Paris in 1780, was offered by an English nurseryman five very expensive young plants of the ginkgo, 'which was still rare in England, and which the gardener

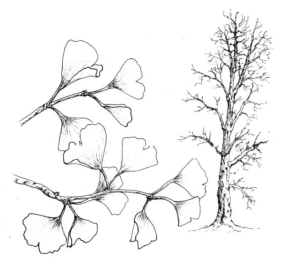

Ginkgo biloba

pretended that he then alone possessed.... However, after an abundant *déjeûné*, and plenty of wine, he sold to M. Pétigny these young trees of Ginkgo, all growing in the same pot, for 25 guineas. ... Next morning, the effects of the wine being dissipated', he tried to buy one of them back for 25 guineas, but was refused. From Pétigny's five trees bought for 40 crowns each, all those in France are supposed to be derived and the French call the ginkgo *l'arbre à 40 écus*. Shortly afterwards, the ginkgo also reached the USA via Philadelphia.

In China the maidenhair tree has been grown since at least the eleventh century AD and was introduced to Japan at about the same period. According to E. H. Wilson, 'this strikingly beautiful tree is associated with temples, shrines, courtyards of palaces, and mansions of the wealthy throughout the length and breadth of China, and also in parts of Japan.' C. S. Sargent, the dendrologist and first director of the Arnold Arboretum at Harvard University, had visited Japan and admired the 'noble great broad-branched specimens in the neighbourhood of the temples in Tokyo fully a hundred feet high', some of which were reputed to be a tremendous age. The ginkgo was assumed to have some religious significance, but the Chinese-American botanist, Hui Lin Li, has recently argued that it did not and that it just happened to be associated with holy places because the priests allowed it to remain with the natural forest in the vicinity.

If the maidenhair tree is secure in cultivation, it is almost certainly extinct in the wild. Its original home is believed to be in the mountains of Chekiang and Anhwei provinces, where it has been found apparently growing spontaneously, and in such abundance that trees were being felled for firewood. But some 200 million years ago, long before its final retreat to eastern China, the ginkgo and its kin were distributed all over the globe. Fossil species of *Ginkgo* have been discovered not only in Asia but in North America, Greenland and the British Isles, and are scarcely different from the existing species. Remarkably, this solitary survivor represents a prehistoric race that flourished in the Jurassic and Cretaceous periods, before the Ice Age and well before the dawn of civilisation. It is a precious and tenuous link with an immensely distant past.

Apart from *Metasequoia glyptostroboides*, another 'living fossil', *Ginkgo biloba* is unique in every sense – the only species in the genus *Ginkgo*, the only genus in the family *Ginkgoaceae*, and the only relic of the ancient group, the Ginkgoales. In its own right it is a magnificent deciduous tree, usually pyramidal in outline though broadening with age, and sending up main branches from fairly low down the trunk which, in turn, produce smaller, slightly weeping branches. These are hung with graceful sprays of distinctive, fan-shaped leaves, which are frequently notched in the middle (hence the epithet *biloba*) and recall those of a maidenhair fern. The foliage is a fresh pale green in spring and darkens before turning to a wonderful bright gold in the autumn.

Most of the ginkgos in Europe are male trees, occasionally bearing flowers like small thick catkins. The fruits of the female tree ripen in late winter in Britain and resemble greenish-yellow plums, with a rancid-smelling sticky flesh. They contain a sweet kernel which is considered a delicacy in the East. When roasted the nuts are said to aid the digestion and diminish the ill-effects of wine. In China the maidenhair tree is known as white fruit, as well as duck's foot, alluding to the shape and colour of the autumn leaves. In Japan it is called *icho*, tree, and *ginnan*, silver apricot, and it has been suggested that the name ginkgo resulted from Kaempfer's inaccurate transliteration of the Japanese. The English botanist, J. E. Smith, thought the name *Ginkgo* was so 'uncouth and barbarous' that he changed it to *Salisburia adiantifolia*, which was frequently used in the nineteenth century despite its lack of botanical standing.

There are at least four cultivated forms of the maidenhair tree available – 'Laciniata', with large, deeply divided leaves, wavy at the margins; 'Pendula', with more pendulous branches; 'Fastigiata', of conical habit, which is especially popular in the USA; and 'Variegata', with faint yellowish stripes to the leaves. The ginkgo is completely hardy, very adaptable and resistant to air pollution. In the cooler West it is slow-growing, often taking thirty to forty years to reach maturity. It is easily propagated from seeds or from semi-ripe cuttings of the young growths.

The ginkgo is an extraordinary monument to prehistory and a living one. Although it is infinitely older than the human race, it apparently owes its continuing existence to man. As Li has written, 'with the aid of man, it now reinhabits ground lost to nature during the past million years' and 'thrives even in a modern urban environment'.

1 *Abutilon ochsenii*

2 *Acer nikoense*

3 *Alstroemeria caryophyllea*

▲ 5 *Allium schubertii*
◄ 4 *Aconitum heterophyllum*

▼ 7 *Amaryllis belladonna* 'Cape Town'

◄ 6 *Acanthus dioscoridis*
▼ 8 *Anemone vitifolia*

9 *Anchusa
caespitosa*

10 *Aquilegia nivalis*

11 *Aspidistra elatior*
   'Variegata'

12 *Bomarea*
   andimarcana

13 *Camellia*
   granthamiana

14   *Asclepias speciosa*

15   *Brassica balearica*

16   *Campanula piperi*

18   *Clematis texensis*

17   *Cardiocrinum giganteum* var. *yunnanense*   20   *Cheiranthus* 'Harpur-Crewe'

19   *Caesalpinia japonica*

21 *Clethra delavayi*

22 *Colchicum*
    atropurpureum

23 *Crocus*
    oreocreticus

▲ 25   *Cyclamen pseudibericum*
◄ 24   *Convallaria majalis* 'Prolificans'

▼ 27   *Decumaria sinensis*

26   *Cosmos atrosanguineus*

28 *Cypripedium*
japonicum

29 *Daphne genkwa*

30 *Dianthus*
'Bat's Double Red'

32   *Dicentra oregana*

31   *Eremurus* 'Highdown Dwarf'

33   *Dierama* 'Blackbird'   34   *Franklinia alatamaha*

▲ 36   *Geranium wallichianum* 'Buxton's Variety'

◄ 35   *Fritillaria michailovskyi*
► 37   *Galanthus nivalis* var. *lutescens*
▼ 38   *Gentiana ornata*

39   *Ginkgo biloba*

40   *Gypsophila* 'Bristol Fairy'

41 *Helleborus*
    'Louis Cobbett'

42 *Hepatica nobilis*
    double red

43 *Hesperis*
    matronalis
    'Alba Plena'

45   *Iris rosenbachiana*

44   *Hemerocallis fulva* 'Kwanso Variegata'

7684

46   *Hidalgoa wercklei*

47   + *Laburnocytisus adamii*

48   *Lardizabala biternata*

50   *Lilium parryi*

49   *Lathyrus nervosus*

52   *Linum arboreum*

51   *Myosotidium hortensia*

53   *Meconopsis grandis* 'Branklyn'   54   *Metasequoia glyptostroboides*

55 *Muscari
macrocarpum*

56 *Mutisia
decurrens*

57 *Ostrowskia
magnifica*

58 *Paeonia
suffruticosa
'Rock's Variety'*

59 *Pamianthe
peruviana*

60 *Papaver
orientale*

61 *Passiflora
      antioquiensis*

62 *Picrasma
      quassioides*

63 *Pleione* x *confusa*

65　*Polygonatum geminiflorum*

64　*Podophyllum pleianthum*

66　*Poliothyrsis sinensis*　67　*Primula vulgaris* 'Alba Plena'

68   *Potentilla* 'Monsieur Rouillard'

70   *Quercus robur* 'Concordia'

69   *Pulsatilla* 'Budapest'

72 *Ranunculus asiaticus*

71 *Scabiosa caucasica* cultivar

74 *Rosa* 'Fortune's Double Yellow'

73 *Stuartia pseudocamellia*

75 *Tulipa saxatilis*

76 *Vinca major*
    'Multiplex'

77 *Viola*
    'Jackanapes'

78   *Worsleya procera*

79   *Tecophilaea cyanocrocus*   80   *Xanthoceras sorbifolium*

Gypsophila

Gypsophila 'Bristol Fairy'

Gypsophila paniculata is one of those indispensable plants whose role is to enhance others – a favourite in flower arrangements, traditionally associated with sweet peas and carnations, and a welcome counter-balance to the bold shapes and often strident colours of the summer border. It is probably the most widely grown member of the genus, together with the alpine *G. repens* and the beautiful annual *G. elegans*. In all there are some 125 species of *Gypsophila*, native mainly to Europe, the eastern Mediterranean and the USSR. As the name implies, from the Greek *gypsos*, gypsum, and *philos*, friendship, they are lime-loving plants and tend to inhabit arid mountains in the wild.

G. *paniculata* is popularly known as chalk plant and baby's breath. It hails from Siberia and eastern Europe and was introduced in 1759. It is a perennial which dies right down in winter and in late spring quickly burgeons into a bushy dome about 3 to 4 feet high and as wide, composed of numerous branching, slender stems and narrow, grey-green leaves. From the end of June to August it is covered in a haze of tiny, grey-white flowers, with a slight but warm scent. After this it becomes rather unsightly and Gertrude Jekyll recommended hiding 'the greater part of the brown seed-spray' with trailing nasturtiums.

A double white variant of *G. paniculata*, 'Flore Pleno', had been grown for some time, but it was not until 1925 that a new and superior garden form made its début. 'Bristol Fairy' (Plate 40) won an Award of Merit two years later, when the RHS *Journal* reported that 'this excellent herbaceous plant is an improvement on the old double-flowered *G. paniculata*. It is more robust and has a stronger constitution, and bears much larger panicles of pure-white double flowers. The height of the plant is about 4 feet, and flowering commences even earlier than in the old form, and continues over a long period.' Another breakthrough came in 1938 with 'Flamingo', which also received an AM. It is similar to 'Bristol Fairy' in height and habit, with large double flowers flushed a pale rose-pink.

Gypsophilas are relatively easy to grow and are hardy except in very severe winters. They resent cold and damp and need a position in full sun, in dry, well-drained soil with some rubble and lime incorporated and sufficient depth for their long tap roots. They should be planted between October and March and left undisturbed. However, both 'Bristol Fairy' and 'Flamingo' are inclined to be short-lived, the latter being especially temperamental. They are also difficult to propagate, the most effective method being by grafting on to seedling *G. paniculata*. Cuttings of side shoots may occasionally root, but seldom result in strong plants.

Such factors no doubt explain why these highly desirable forms have become so scarce in gardens and in commerce. They seem to have been largely superseded by the dwarfer cultivars of *G. paniculata*, the white 'Compacta Plena' and 'Rosy Veil' or 'Rosenschleier', which are more reliable garden plants and easier to increase. Although 'Bristol Fairy' and to a lesser extent 'Flamingo' were fairly standard items in catalogues until the 1960s, they are now offered by only a few nurseries. Unless they continue to be made available and grown, they could be in danger of disappearing from the garden scene for ever.

Helleborus   *Hellebore, Christmas or Lenten rose*

There are probably some fifteen to twenty species of *Helleborus*, depending on taxonomic opinion, confined to Europe and Asia. Perennial and evergreen or deciduous, they have distinctive, deeply lobed or divided leaves and large cup- or saucer-shaped blooms, consisting of five sepals with a central boss of stamens and pistils surrounded by nectaries derived from the true petals. Hellebores are greatly valued for their presence at a bleak season, the earliest appearing in late winter and the Lenten roses continuing into March and April. The 'flowers have the most beautiful aspect, and at the time of his flowering most rare', wrote Parkinson of the Christmas rose. Like the majority of hellebores this has black roots, whence its name *Helleborus niger*, which was given by Linnaeus.

The identity of the true black hellebore is uncertain, though it was possibly the variant of *H. orientalis* known as *H. olympicus*. Similarly, the derivation of the Greek generic name is obscure and the word *helleboros* was also applied to species of *Veratrum*. The Greeks, however, recognised the poisonous properties of the hellebore. It apparently enabled Attalus of Pergamum to

Helleborus orientalis 'Dr Moore'

pursue his hobby of disposing of unwanted friends. The ancients endowed it with extraordinary powers and the belief that it cured insanity persisted into the sixteenth century. Gerard recommended it 'for mad and furious men, for melancholy, dull, and heavie persons' and Paracelsus, the sixteenth-century Swiss physician and chemist, claimed that, powdered and mixed with sugar, it renders 'old people younger and more vigorous'. In Britain the native setterwort *H. foetidus* and the bear's foot *H. viridis* were used to treat sick cattle, while *H. niger* was planted near the front door to ward off evil spirits.

H. niger may have been brought over by the Romans, although some authorities fix its arrival in the late sixteenth century. Distributed in central and southern Europe, it is variable in nature but normally up to 12 inches high, with leathery dark green leaves and red-spotted stems. The flowers, from 2 to 5 inches in diameter, semi-erect or nodding, are borne singly or severally and range in colour from white tinged with green or pink to pure white. A subspecies, *macranthus*, is distinguished by its dwarfer stature, green stems and very large, clear white blooms, often overtopped by the spreading bluish-green foliage. The form sold today as 'Potter's Wheel' is almost certainly descended from this.

The nurserymen of the late Victorian period maintained a broad selection of *Helleborus* species and cultivars, as a glance at their catalogues shows. Of *H. niger* alone there were at least eight forms. Prominent among them was 'St Brigid', always presented in glowing terms with its 'snow white wax-like petals' and 'fresh green foliage'. It was named by F. W. Burbidge, plant collector, writer and at the time curator of the botanic garden of Trinity College, Dublin. He spotted it growing in the garden of Mrs Lawrenson, who had adopted the name of St Brigid, the patron saint of Co. Kildare, as her pen name and was later to breed the famous double St Brigid anemones. 'St Brigid' was probably a form of *H. niger macranthus*, and, according to another hellebore specialist,

William Brockbank, in an article in the *Gardeners' Chronicle* of 1884, it was the same as the form called 'Brockhurst'. He argued that it had been established for many years in England as well as Ireland and may have been the 'true' Christmas rose extolled by Gerard and Parkinson, which had been introduced by Dutch gardeners in the reign of Elizabeth I. Whatever its origins 'St Brigid' was offered by many nurseries until well into the next century. It was often planted in the kitchen garden for cutting and was also cultivated on a commercial scale. As Shirley Hibberd, the popular Victorian gardening author, wrote 'it is quite a proper thing . . . to visit Covent Garden Market at an early hour on a morning of December to see the Christmas roses.' But by 1932 'St Brigid' was ominously 'scarce' even in the catalogue of the noted hellebore nurserymen Barr & Sons of Covent Garden and it had been dropped from their list within a few years. This historic and once so well known cultivar is now lost to cultivation.

Other forms of *H. niger* had a much more fleeting existence. 'Mr Poë's Variety', for instance, commemorates a hellebore enthusiast and friend of Burbidge, John Bennet-Poë of Tipperary. But it does so only in a lovely painting of 1887 by Lydia Shackleton for the Irish National Botanic Gardens, Glasnevin. Another one, 'Apple Blossom', had 'flowers rosy white, outside of petals rosy purple'. It received a brief mention in Barrs' catalogue in the 1890s and then disappeared. It is to be hoped that the same fate will not befall one of the outstanding modern cultivars, the pink-flushed 'Louis Cobbett' (Plate 41, not Lewis Cobbett as it is sometimes written). This gained a Certificate of Preliminary Commendation in 1962 when shown by Anna Griffiths of Cambridge. Its white blooms are sufficiently tinted to suggest that it could be the progenitor of a race of blush-pink forms of the Christmas rose. But it is still rarely seen even in the gardens of hellebore aficionados.

Many of the hellebores grown in gardens today are derived from *H. orientalis* and its allies. The species reached Britain from Asia Minor in 1839, but the Lenten roses as we know them date from the 1850s onward and the pioneering work of T. Archer Hind of Devon. Their exact origins are now impossible to disentangle and *H. orientalis*, *H. abchasicus*, *H. guttatus* and other variations on a similar theme all had a role in the breeding. Modern botanists tend to lump these 'species' under *H. orientalis*, although from the gardener's viewpoint they are reasonably distinct. Members of this group do, however, hybridise very freely between themselves and with the *H. dumetorum* complex. Generally speaking the Lenten roses are about 2 feet high with flat or slightly cupped blooms up to 2 inches across, often freckled and ranging in shade from creamy pink to pink and deep plum. The deep purple colouring is provided by *H. abchasicus* and the attractive carmine spots by *H. guttatus*, both from the Caucasus.

In addition to Archer Hind and others in Britain, breeders on the Continent were busy in the late nineteenth century. An anonymous article of 1884 recounts how 'within the past few years these half dozen so-called species have been taken in hand by hybridists, the result being that a numerous race of seedling varieties has been obtained by inter-crossing ... carried out chiefly in continental nurseries and gardens.' The British horticultural press endlessly discussed the new hellebores and the nurseries kept pace in their catalogues, with Barr foremost among them. The hellebore craze was closely linked to the daffodil boom of the time and involved many of the same people such as Burbidge, Bennet-Poë and especially Peter Barr, 'the daffodil king'. At 'Mr. Barr's bulb grounds at Tooting ... is to be found the most complete collection of Hellebores which at present exists', reported the *Gardeners' Chronicle* in 1879. They included 'one of the finest forms known in cultivation', 'Dr Moore', which had been raised by David Moore, curator of Glasnevin until 1878 when he was succeeded by his son Frederick. *The Garden* was equally admiring: 'it is an abundant bloomer of vigorous habit with greenish stems spotted with purple. The flowers are larger than those of the type, of a lively rose tint, with the edges and inner face of the sepals of a lighter hue.' This too was painted by Lydia Shackleton for Glasnevin, but is now feared to be extinct.

Possibly of German origin was the striking 'Black Knight', which won an Award of Merit in 1927. It was described as having 'very dark purple flowers, covered with a rich bloom, foliage dark bronzy green, very handsome'. It was available from Barrs in the 1930s and was grown by the plantsman Eliot Hodgkin in Berkshire in the 1970s, but has remained a great rarity. Another unusual and sought-after form is 'Ballard's Black'. It was raised in Hereford-shire by Ernest Ballard, the celebrated breeder of Michaelmas daisies, whose daughter-in-law continues the tradition by collecting and hybridising helle-bores. In his catalogue it was said to have huge, well-shaped flowers, nearly black in colour with clusters of pale anthers in the centre.

Several attempts have been made to obtain yellow-flowered hellebores by selecting seedlings of Lenten roses. Among those raised by Archer Hind were 'Primrose Dame' and 'Coombe Fishacre Yellow', both more yellow-green than white. A pale lemon-yellow was achieved in 'Luteus Grandiflorus' from Glasnevin, which has probably not survived, and in 'Bowles' Yellow'. At present very uncommon, this is worth every effort to acquire, not only for its exceptional shade but for its valuable early flowering, at the same time as *H. niger*. Some of the best yellows, with potential for improving the colour depth of hellebores, are grown by Mrs Ballard.

One of the most interesting *Helleborus* hybrids is *H. × nigericors*, a cross between *H. corsicus* and *H. niger*. The latter had never been recorded as a parent until this spontaneous hybrid occurred in the garden of J. E. H. Stooke of Hereford in the 1930s. It was grown at Wisley up to the 1950s, but subsequently lost. However, in 1958 the plantsman E. B. Anderson repeated the cross and called the result 'Beatrix' after his wife. This magnificent plant produces stout stems about 12 inches high, carrying trusses of a dozen or more flowers about 2 inches across, of cream with a green tint. It was also grown by Hodgkin, a friend of Anderson's, but unfortunately has not gained wider circulation, mainly because it is difficult and slow to propagate. The cross has again been made by Elizabeth Strangman of Washfield Nurseries in Kent, who has introduced a number of very fine forms of *H.* × *nigericors*, such as 'Alabaster', which are gradually reaching the public.

The reasons for the loss of many named forms of hellebore in the past and their comparative scarcity in the trade today are not hard to find. They can only be propagated true by division and, since they are slow to increase, this diminishes their value in the eyes of the commercial grower. Most hellebores also seed themselves freely and the seedlings can be just as desirable and worthwhile and less trouble than perpetuating a particular selection. On the whole hellebores are easily grown in moist, well-drained, fertile soil, whether alkaline or acid, and preferably in some shade. The Christmas roses are more demanding than the Lenten roses, doing better in alkaline soil with sharp drainage. All resent disturbance and should not be allowed to dry out in summer and autumn. Division is best carried out in early autumn when the ground is still warm enough for the divisions to re-establish readily.

The species of *Helleborus* are generally much less familiar than the Christmas and Lenten roses, although they attract a small but devoted following among gardeners. Of the green-flowered hellebores, many are quite common in the wild and of easy culture. But, apart from *H. corsicus* and *H. foetidus*, they rate only an occasional entry in catalogues. *H. cyclophyllus* from southeastern Europe, with large, scented blooms, the distinctive *H. multifidus* from Yugoslavia and Albania, with multipartite, palm-like leaves, and *H. bocconei* from southern Italy, which often flowers in December, are all worthwhile plants for the woodland garden and seed around once settled.

The taxonomically difficult *H. dumetorum* group, which includes plants grown as *H. purpurascens*, *H. atrorubens* and *H. torquatus*, again presents no problems in cultivation. Rather smaller-flowered than *H. cyclophyllus* and its allies, they have injected into their hybrids the characteristic purple found especially in *H. purpurascens*. While not the showiest of hellebores, they have a peculiar fascination with their sombre colours.

H. vesicarius bears small green flowers with brownish rims akin to *H. foetidus*, but its extraordinarily swollen seed pods are unique to the genus. It is perhaps the rarest of all the species in gardens. Archer Hind, writing in 1900, believed that it had 'never been seen in England' and the introductions in the 1950s by Dr Peter Davis and Oleg Polunin have not survived. Native to southern Turkey and northern Syria, like many plants from that region it becomes dormant during the summer months and dies off completely above ground, not reappearing until the autumn rains. Bulb frame treatment or a position under the eaves of a house are likely to provide the most suitable growing conditions should this remarkable species be reintroduced.

Hemerocallis   *Day lily*

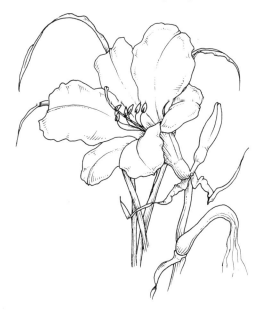

Hemerocallis minor

The day lily is one of the oldest plants known to man. Cultivated thousands of years ago in China for its edible flowers, which are still considered a delicacy, *Hemerocallis fulva* may well have originated there as Linnaeus believed. It has been propagated by division for centuries, since it does not set seed. *H. flava* is equally ancient. It was familiar to the Egyptians and Romans and was included as a medicinal herb in the influential *Materia Medica* by the Greek Dioscorides in the first century. Both these lily-asphodills, as they were then termed, reached England in the 1570s and were grown by Gerard and 'also in the gardens of Herbarists, and lovers of fine and rare plants'.

In his *Garden Book* of 1659 the gentleman gardener Sir Thomas Hanmer noted that 'we have only the Orenge, which is called the Day Lilly, continuing in flower but a day, and the Yellow.' The generic name, from the Greek *hemera*, day, and *kallos*, beauty, also refers to the brief life of the bloom. A hundred years later, these two day lilies were joined by a third, *H. minor*, from eastern Asia. As the epithet suggests, it is less tall than the others, about 10 to 18 inches high, and was at first considered a dwarf variety of *H. flava*. It bears large, trumpet-shaped flowers, lemon-yellow tinged with brownish red on the outside and faintly scented, above a dense clump of long slender leaves. The blooms, from two to five per spike, open on successive days and appear in May and June. *H. minor* was recognised as a separate species by Philip Miller in 1768. It is distinguished from *H. flava* by being smaller in every feature except the flower, having fine rather than fleshy roots and dying down earlier in the autumn. The *Botanical Magazine* of 1805 portrayed it as the 'narrow-leaved day-lily' with two illustrations, 'the more entire one from a specimen actually raised from Siberian seeds'. According to William Robinson in 1883, it was 'also known in many gardens under the highly characteristic name of *H. graminea*, from its grass-like foliage.' His implication that it was a fairly common plant is no longer true, although it has everything to recommend it, especially for smaller gardens.

'Quite hardy and of easy culture' as the *Botanical Magazine* stated, *H. minor* shares the tolerant nature of all the day lilies. They thrive in any reasonable situation and ordinary, not too dry soil and can be naturalised in grass. *H. fulva* and *H. flava* are particularly prolific, spreading by means of rhizomes, while others form a thick mass of roots and need division after about five years to prevent them becoming congested and less floriferous. This is the simplest method of increase and may be carried out in early spring or autumn.

There are countless modern cultivars, many of them from the United States and Australia where day lilies are very popular. These often represent an improvement in colour range and size of flower, but they have tended to detract from the merits of the species themselves and of some of the older and equally desirable garden forms. One old favourite less often seen today is a semi-double form of *H. fulva* known as 'Kwanso Flore Pleno'. About 3 to 4 feet high, it has large blooms of orange mingled with red and copper. A version with variegated as opposed to plain green leaves (Plate 44), apparently the original holder of the name, was imported from Japan at the same time in the 1860s. This beautiful plant with its distinctive silver-striped foliage is now a collector's item.

The nurseryman Amos Perry, of Enfield in Middlesex, was a pioneer in the development of day lilies, as well as of bearded irises and poppies, and a few of his cultivars survive, remarkably, in gardens. A notable casualty, however, was 'E. A. Bowles', which he named in honour of his great gardening neighbour. It was selected for trial at Wisley in 1931 and had well-expanded flowers nearly 6 inches across in 'a delightful shade of orange-apricot, with a faint reddish zone'. It is sad to think that this lovely plant with its associations should have been lost.

'One of the finest new hardy plants obtained within recent years' was how *The Garden* of 1885 welcomed *H. aurantiaca*. It was said to have been found in Japan among a clump of *Iris kaempferi* and was named in 1890 from a plant growing at Kew by the botanist J. G. Baker, who thought it 'worthy to be regarded as a distinct species', although it is probably no more than an ancient garden form. It produces up to fifteen funnel-shaped flowers, about 4 inches across, which open successively and are clustered at the top of the 3-foot stalk, well above the narrow green leaves. Rich orange in colour, often with a reddish-brown flush, they appear in June and July. *The Garden* noted that it was 'now being distributed, and no doubt ere long will be plentiful'. Up to the 1930s it was listed regularly in catalogues but since then, inexplicably, has almost disappeared.

Baker reserved his highest praise for *H. aurantiaca* 'Major', which he called 'the finest Hemerocallis I have seen'. It is a more vigorous form with bigger, more abundant flowers of deep orange-yellow, although it is reputed to be less hardy than *H. aurantiaca* itself. It was imported from Japan in about 1890 by Wallace & Son of Colchester. It too has become lamentably scarce.

Hepatica

Hepatica nobilis, double

Hepatica nobilis (or *H. triloba*), which has long been grown in our gardens as *Anemone hepatica*, is now dignified with its own small genus. The curious name comes from the Greek *hepar*, liver, and like the English equivalent, noble liverwort, and the alternative name, trinity flower, it alludes to the shape of the three-lobed leaves. The plant was also valued in the Middle Ages for its supposed curative effects on the liver and 'specially for the liver of newly married young men which are desirous of children'. From the time of Gerard onwards, writers have agreed on the garden merits of this dainty plant. No more than 6 inches high, its anemone-like flowers appear in February, just before the tufts of new leaves emerge – 'the most welcome early guests' as Parkinson described them. The petals are usually lavender-blue, surrounding the pale yellow stamens, but white, pink, red and deep blue forms are recorded if seldom obtainable today.

The double hepatica was especially prized. Like the single, which is native to Europe, it was believed to have originated on the Continent. At the beginning of the seventeenth century, Parkinson grew ten forms of hepatica, including a double purple 'sent from Alphonsus Pontius out of Italy, as Clusius reporteth and which was also found in the woods near the Castle of Starnberg in Austria'.

According to Sir Thomas Hanmer in his *Garden Book* of 1659, 'there are only Two with Dowble Flowers, one of a rich Blew color, the other a red or flesh color.' These, the blue or purple and the red, sometimes called pink or peach, remained common well into the twentieth century. But the double white has always been a rarity and some even doubted its existence. The Victorian parson Canon Ellacombe, famous for his garden at Bitton in Gloucestershire, admitted he had never seen it, 'but I was assured by the late Mr. Wheeler of Warminster . . . that it only occurs as the autumnal form of the single red.' Reginald Farrer mentions 'a very miffy and expensive double white' and it was very occasionally offered in catalogues up to the 1930s.

With the exception of the double white, hepaticas in all their colours and forms were widely available from the nursery trade up to the Second World War. Messrs Van Tubergen, the Holland-based nursery, continued to list the double blue and red (Plate 42) until the 1960s. The single kinds, while not difficult to grow, are slow to settle down and flower which is probably one explanation for their slump in popularity. As Farrer pointed out, the hepatica 'luxuriates in damp rich woodland soil, and forms, in time, huge clumps; and it acutely resents being divided and disturbed.' They should be planted in March in leafy soil and semi-shade, taking care not to bury the crown below the soil surface, and will need a year or two to establish before blooming freely. Single-flowered plants may be increased by division, or from seed sown as soon as ripe, preferably in small pots of seed compost plunged outside to undergo winter-freezing. Germination should occur in spring and the young seedlings are then planted into a leaf-rich soil to grow on, prior to planting in their final positions.

The double forms are more awkward to grow and 'in many gardens almost an impossibility' in Ellacombe's view. The double white in particular 'seems never to be of strong constitution', according to Gertrude Jekyll. Division is the only current method of propagation and is carried out immediately after flowering. The young divisions should be grown in partial shade and kept well-watered until they become established. As Hammer noted in 1659, perhaps identifying another reason for their decline in gardens, 'the Dowble kind never bears fair large flowers in smoky towns, but delights in a pure ayre.'

A few plants of the double forms remain in private collections and some can be seen in the Queen's Garden at Kew. But they are rare and likely to disappear completely unless micropropagation techniques can be developed to increase them in quantity and ensure their wider distribution.

Hesperis *Sweet rocket*

Hesperis matronalis 'Alba Plena'

'Double White Rocket is in full blow, and its soft tone of white is a thing of its own . . . whiter than the grey of an oyster, and greyer than the greenish gleam of Lowestoft china.' Of the several double forms of *Hesperis matronalis*, the white so lovingly described by E. A. Bowles was always the most common. It is still just in cultivation and a plant exhibited as 'Alba Plena' (Plate 43) won an Award of Merit in 1972. But this cottage garden favourite had already become 'a rare old-world plant' in catalogues at the beginning of the twentieth century, when Gertrude Jekyll lamented the fact that it was 'no longer in general cultivation'.

Known as sweet rocket, dame's or damask violet, queen's or rogue's gilliflower, *H. matronalis* has been grown in Britain since at least the sixteenth century. Like the other gilliflowers it was highly esteemed for its fragrance, which is strongest in the evening and accounts for the generic name, from the Greek *hesperos*, evening. Parkinson, unusually, thought that it had 'neither sight nor scent much to commend it' and the single form, with the characteristic cross-shaped flowers in May and June, is pleasant rather than spectacular. Tolerant of poor soil and seeding itself freely, it is often advocated dismissively for the wild garden.

However, the double rocket is 'one of the handsomest and certainly one of the sweetest of garden flowers' in Miss Jekyll's words. It is supposed to have been introduced to England by Huguenot refugees and was also apparently a favourite flower of Marie-Antoinette. As Sir Thomas Hanmer portrayed it in his *Garden Book* of 1659, 'the leafe is of a darke color, with teeth in the edges like a saw. The flowers grow many on a stalke like stockes, but closer together. Their color is either White or Red, and their sent in hott yeares and countreys very sweet.'

The double white and the double red, by which he no doubt meant purple, remained the most familiar. But there were other variants too, in the three basic colours of white, purple and lilac and differing in size and vigour. William Robinson distinguished two of the whites, a tall one shading to pale pink; and a dwarfer one with more compact flowers which (in 1883) 'is met with in the North, but little known in the South' and had a reputation for being particularly capricious. There seems to have been a third, perhaps the true old pure double white. The pale lilac was very robust and is thought to have been the one that received an Award of Merit in 1904, when the true old lilac was already almost extinct. Of the two purples, one had a reddish tinge and was a strong grower and coarsely leafed. A 'variegated' or purple and white striped was never more than a rarity.

At least four of these cultivars were grown regularly by Victorian gardeners. They were popular bedding plants, especially in northern England, and in Ireland where they can sometimes be traced today. But by 1901 the RHS *Journal* was mentioning two of them as 'old and rare', the double lilac and the double purple. The rest were seldom offered in catalogues of the day and have now totally disappeared from commerce. Perhaps the last time the double sweet rocket was seen in any quantity was when Thomas Hay was in charge of Hyde Park in the 1920s and 1930s: 'The Guildford Hardy Plant Co ... supplied them at a very cheap rate, so that huge beds of the white and purple graced our London Parks ... and the Royal Gardens, Kew.'

The double *H. matronalis*, like so many desirable double forms, is difficult both to cultivate and to propagate, almost certainly because of debilitation by virus infection. It requires 'good earth', rich and moist but well-drained and preferably limy, in sun or partial shade, and even then may not be satisfied. Nor is it always completely hardy. Hanmer observed that it ought to 'stand in a warme place abroad all wynter, otherwise to be kept in potts', although in many gardens it has survived severe weather without trouble. However, plants quickly deteriorate after a year or so in one position and should be propagated regularly to maintain stocks. If the flower heads alone are removed after blooming, instead of cutting down the stems, new side growths will develop which can be used as cuttings and rooted in a cold frame.

Hidalgoa

Hidalgoa wercklei

The arrival of this new climbing dahlia in 1898 caused quite a stir in the horticultural press. It had been discovered by a Costa Rican collector, Carlo Werckle, in the mountains of his homeland and was distributed by the New York nurseryman, J. L. Childs, as *Childsia wercklei* or treasure vine. A plant sent to Kew flowered in 1899 and was then assigned to the genus *Hidalgoa*. This contains only three species, native to Brazil and Costa Rica, and is closely related to *Dahlia*, differing chiefly in the climbing habit. The name commemorates a Mexican naturalist of the early nineteenth century, M. Hidalgo.

Hidalgoa wercklei (Plate 46) is a tender greenhouse perennial and in cultivation can reach a height of 20 feet, as it did in the Temperate House at Kew. It clings in the same way as a clematis, twisting the leaf stalks round any available support, and branches freely, with its divided leaves 'of a cheerful green' tipped reddish brown. Flowering throughout the summer, it has dahlia-like blooms up to $2\frac{1}{2}$ inches in diameter, of brilliant scarlet with a yellow centre and underside.

Despite its exotic appearance, *H. wercklei* is easy to grow in ordinary soil and readily increased by young stem cuttings, rooted in gentle heat. 'Doubtless it is a plant come to stay' remarked *The Garden* in 1900. Three years later it won an Award of Merit, when it was described as 'a rampant climber suitable for clothing rafters and pillars in lofty greenhouses'. There perhaps lies the reason for its subsequent decline into obscurity. The days of lofty greenhouses were already passing and there are now very few gardeners who could find room for such a beautiful and vigorous plant even if they were able to obtain it, which is unlikely.

Iris

Iris winogradowii

'Let me hear from thee; for where so'er thou art in this world's globe, I'll have an Iris that shall find thee out.' Iris was the amiable messenger of the gods and here, in Shakespeare's *Henry VI*, of mortals too, whose rainbow spanned the gap between heaven and earth and whose name was applied by Linnaeus to this rich and beautiful genus. Gerard ably expressed its extraordinary diversity:

> There be many kindes of Iris or Floure-de-luce, whereof some are tall and great, some little, small and low; some smell exceeding sweet in the root, some have no smell at all. Some floures are sweet in smell, and some without; some of one colour, some of many colours mixed; vertues attributed to some, others not remembred; some have tuberous or knobby roots, others bulbous or Onion roots; some have leaves like flags, others like grasse or rushes.

The 250 or more species of *Iris* now recognised are distributed throughout the northern hemisphere from high mountains to sea level and from deserts to watersides. Some have been cultivated since man first made use of plants. The ancient Egyptians regarded the iris as a symbol of eloquence and one species, possibly *Iris albicans*, is represented on the walls of the temple of Thutmosis III at Karnak. The iris also has a special place in Moslem culture, for it is believed to signify wealth and is planted on graves to ensure that the dead will be well-endowed in the next world. *I. albicans*, one of the flag group of irises and originally native to Saudi Arabia and the Yemen, is naturalised in virtually all countries conquered by the Saracens and often found on the sites of cemeteries. It is even recorded from Mexico, presumably having been transported there by the Spanish.

An attractive garden plant, *I. albicans* produces its sweetly scented white or blue flowers on stems 1 to 2 feet high. In general aspect it is a typical bearded iris and has been much confused with *I. florentina*, which is today considered to be an albino of the ubiquitous *I. germanica* or common iris whose blue-purple perfumed flowers adorn many a back yard in May. The white iris of William Turner's *New Herbal* of 1551, with roots 'whyche are cut in little shives or cakes, and are dried in the shadow, and then are put upon a threde, and so kept', is almost certainly *I. florentina*. It is the source of the orris root with its violet fragrance, which was valued in the Middle Ages as a basis for toilet waters and cosmetics.

The iris was credited with a fantastic assortment of medicinal properties in the past, from assistance in childbirth and the removal of freckles to the healing of broken bones and ulcers. But perhaps it is most celebrated as a heraldic device, the fleur-de-lis of the French monarchy which Louis V I I adopted as his emblem during the Crusades. This was the yellow flag iris *I. pseudacorus*, a common plant of marsh and pond in Britain and spread across Europe to western Siberia. Its royal associations stretch further back, to an incident in the sixth century when the Frankish king Clovis I was cornered by the Goths near Cologne. He noticed irises growing far out in the Rhine and, realising that the water must be shallow there, was able to escape across the river. It also became a flower of chivalry, with 'a sword for its leaf, and a lily for its heart'. In Gerard's time, the roots were supposed to 'take away the blacknesse or blewnesse of any stroke or bruse', while the seeds, despite their purgative powers, later enjoyed some vogue as a coffee substitute.

A number of species of the bearded or Pogon irises have been hybridised to provide the marvellous range of colourful cultivars available today. These and most members of the group are relatively easy to grow, preferring well-drained, slightly alkaline soils and a sunny, open position. They are readily propagated by division of the thick fleshy rhizomes, which is best carried out in August or early September just before the new roots are produced. Vigorous, healthy leaf fans with short pieces of rhizome should be selected and replanted with the upper surface of the rhizome slightly above ground level, old withered leaves removed and any remaining foliage clipped back to reduce water loss while the plants are becoming established.

The distinctive *I. aphylla* is seldom seen, although it can be recommended for small gardens where the robust *germanica* hybrids may prove too large. It grows wild in central and eastern Europe and bears up to five deep purple or violet-blue flowers on branched stems under 1 foot high. It is not difficult to raise from seed, blooming in the second or third year after sowing like most others in this section of the genus. *I. pumila*, another small bearded iris as the name suggests, reaches about 5 or 6 inches in height and is very variable in colour. Yellow-, purple- and blue-flowered forms, richly scented, are found in different parts of its habitat, through the Balkans and central Europe to the

Urals in the USSR. This species and the related *I. attica*, from the southern Balkans and western Turkey, have been used with others such as the exceedingly variable *I. lutescens* (*I. chamaeiris*) and the delightful *I. suaveolens* to breed the free-flowering dwarf hybrids popular with growers in recent years.

Often better known as *I. mellita* and *I. rubromarginata*, *I. suaveolens* is again only a few inches high and variable in flower and colour. Yellow, purple, brownish-purple and yellow and purple forms occur on the open, grassy hillsides of its homeland in Bulgaria and northwestern Turkey. Useful, quietly attractive plants for the rock garden, all these diminutive irises deserve greater recognition from gardeners, but are not easily obtainable. They are only occasionally grown by specialists, notably by enthusiasts of the British Iris Society who maintain small stocks of many species and their variants.

The taller lilac-blue and yellow-bearded *I. pallida*, with pleasant greyish-green foliage and branched flower stems 3 to 4 feet high, has long been familiar in gardens. Sometimes called *I. dalmatica*, it was Gerard's 'Great Flower de Luce of Dalmatia', whose 'flowers do smell exceeding sweete, much like the Orenge flowers'. Given open, sunny conditions similar to those of its native limestone slopes in western Yugoslavia, there is no problem in growing *I. pallida*, nor its lovely variegated forms, one yellow- and one white-striped. Yet sadly this elegant plant, a basic parent of the early flag irises, is fading from the scene, except in some National Trust gardens where it is still treasured.

In the same way, *I. variegata*, another Balkan and central European bearded iris, is now confined to a few collections, although it is much sought after by anyone who sees it in full bloom. The flowers have yellow standards contrasting with dark falls of violet-purple or red-brown, veined in yellow or white. It too had a role in breeding work and passed on these features to many of its hybrid offspring. Scarcely any have survived, apart from one or two like 'Emily Grey' which can be traced by diligent search. However, another form of *I. variegata*, described as a separate species *I. reginae* only in 1947, is happily still extant. With its white ground colour and striking violet veining on both falls and standards, it is to be hoped that this will be propagated and circulated more widely to secure its place in gardens.

Sometimes called cushion irises, those belonging to the Oncocyclus section of the genus are among the most beautiful of all bulbous plants, but much more demanding in their cultural requirements. Also rhizomatous, they come mainly from dry regions with cool winters and hot summers and do not take kindly to the British climate. Regrettably, despite frequent introductions to our gardens, they will always remain plants for the specialist. However, numerous hybrids have been raised in the southern United States, where they flourish in conditions akin to those of the species in their native homes. Oncocyclus irises occur wild from the Caucasus to central Turkey, eastwards to Iran and southwards to Lebanon, Syria and Israel and generally flower in

March and April or, in mountain areas, in May and June as the snows melt. Their individual populations tend to be fairly localised. A few will grow and flower well in a bulb frame, in sharply drained but fairly rich soil into which the strong roots can thrust. They should be kept dry during the dormant period from June to October, then thoroughly soaked to encourage root growth, before watering is further reduced over the winter. In early spring they are watered again and if necessary given liquid feed to induce strong rhizomes for the following year's flowering. Contrary to the assumption that they prefer near starvation because of their dry, almost desert-like habitat, they are often greedy feeders. This basic misunderstanding of their needs has led to the loss of many an Oncocyclus iris obtained at considerable cost to the gardener – and possibly to the original colony in the wild.

Nevertheless, the mourning iris, *I. susiana*, has been cultivated for over 400 years and is still grown, although the present stock is probably clonal and debilitated by virus. Brought to Europe via Constantinople before 1573, it was called the 'Turkie flower de luce' and was highly prized for its curiously mournful flowers. The greyish-white ground is almost obscured by heavy purple-black veining and stippling, with a velvet black signal patch at the throat. W. R. Dykes, one of the foremost authorities on the genus this century, compared it to 'newspaper on which the ink had run'. No longer known in the wild, *I. susiana* is reputed to have come from Persia but more likely originated in Lebanon where the very similar *I. sofarana* and *I. basaltica* are found.

One or two Oncocyclus irises seem to be slightly more amenable to cultivation than their fellows. Among them is the extraordinary variable *I. paradoxa*. The form referred to as var. *choschab* is most attractive, with upright white standards, delicately veined dark violet, and small blackish-violet falls like velvet footstools above the short, curved foliage. Another of the 'possibles' is *I. iberica*, whose large bicoloured blooms have creamy, brown-veined standards and more intensely coloured purplish-brown falls with darker throat patches. It too is extremely variable, from rosy-purple to brownish-red in colour, and desirable in all its forms, though these have merely a foothold in cultivation.

Growing in similar habitats in the wild, the Regelia irises are closely related to the Oncocyclus group but, unlike them, mostly carry more than one flower per stem. They are also less difficult to cultivate. Some such as *I. hoogiana*, with scented lilac-blue, yellow-bearded flowers, and the ivory, maroon-veined *I. korolkowii* succeed in the open garden in dry, well-drained positions. Unfortunately, very few species are in cultivation, while even the handsome Regelio-cyclus hybrids stocked by Dutch nurseries are dwindling fast. These hybrids have generally proved much easier than their parents and with their striking colours and elegant shape make excellent flowers for the house if cut in tight bud. In 1974 the well-known Dutch bulb specialists, Van Tubergen, offered eighteen distinct Regelio-cyclus cultivars in their wholesale list; by

1984, this number had been halved. A number, such as 'Barcarole', 'Camilla', 'Clara', 'Lutetas', 'Medea' and 'Mercurius', may still be grown by the occasional gardener, but their chances of survival are slim now that they have been discarded commercially.

The Evansia irises are among the most distinctive of their race and of considerable garden value, though not all are fully hardy. *I. japonica*, from central China and Japan, has dark evergreen leaves and branched sprays of frilled white or pale blue flowers, embroidered with orange and purple crests. It and its near allies, *I. confusa* and *I. wattii*, which are usually somewhat tender, can be found in gardens but seldom, in the case of the latter two species, in the trade. In nature they tend to be woodland plants, creeping through damp, leaf-rich soil by wide spreading stolons and flowering throughout April and May. Of similar stature at $2\frac{1}{2}$ to 3 feet tall is the Himalayan *I. milesii*, whose gracefully branched stems produce blooms of delicate lavender-pink marked with purple over a period of several weeks. It is an easily grown species with rather fat rhizomes resembling those of the common bearded irises and it is simple to propagate from division or from seed. Why it is not more familiar to gardeners is hard to understand.

Some of the charming dwarf irises in this section are fine rock garden or peat bed plants. The diminutive *I. cristata* from eastern North America is only a few inches high and has neat leaf fans and May-borne flowers ranging from white to lavender through blue to violet, the white patches on the falls variously marked yellow to orange-brown. Its sky blue relative, *I. lacustris*, is even smaller. Both are very easy to grow and increase but rarely available. The same applies to *I. gracilipes*, from the mountains of Japan. It is a vigorous plant with narrow grassy foliage and branched stems no more than 6 or 7 inches high, carrying the dainty lilac-blue blooms with white and yellow crests in late spring. It thrives in woodland conditions and, together with its lovely albino form, is worth every effort to acquire.

The Siberian iris *I. sibirica* and several of its allies are popular free-flowering plants for virtually any position in the garden, performing best in moist soil in open, sunny situations. The closely related *I. sanguinea* is often confused with *I. sibirica* and each has contributed to the range of good hybrids now obtainable. However, two other species in this group, both from China and both yellow-flowered, are too seldom seen in their own right unadulterated by hybridisation. *I. forrestii*, a mere 15 inches high when in flower and with slender glossy leaves, produces two neat, scented, clear yellow blooms on each stem, with erect standards and falls pencilled red-brown. It was collected early this century by George Forrest from alpine pastures in western Yunnan and is happy in any reasonable soil. The larger and more robust *I. wilsonii*, the name commemorating another famous plant-hunter who secured it in 1907 in western Hupeh, has broader leaves which are greyish-green on both surfaces and bigger, slightly paler, flowers with the standards held obliquely. It is a most floriferous plant of great garden merit, requiring moist, fertile soil to excel.

More widely available but still only occasionally encountered, *I. chrysographes* is 15 to 18 inches high, with flowers of velvety, dark-reddish violet, sometimes almost black, and delicate gold pencillings on the falls. It is yet another of the excellent garden plants we owe to 'Chinese' Wilson and was described by Dykes in 1911 from material collected in the high pasture land of western Szechuan three years before. *I. dykesii*, featured in the *Botanical Magazine* in 1932, is akin to *I. chrysographes* but has broader leaves and taller flower stems, with the violet-purple blooms prettily veined white and yellow on the falls. It flowered in the garden of Charles Musgrave in Hascombe, Surrey, in 1926, from seedlings given by Dykes in about 1922. Unfortunately, the latter died without seeing it in bloom and his theory that it might be an unnamed Chinese species has not been proved. It may, alternatively, be a hybrid of *I. chrysographes*. Although easily grown, this choice plant seems to have disappeared. However, it is still worth searching for in the hope that it might be growing anonymously in the gardens of past iris enthusiasts who were in contact with Dykes.

All the Sibirica irises flower in early summer and are readily propagated by division of the tough rhizomes in September, giving the transplants warm, moist conditions to establish them quickly. The Spuria group are similar in their cultural demands and, apart from some admittedly dull and uninspiring members, include a number of species that can be thoroughly recommended for general garden use. *I. orientalis* (usually under the name *I. ochroleuca*), 3 to 4 feet high with stiff foliage and abundant, well-shaped white blooms marked yellow on the falls, is not uncommon. Probably derived from it and the newly described *I. xanthospuria* from Turkey, is *I. monnieri*. This delightful, clear lemon-flowered iris, some 3 feet in height, is unknown in the wild and was found in the garden of Monsieur Lemonnier in Versailles, after whom it was named. It was also called 'Iris de Rhodes' and has been linked incorrectly with Crete. Its hybrid 'Monspur', with blooms of a soft Spode blue, was raised by Sir Michael Foster, the eminent Cambridge physiologist and amateur iris grower. Both are vigorous and tractable plants but are today unaccountably difficult to trace.

Strangely neglected too is the superb hybrid 'Ochraurea', derived from *I. orientalis* and *I. crocea*, with soft yellow flowers marked in darker yellow borne several to each stem. *I. crocea* (*I. aurea*), the other parent, is found in Kashmir where it is often associated with cemeteries. Just as robust as *I. orientalis*, it differs in its rich golden yellow flowers and, once again, eludes all but the very diligent plantsman. Yet these, like many of the Spuria species and their hybrids, are among the most troublefree and rewarding of irises to grow.

The well-known Dutch and Spanish irises with their bulbous rootstocks are descended from *I. xiphium*, an inhabitant of Spain, Portugal and North Africa. Colour forms and variations have been cultivated since the late sixteenth

century – Parkinson listed thirty-one variants in his *Paradisus* – and continue
to be selected, particularly in Holland. Less frequently seen is the Pyrenean
I. latifolia (*I. xiphioides*). This is still referred to as the English iris and was
grown so extensively around Bristol in the late sixteenth century that Dutch
bulb merchants purchased their stocks from there. A handsome garden plant
which produces its violet-blue, yellow-touched blooms on 2-foot stems during
June, neither it nor its cultivars are regularly offered now.

The Juno irises, also bulbous but with thickened fleshy roots which are
replaced each year, are undeniably beautiful though much more difficult to
grow. With the exception of *I. planifolia*, from Europe and North Africa, they
occur wild in western and central Asia, notably from central Turkey to the
Caucasus, and often in mountainous regions and semi-arid steppe. A few
species such as the golden or pale yellow *I. bucharica*, the lilac-blue *I. magnifica*
and darker blue *I. graeberiana* prove quite successful in the open garden, given
good drainage and friendly neighbours with spreading summer foliage to
prevent excess rain gathering round the dormant bulbs.

However, most are definitely bulb frame plants in this country and their
sumptuous colourful flowers are attainable only by experts. Some of the most
exquisite include the glittering yellow *I. doabensis*, introduced in the 1960s
from the Hindu Kush in northeast Afghanistan by Admiral Paul and Mrs Polly
Furse, who made extensive plant collections in that area; the striking
bicoloured purple and yellow *I. fosteriana*, known for nearly a hundred years
from the Kopet Dag mountain range on the Iran–USSR border; *I. nicolai*,
pale lilac with deep violet falls; and the closely related but horticulturally
distinct *I. rosenbachiana* (Plate 45), with deep red-purple, orange-crested
flowers, which has been in and out of cultivation for over a century. But they
are unlikely to be accessible to the average gardener unless effective
micropropagation and improved cultural techniques can be achieved in the
future.

The Reticulata irises with their fat bulbs and netted tunics will be familiar to
every gardener. At least two of their number, the charming *I. danfordiae* and
I. reticulata, have reached the chain-store. Easily grown in the open garden in a
well-drained, sunny position, they flower in February and March and increase
steadily from bulblets. Probably the most reliable of this group of dwarf irises
is *I. histrioides*, with large, bright to dark blue flowers variously marked around
the yellow crest on 3- or 4-inch stems. Confined to a relatively small area of
central-northern Turkey, it makes an excellent rock garden plant, flowering
regularly each season and increasing well from offsets.

By contrast, the magnificent *I. winogradowii* is surprisingly rare in gardens
and very expensive when it can be procured. In general aspect it resembles
I. histrioides, but has primrose-yellow flowers with greenish markings on the
falls. It is hardy and readily grown in the open garden. It also produces plenty
of bulblets and is easily raised from seed (if obtainable), flowering the third or

fourth year after sowing. Its scarcity in cultivation is inexplicable and since it is of very limited distribution in the wild and on the verge of extinction in its native Abkhazia in the USSR, it is doubly important that this lovely plant should be maintained and circulated by gardeners.

With *I. histrioides*, *I. winogradowii* has been responsible for two fine offspring. 'Katharine Hodgkin' was raised by E. B. Anderson, whose knowledge and skill as a bulb grower were unequalled in his generation, and named after the wife of another great plantsman, Eliot Hodgkin, while 'Frank Elder' was produced in Scotland by the enthusiastic gardener whom it commemorates. The flowers are intermediate in colour between the parents, a cool mix of blue and yellow which is unusual and attractive. Both are hardy and vigorous, flower prolifically and multiply from offsets, yet remain extremely expensive, if available at all.

The chief enemy of the Reticulata irises is ink disease, which can quickly decimate colonies if undetected and untreated. It appears as black spots on the outer scales of the bulb and spreads and eats into it until it rots away. Systemic fungicides should be used for protection, either soaking the lifted bulbs or watering the plants *in situ* in the autumn. However, although so many members of this group are of comparatively simple culture, others are more exacting in their needs. The beautiful early-flowering *I. histrio* and its variants, from southern Turkey, Lebanon and Syria, has large pale blue flowers with darker splashes on the blade of the falls. They may be grown in a bulb frame, but are not fully hardy and they are seldom offered in the trade. The fairly recently described *I. pamphylica* is a bizarre mix of brownish-purple, bright yellow, green and purple and may be somewhat insignificant in garden terms. But like many of these dwarf irises, it is restricted to a very small locality in the wild, in this case around Antalya in Turkey. In the same category, the pale lilac-blue and purple *I. kolpakowskiana* grows on stony mountain slopes in the Tien Shan range in the USSR. Known and cultivated for over a century, it is not easy to maintain and appears only fitfully in the gardens of specialists.

Quite apart from any inclination to try these unusual and attractive irises in our gardens, it is vital that we grow, multiply and distribute them if they are not to be totally lost like many other rare and endangered species in the past. While conservation of their natural habitat may be the ideal, it is not always practicable. The example of a plant such as *I. winogradowii* highlights the importance of the gardener's role in maintaining them in cultivation.

+Laburnocytisus

+Laburnocytisus adamii

The art of grafting, in which the shoot or scion of one plant is united with the root system or stock of another, has been practised since the most ancient times as a method of propagation. Normally, only the size and vigour of the scion are affected, as in the creation of a standard rose or a cordon apple, while the essential characteristics of flowers, fruit and growth are retained. In a few very rare instances the process has led to the formation of a graft hybrid in which an inner core of tissue from one parent is surrounded with an outer layer from the other. This is called a chimaera, after the mythological monster with its lion's head, goat's body and serpent's tail. It is represented in script by a plus sign before the name to distinguish it from a true hybrid where a multiplication sign is used.

One of the most celebrated examples of this phenomenon is *+Laburnocytisus adamii* (Plate 47), also known in the past as *Cytisus adamii* and *Laburnum adamii*. Jean-Louis Adam, a nurseryman at Vitry near Paris, had grafted the dwarf purple broom *Cytisus purpureus* on the common laburnum *L. anagyroides*, which was a normal technique for obtaining a standard of the former. In 1825 a branch developed with foliage intermediate in size between the two, later followed by long clusters of blossom like the laburnum but smaller and of purplish brown. Adam paid little attention and put it on the market under the name of great Austrian broom, always selling the trees before they flowered. In 1831, astonishingly, it produced branches of pure laburnum with the typical hanging golden yellow blooms, and in 1833 of pure *Cytisus*, with its tufts of purple pea-type flowers, both in addition to the curious mixed blossom.

+L. adamii has the general habit of the common laburnum, reaching a

height of up to 25 feet, and similar leaves overall, though smaller and smooth. It is of equally easy culture, hardy and thriving in any soil and situation. Fertile seed is apparently only set by the laburnum flowers and seedlings from this result, as might be expected, in typical laburnums. The graft hybrid is therefore propagated by grafting scions onto *L. anagyroides*. Thus all the plants in existence are derived from Adam's original branch. No one has managed to repeat his particular graft hybrid, but further graft hybrids have been raised, notably between the medlar and the hawthorn, to quash earlier doubts about the origins of Adam's plant.

As 'the purple Laburnum', + *L. adamii* was figured in the *Botanical Register* of 1837 'merely for the sake of dispelling the false impression that still exists as to its appearance'. It seems that 'every body was anxious to obtain a plant with so promising a name', heedless 'of the tricks of foreign dealers', and were then disappointed by 'such dull, dingy, dirty-purple clusters'. But when its remarkable tricolour effect did emerge, it soon became popular in Britain and on the Continent. According to *La Belgique Horticole* in 1871, it was to be found in many European gardens and the RHS *Journal* twenty years later said that it was available 'from all good nurseries'.

Sadly, this no longer applies, although + *L. adamii* has been grown at Wisley for a number of years and is still to be seen there and in other parts of Britain. It is a fascinating rather than beautiful plant and 'much inferior to either of the common laburnums' in W. J. Bean's opinion. Perhaps it was more to Victorian taste than our own. However, it would be a pity if it were allowed to die out completely, if only because of its value as a botanical and horticultural freak.

Lardizabala

One of the earliest arrivals from Chile at the celebrated Exeter nursery of James Veitch & Son, *Lardizabala biternata* (Plate 48) was an example of the riches soon to come from that country. It had been closely preceded by *Desfontainea* and was followed by *Embothrium*, *Lapageria* and *Berberis darwinii*, all resulting from trips in the 1840s on behalf of the firm. However, *L. biternata* was originally obtained not by their famous collector William Lobb but by George Thomas Davy, who described the circumstances in a latter to Veitch: 'When I first saw it in the Province of Concepcion, I was so much struck with the singularly dark colour of the flowers, and the beauty of the foliage, that I gave instructions to have a root sent to me at Valparaiso.' It was then brought home by Lobb in 1844 and flowered five years later in December at Veitch's premises.

A native of southern Chile, where it grows in damp woodland, *L. biternata*

Lardizabala biternata

belongs to a genus of one or possibly two climbing shrubs. The name commemorates a Spanish naturalist, M. Lardizabal y Uribe. It is a plant of vigorous and rapid growth, attaining 6 to 10 feet in a single season. The collector Harold Comber, who encountered it in the wild in 1926, recorded a height of 20 to 50 feet in his field notes. The copious evergreen leaves, glossy dark green and leathery with an occasional sharp point to the oval outline, consists of three, six, or nine leaflets (whence *biternata*). From their axils the male flowers hang in dense clusters up to 4 inches long, of an unusual deep purplish chocolate shade. The female flowers are individually larger but solitary and Comber considered the male 'a much better garden plant' than the female. It was the former that first reached Britain. *L. biternata* blooms in late autumn or early winter and may ripen fruits if the two sexes are grown in close proximity. These resemble long, dark purple peppers containing a sweet edible pulp, and in Chile are sold in the markets. Cordage is also made from the stems 'by simply passing them through fire and macerating them in water', according to *The Garden* in 1885.

L. biternata was assumed to be hardy when it was introduced. At Veitch's nursery it grew to 12 feet against a wall, while at Kew it survived three winters outside. However, as *The Garden* sagely remarked, the flowers are liable to damage from autumn frosts since they develop so late and many authorities now recommend it for the greenhouse, except in the mildest areas. It is otherwise quite amenable to cultivation and may be propagated either by cuttings of semi-ripe shoots rooted under mist or in a closed case, or by evergreen cuttings taken in late summer and rooted in a cold frame. These should then be grown on in a well-drained compost, before planting out in a similarly well-drained sheltered site.

This striking shrub can be seen at Mount Stewart, Co. Down, and a few other places in the British Isles, and is sometimes grown in Mediterranean gardens. Its slight tenderness, together with its rampant habit, no doubt explain why it has remained such a horticultural rarity.

Lathyrus

Lathyrus pubescens

The genus *Lathyrus* is named from the ancient Greek for pea and numbers at least one hundred species distributed across the temperate regions of the world. The more familiar ones came from Europe at an early date – the perennial *Lathyrus latifolius*, a cottage garden favourite since the sixteenth century; the clump-forming spring vetch *L. vernus*; the annual chickling pea *L. sativus*; the sweet pea *L. odoratus*, which was sent from Italy in 1699 and soon eclipsed all the others in popularity; and the everlasting pea *L. grandiflorus*, a later arrival in 1814. Annual or perennial, the species are mainly climbers clinging by tendrils and producing their characteristic butterfly flowers over a long period. The majority are hardy, vigorous and easily grown in ordinary, well-drained soil and a sunny position. But the minority, the tender or less amenable species, include some of the loveliest. Out of the forty or so members of the genus in general cultivation, these hover on the fringes.

First described in 1876 and introduced in 1881, *L. splendens* attracted fulsome praise from Reginald Farrer. It is known as pride of California, somewhat misleadingly since it is restricted to the southern part of the state where it occurs very locally scrambling over bushes. It is a rambler rather than a climber, about 1 foot or more in height, and bears clusters of large flowers 'of the richest and most gorgeous crimson throughout', according to the *Botanical Magazine*, or sometimes lilac-purple or rose. These have 'such a superb air that it is difficult to believe that they are not the product of centuries of careful selection by the gardener'. It blooms profusely throughout the summer if liberally watered and, although usually recommended for the greenhouse, it has been grown successfully outside in warmer areas such as Cornwall and the Isle of Wight. It also flourished on a south wall at Kew and won an Award of Merit when exhibited in 1899. *L. splendens* does not set seed readily in cultivation, but may be propagated by softwood cuttings of the young growth taken after flowering.

Another American species which unfortunately seems to have made little horticultural impact is *L. ornatus*. Thomas Hay, superintendent of the royal parks in London, could find no record of it in cultivation since its discovery in 1838. He located a farmer in North Dakota on whose land a few plants grew among the rocks and through him eventually managed to obtain seeds, when they could be rescued from greedy cattle. The resulting plants flowered in the summer of 1935. Hay reported that it was hardy, a rambler but 'by no means a ramper' up to 2 feet high, with 'particularly light and graceful' foliage. The typical pea flowers, in groups of four to seven, were a deep rosy purple with paler central petals. He concluded that it was 'a very distinct and showy species'.

Thomas Hay was also involved in the reintroduction of the famous but elusive blue pea *L. nervosus* (Plate 49). Its muddled history starts in 1744, when Lord George Anson put into Cape Horn during a four year round-the-world voyage and 'these Peas were a great relief to the sailors' starved of fresh food. The admiral returned with a captured ship and extended the family home of Shugborough in Staffordshire on the proceeds, while his cook brought back seeds of the plant. These were grown in the Apothecaries' Garden at Chelsea before apparently dying out. Philip Miller named the plant *Pisum americanum* and referred to it as the Cape Horn pea. It was later called Lord Anson's pea. It was introduced again in 1834 'from the Brazils' and wrongly identified as *L. magellanicus* and yet again a few years later by a Scottish settler in the Argentine, John Tweedie, who sent seeds to the duke of Bedford 'from Puerto Bravo in south Brazil'. In both cases Brazil was probably the present Uruguay. In the *Botanical Magazine* of 1842 it was figured correctly as *L. nervosus* by Sir William Hooker, director of Kew, and his son Joseph, who greeted it as 'a handsome and very desirable greenhouse plant'. It seems to have survived in cultivation until the 1890s, but was still confused with *L. magellanicus*. To make matters worse, supposed seeds of 'the blue pea' offered in catalogues turned out to be the humble chickling pea, *L. sativus*.

In 1926 *L. nervosus* was reintroduced under its rightful name through

Thomas Hay. From these seeds one plant flowered at Kew in 1927 and another received an Award of Merit when shown by Hay the following year. It is a climber to about 5 feet in height and has very long tendrils and smooth, grey-green, rather hard leaves which are distinctly nerved and with thickened margins. Its sprays of fragrant blossom are carried from June to September and consist of four to five flowers each about 1 inch in diameter. The colour is often stated to be clear blue, although the Kew plant had blooms of deep purplish blue fading to pale blue and almost white in the centre. *L. nervosus* is a native of Argentina, Chile, Uruguay and south Brazil and inhabits coastal districts and lakeland, growing in open soil and scrub. This maritime habit is probably the reason for its poor record in cultivation. At Kew it was tried in the open and in large pots in a cool greenhouse, and the sole survivor was placed at the foot of a south wall. James Comber, head gardener at Nymans, Sussex, found that the plants tended to die in the second year and were prone to mildew.

A fresh introduction was made in the early 1970s, when seed of *L. nervosus* (under the name *L. magellanicus*) was sent to Wisley from a South American botanic garden. This was raised successfully, the plants flowered well and seeded freely. As a result, Lord Anson's blue pea is now installed in a number of gardens, including Shugborough – a fitting tribute to its instigator.

The true *L. magellanicus* was finally collected in Argentina by Comber's son, Harold, and gained an Award of Merit in 1929. Judging from his field notes, it is a variable plant, ranging from 18 inches to 4 feet high, rambling or spreading, with clustered flowers of purple or lilac and white. The leaves are greyish-green like those of *L. nervosus*, but sparsely hairy beneath and lacking the prominent nerving. This 'handsome herbaceous perennial' grows in the wild at altitudes above 2,500 feet and is said to be hardy and perhaps of easier culture than its relative. It is not easy to tell the two species apart and both are still scarce in cultivation.

The most tractable of the rare South American species is *L. pubescens*. The same Mr Tweedie was responsible for its introduction from Buenos Aires in 1840. It is covered in hairs, as the name implies, and is a strong climber with dense groups of large, pleasantly scented flowers. The colour is lavender or, in the variety discovered by Harold Comber in Chile in 1927, creamy white. It blooms from May onwards and produces seed which germinates freely. Unfortunately, it is not completely hardy in this country and James Comber maintained that it could only be grown outside in favoured districts, protected in winter with matting and ashes around the roots. *L. pubescens* gained an Award of Merit in 1903, when it was described as 'a wonderfully pretty and uncommon perennial species from Chili, suitable for cool-house culture'. In the 1920s it was occasionally listed by nurserymen, but unfortunately has never become well known to gardeners.

Lilium *Lily*

Lilium mackliniae

One of the most sumptuous of horticultural works is the *Monograph of the Genus Lilium* by H. J. Elwes, published between 1877 and 1880. Such is its authority that it was revised by Patrick Synge a century later and several supplements were added in the interim to cover recent introductions. The genus as presently recognised contains over eighty known species (as well as innumerable hybrids), distributed in Europe, Asia and North America. While some have never proved amenable to cultivation and will remain collectors' pieces, many more can be accommodated in the average garden. *Lilium martagon*, *L. regale*, *L. pardalinum*, *L. lancifolium* (*L. tigrinum*) and *L. pyrenaicum* are all reliable species and the hybrid lilies are usually quite easy to grow, if martyrs to virus, which has been a major cause of the disappearance of some of the finest lilies from our gardens.

The venerable *L. candidum*, native to Greece and western Turkey, has probably been in cultivation for at least three thousand years and was brought to this country by the Romans. It was valued both for its beauty and for its curative powers against such ailments as boils, corns, dropsy and wrinkles. It was one of the few foreigners included in *The Feate of Gardening*, a list of plants recommended for English gardens by Jon the Gardener at the beginning of the fifteenth century. Virgil had dubbed it *candidum*, shining white, and the epithet was adopted by Linnaeus. It was more familiarly known as the cottage lily and later as the Madonna lily, having long been identified with the Virgin Mary. Three main variants of *L. candidum* were grown, with double flowers, with flowers spotted with purple, and with yellow-margined leaves. The first two were mentioned 'merely as curiosities' in the *Botanical Magazine* of 1794 and are not greatly missed today. However, the third, 'Aureo-marginatum', was considered by Elwes to be 'a very handsome object' and especially useful in winter because of its attractive rosettes of leaves with their broad yellow bands. It was scarce even then and is now apparently lost to cultivation.

The pure white trumpets of the Madonna lily are still to be seen at midsummer, often gracing an old garden where the plants have been left undisturbed. William Robinson maintained that it 'dislikes coddling or being meddled with' and Gertrude Jekyll found it 'the most capricious' of lilies. It is best split and transplanted when dormant in August, contrary to the standard practice with *Lilium* species. It is also particularly prone to virus infection and normally sterile in cultivation. We cannot afford to be complacent about this much-loved plant.

Another old favourite of European origin, *L. chalcedonicum*, was once so common that Parkinson did not 'bestow many lines upon it' in his *Paradisus* of 1629. The 'Red Martagon of Constantinople', as he called it, displays its abundant bright-red Turk's cap flowers in July and is easily grown in well-drained, leaf-rich soil. It also produces seed freely, which results in bulbs of flowering size within about four years from sowing. Partly owing to its susceptibility to virus and diseases, *L. chalcedonicum* has recently become quite scarce in gardens. However, it received a First Class Certificate in 1978 and, thankfully, has returned to the list of at least one specialist nursery.

Among the earliest of the Asiatic lilies to reach the west was *L. brownii*. In Elwes's words, it was 'introduced to Europe from China as long ago as 1804 by Capt. Kirkpatrick of the East India Company's service'. The first record of it flowering here is with the nurseryman F. E. Brown at Slough in 1837, whence its most appropriate name. The long, funnel-shaped, slightly scented blooms, up to four per spike, are held almost horizontally and the petals are a distinctive purplish-mahogany on the outside, the same colour as the stem, contrasting with the pearly white interior and set off by reddish-brown anthers. The form of *L. brownii* originally introduced has never been traced in its native habitat and may already have been a cultivated plant in China. But its two varieties occur wild in China and Hong Kong – *australe*, which is taller than the type, up to 5 (or occasionally 10) feet tall, with more open, faintly coloured trumpets; and the fragrant *viridulum*, with a mauvy outer surface to the petals. The latter is, or was said to be, native to 'every one of the eighteen Chinese provinces', where it was esteemed for its edible bulbs, and it was also widely grown in Japan.

'Hardy and vigorous, and succeeds without giving much trouble' was Robinson's verdict on *L. brownii*, while Elwes considered it 'one of the finest species we have'. However, like *L. candidum*, it seldom sets seed and is also 'rather particular as to the quality of the soil'. Elwes complained that it 'has never become at all common in England', although it was certainly better known in the past. It was mentioned in many popular gardening books at the turn of the century, so must have been quite easily obtainable, whereas today stock is only occasionally to be had from Holland and elsewhere. It is doubtful whether any nursery will ever repeat the magnificent exhibit of 150 cut spikes of *L. brownii*, staged by W. A. Constable & Sons at the RHS lily show in 1935.

One of the loveliest but most elusive of North American lilies is *L. parryi* (Plate 50). It was first collected by a US government botanist, Dr Charles C. Parry, near San Bernardino in July 1876. It carries twelve or more perfumed flowers to a stem, of clear yellow and narrowly trumpet-shaped with the petals folded back and often spotted with maroon. Haunting shady valleys in the arid mountains of southern California and Arizona, its numbers have diminished and the actual sites, as the *Arizona Flora* put it, are 'something that one kept to oneself'. In cultivation, the lemon lily has remained equally rare, although it won an FCC in 1885 soon after its introduction to Britain and was successfully grown at Kew, where it may still be seen, and in other gardens. It requires a very rich soil and sharp drainage, with plenty of moisture, coolness at the roots and some shade. It may be increased readily, if slowly, from fresh seed.

The Far East is a tantalising source of several species yet to be secured in cultivation, although some have made a fleeting appearance. *L. souliei*, for instance, was discovered in 1898 in Szechwan, China, by the French missionary J. A. Soulié (who was murdered in 1905). It was subsequently sighted in Tibet in 1936 by Frank Ludlow and collected by him in 1947. It resembles a fritillary or tulip and has nodding, bell-shaped flowers of a distinctive dark crimson maroon. This did not endear it to another great collector, Frank Kingdon Ward, who dismissed it as 'a plant of slight garden merit'. In Britain this unusual dwarf lily has flowered at the Royal Botanic Garden, Edinburgh, but it is probably no longer in cultivation.

Also reminiscent of a fritillary is *L. sherriffiae*. It was found in memorable circumstances on one of the Himalayan expeditions conducted by the celebrated modern collectors Frank Ludlow and George Sherriff. Mrs Sherriff and Dr J. H. Hicks, who were members of the party, caught the first glimpse of the plant on the banks of a stream near Lao in Bhutan at an altitude of almost 9,000 feet. Mrs Sherriff then broke her arm in a fall. Later that year, 1949, and in the same locality, Ludlow and Sherriff came across the lily growing in profusion over a tiny area. Each plant carried a single bell-shaped flower, 'maroon with inside of corolla chequered with gold', according to their field notes. *L. sherriffiae* was named for Betty Sherriff and, following its introduction, was grown in the north of England, Scotland and at Wisley. Unfortunately, it no longer survives at the RHS garden and is only just represented in cultivation today.

One of the most exciting modern plant discoveries took place in 1953 in northern Burma when Kingdon Ward, that thorough explorer of eastern Asia, met with a unique and quite unexpected species of *Lilium*. As he recounted, 'I caught a glimpse of what looked like a bunch of dry capsules high up in a tree and half smothered by epiphytes. It wasn't exactly the place to find a lily, so I studied it for some time through field glasses before finally deciding that it really *was* a lily.' *L. arboricola* is the only known tree-dwelling or epiphytic species and is noted for other peculiarities such as the minute bulbils in the leaf axils. Its flowers are pendulous with folded-back petals and the colour 'a delicious Nile green in startling contrast with the orange-vermilion anthers', with a strong perfume of nutmeg or cloves. A few bulbs of this remarkable plant reached Britain in January 1954 and one of those grown in a heated greenhouse at Wisley flowered on 17 July. Others were tended by the RBG, Edinburgh and the Liverpool Parks Department with varying results. But eventually all living specimens of *L. arboricola* in cultivation perished.

A happier outcome attended Kingdon Ward's introduction of *L. mackliniae*. It was named in honour of his wife Jean, *née* Macklin, and first recorded in 1946 from Manipur, between Assam and Burma, growing at an altitude of nearly 9,000 feet. The graceful Manipur lily bears hanging lampshade blooms, up to six per spike, of 'a delicate shell-pink outside like dawn in June, with the sheen of watered silk' and inside 'faintly flushed alabaster'. It is hardy, vigorous and long-lived when not attacked by botrytis or virus and produces plentiful seed, which germinates readily and may attain flowering size within two to three years. *L. mackliniae* flourishes in a number of British gardens, as well as in Oregon, USA, and Australia, and is offered by a few nurseries. But it is still not grown to the extent that it deserves.

Most lilies thrive in gardens where the soil is well-drained and the acidity or alkalinity not too extreme. Several species, including *L. candidum*, *L. martagon*, *L. henryi*, *L. pyrenaicum* and *L. chalcedonicum*, grow contentedly in alkaline soils. On the other hand, *L. sargentiae*, *L. rubellum* and *L. superbum* and its relatives require lime-free conditions, while some such as *L. parryi* will tolerate a little lime. A neutral, friable open loam with leafmould incorporated suits the majority of species and hybrids and they are not affected by mild drought, provided their bulbs and roots have a cool root-run. If they are to flower freely, an open, sunny situation is generally desirable, although *L. martagon* and *L. szovitsianum* and its allies will stand fairly deep shade. An excellent combination can be achieved by grouping lilies between dwarf shrubs with low protective canopies, like rhododendrons and daphnes, allowing them to project their flowering stems into the sun and air above. However, they should not be planted among vigorous shrubs and herbaceous plants which would compete for available food and contribute to their eventual decline.

Lilies sometimes continue to flower and increase steadily if left to their own devices, but in most cases it is wise to lift clumps every few years and replant the bulbs on a fresh site where lilies have not been grown recently. On the poor, sandy soils of Wisley, a wide range of species and hybrids is maintained through a triennial programme of lifting and moving to new leaf-rich soil. This is best done as soon as the flowering stems start to die down, although some growers prefer to carry it out just after flowering. An annual mulch of leafmould and dressing of general fertiliser as growth begins in spring, together with appropriate control of lily disease (*Botrytis elliptica*) using a copper-based fungicide, should ensure a fine succession of bloom each season.

Propagation by division of clumps of bulbs or from bulb scales is a useful method of increase. Most species and many hybrid groups may also be raised satisfactorily from seed, but may take as much as five or six years to reach flowering size.

Virus is the major problem with lilies apart from botrytis and can rapidly debilitate stocks, although the effects are masked in a few species such as *L. lancifolium* and hybrids like 'Enchantment'. The only practical solution with virused plants, and with bulbs showing symptoms of being already infected when purchased, is to burn them and try again.

Linum   *Flax*

Linum narbonense 'Six Hills'

The genus *Linum* numbers at least one hundred species of annuals and perennials, of global distribution and concentrated in southern Europe and the Middle East. Pre-eminent among them is the common flax, *Linum usitatissimum*, which has been valued by man since earliest times as the source of linen thread and linseed oil. Of the rest comparatively few have found a place in gardens, although they include such excellent alpines and border plants as *L. austriacum*, *L. flavum*, *L. monogynum* and the native British *L. perenne*, in addition to the crimson-flowered hardy annual, *L. grandiflorum*, and a small shrub, *L. arboreum* (Plate 52).

Known as the tree flax, *L. arboreum* deserves much greater recognition from gardeners, particularly in view of its restricted natural habitat. It occurs wild in the gorges of Crete and, according to the *Botanical Magazine*, was 'introduced to this country in the year 1788, with a profusion of other vegetables, by John Sibthorp, M. D., the present celebrated Professor of Botany in the University of Oxford'. It grows up to 18 inches high and produces masses of clear yellow flowers throughout the summer, which are set off by the vivid blue-grey, compact foliage. It needs a very sharply drained position in full sun to thrive and is probably best grown in an alpine house, although it is hardy except in severe winters. It is also readily propagated by softwood or semi-ripe cuttings in a propagating frame. Despite its ease of culture and undoubted charm, the tree flax has never been common in cultivation and is now very rarely offered in the trade.

Of the taller perennial flaxes, *L. narbonense* is arguably the finest. Possibly grown by Philip Miller at Chelsea in 1739, its introduction is usually dated twenty years later. It forms a bush about 18 inches high of delicate spreading branches and narrow, greyish-green leaves and is covered with large, rich blue flowers for several weeks in midsummer. Like other hardy perennial flaxes, it requires well-drained soil and a warm, sheltered position in full sun for the flowers to open and, as a native of the Mediterranean region, it resents extreme or prolonged cold. It is short-lived, but can be propagated with ease from the amply produced seed, sown in spring to flower the following year. Alternatively, softwood or semi-ripe cuttings may be rooted under mist or in a cold frame.

Beautiful in its own right, *L. narbonense* has been improved in a number of garden forms such as 'June Perfield' and 'Heavenly Blue'. The most sought-after is the 'Six Hills Variety', which is named after the famous nursery at Stevenage, Hertfordshire, founded in 1907 by Clarence Elliott. In an article in 1923, he told its intriguing story:

> Some few years ago a friend sent me from the West of Ireland a plant of Linum narbonense of a very special form which he called Peto's variety. . . . I had long grown ordinary Linum narbonense, and greatly admired it as the handsomest and most reliable blue Flax of my acquaintance, but Peto's variety quite put me out of conceit with the ordinary form. The plant was very much more vigorous, and its flowers much larger; great funnel-shaped trumpets of thick satin texture and deepest, richest sapphire-blue.

Elliott began to sell 'Peto's Variety' and shortly afterwards was approached at the Chelsea Flower Show by a Mr Peto, who said he had no connection with it. Elliott therefore rechristened it 'Six Hills Variety', but then began to wonder whether he might have offended another Mr Peto. If he did exist, the real Mr Peto was not a reader of the *Gardeners' Chronicle*. There was no response to Elliott's article and the origin of the plant remained unresolved.

Elliott wrote of the 'Six Hills Variety' that it 'takes a year or two to establish, and form a typical bush, but once it has taken hold, its flowering is an astounding performance'. It does not breed true from seed, though it apparently has fine offspring, but it can be propagated by cuttings or division. Elliott recommended the second method, since 'the plant has a good-natured way of spreading steadily and sedately, underground, and it is a simple matter to lift and detach rooted suckers.' The 'Six Hills Variety' was listed regularly by his nursery and others throughout the 1920s and 1930s and made a brief reappearance in his catalogue after the war. Subsequently, it seems to have become very scarce and one can only hope that it did not share the fate of the nursery whose name it bears, which came to an end in 1946 when it was forced to close.

Meconopsis *Himalayan poppy*

Meconopsis bella

Elusive both in and out of cultivation, the Himalayan poppies have fascinated plant collectors and gardeners alike. Even *Meconopsis betonicifolia*, which is now the most popular, escaped its pursuers for nearly forty years until it was successfully introduced by the renowned collector Frank Kingdon Ward in 1924. It arrived at a time when the full extent of the genus was just beginning to emerge, following a spate of discoveries in the 1900s to add to the few introductions dating from the mid-nineteenth century.

The genus is named from the Greek *mekon*, poppy, and *opsis*, like, and is thought to contain some forty-three species, two more than the number recognised by Sir George Taylor in his monograph of 1934. About half of these are, or have been, in cultivation. With the singular exception of the Welsh poppy, the European *M. cambrica*, all are native to the Himalaya and surrounding region. Their vivid, poppy-like blooms are produced, often above a rosette of basal leaves, from late spring into summer. Some are monocarpic, dying once they have flowered, the rest are perennial. They tend to occur naturally in light woodland and high pastures and respond to similar conditions in the garden. As Taylor points out, the misconception that they are rock plants requiring full sun has led to many failures and a reputation, not always well founded, of being difficult to grow.

'Supreme among the Tibetan poppies' in his opinion, *M. grandis* is found in four of the Himalayan states and has been introduced on several occasions. It was originally discovered in 1881 close to the Nepalese border in Sikkim, where it was cultivated by local shepherds for the oil extracted from the seeds. For many years it was believed to be confined to that site. It was described by Sir David Prain, director of the Calcutta Botanic Garden and subsequently of Kew, and probably through him reached this country in 1895. Its stout flowering stems are 2 to 5 feet high and arise from a clump of pale green, coarsely toothed, bristly leaves, with another scatter of leaves mid-way up. In Reginald Farrer's words, each carries 'a stately cup-shaped bloom of handsome size – about 4 or 5 inches across – and varying in colour from rich violet and clear-blue to duller slatier tones'.

This Sikkim form has been reintroduced very recently. However, *M. grandis* is more variable and has a broader distribution than was at first supposed. In 1921 it was collected in Tibet by the Mount Everest expedition and ten years later turned up in Nepal in somewhat different guise. The Nepalese form is a less robust plant about 18 inches high, with smaller, wine-purple flowers. It received an Award of Merit in 1968 and the name 'Keillour Crimson'. Keillour Castle in Perthshire is also associated with a magnificent white form, 'Miss Dickson' or 'Puritan', which has creamy blooms up to 6 inches in diameter.

The most outstanding version of *M. grandis* originates from Bhutan, where it was sighted in 1933 and collected by George Sherriff the following October as GS 600. Named 'Branklyn' (Plate 53) in 1961 after Branklyn Garden in Perth, it won both an Award of Merit and a First Class Certificate in the next two years. It is about 7 feet in height and bears as many as a dozen wide flowers up to 7 inches across, which open purple before turning to a translucent satiny blue. The leaves are also a distinctive deep purple in spring and the flowering season is later and longer than in the Sikkim form. These differences have led to the suggestion that it may be a natural hybrid of *M. grandis*.

A charming story is attached to a reintroduction of *M. grandis* from Bhutan in 1949, which became known familiarly as 'Betty's Dream Poppy'. Mrs Betty Sherriff was accompanying her husband on his last Himalayan expedition, but was temporarily separated from him since he was travelling elsewhere. One night he appeared to her in a dream and gave detailed directions as to where she might find a new poppy. She followed these instructions the next morning and discovered *M. grandis* 20671, which was secured by Dr J. H. Hicks, the medical officer to the expedition. Betty then wrote to Sherriff to ask whether he had been thinking of her or the poppy on the night of the dream and got for reply a laconic 'Neither'.

M. grandis is perennial and one of the easier species to grow. Like most of the others, it needs moist, humus-enriched soil, with a porous top layer and very sharp drainage to minimise the risk of crown rot, and a cool, partly shaded position sheltered from the wind. It resents dry summer heat and therefore performs better in northern Britain. The crowns should be planted in April or August, level with the soil surface, and division or replanting should be carried out in those same months every few years. It seldom sets fertile seed, but can be propagated without difficulty by separating side shoots from the parent plants.

M. grandis hybridises freely with other species and notably with *M. betonicifolia*, the latter resulting in the superb *M. × sheldonii*. The cross has been repeated several times, using both the Nepal and Sikkim *M. grandis*, and has also arisen spontaneously. *M. × sheldonii* is vigorous and free flowering and ranges from 3 to 5 feet in height, with sky blue blooms either open and saucer-shaped or slightly ruffled and pendulous. Writing in 1949, the president of the RHS, Lord Aberconway, maintained that it has, 'in its finest form, the best blue colour of any Meconopsis, and the largest flower'. The original cross was made in 1934 by W. G. Sheldon of Oxted, Surrey, and gained an Award of Merit three years later. It then seems to have disappeared, although it was offered in the Slieve Donard catalogue for 1953. The Co. Down nursery listed another form of *M. grandis* as 'Prain's Variety' which, according to one account, they had acquired from nearby Mount Stewart. However, it has now been argued that the plant was really the same as *M. × sheldonii* and had been raised by Dr Alexander Curle of Edinburgh in about 1935. The name was changed to *M. grandis* 'Slieve Donard' in the 1960s and later to *M. × sheldonii* 'Slieve Donard'. Up to 5 feet high, it is covered with gingery hairs and produces many nodding flowers of brilliant blue with crinkled petals. It thrives in Ireland at Rowallane, Mount Stewart and Castlewellan. A paler blue sister seedling is still grown in Scotland under the name 'Ormswell'.

As one of the loveliest and most tractable species, *M. grandis*, together with its hybrids, certainly merits wider recognition from gardeners. By contrast, *M. bella* is awkward both to obtain and to grow and is unlikely to rise from the ranks of obscurity. All who have seen it are united in their admiration for this dwarf poppy. A mere 4 to 5 inches high, it has tufted leaves, normally bristly and deeply cut, sometimes entire, and huge flowers of pink, pale blue or purple, with contrasting dark blue and yellow centres. Native to the eastern Himalaya at altitudes of 12,000 to 16,000 feet, it clings to cliff faces and rock crevices by means of a long tap root – in one case 56 inches in length was recorded. It was first encountered on the Nepal–Sikkim frontier in 1888 and described by Prain, but was not introduced until a later collection, flowering at the Edinburgh Royal Botanic Garden in 1906. After a gap when it seems to have been lost, it was reintroduced from Bhutan by Sherriff and won an Award of Merit in 1938. He considered it 'a beauty', which 'should do well at home in rockeries'. Farrer had been more realistic in saying that 'the plant, however perennial, yet needs the most careful care'. Kingdon Ward dismissed it as 'quite hopeless'.

Another species which has had a similarly fitful career in cultivation is *M. punicea*. It was discovered in Tibet in 1884 and in Szechwan in 1885, but was introduced only after E. H. Wilson had made a special six-week trip in northwest Szechwan for that purpose. Seeds were sent home by him to his employers James Veitch & Sons and flowered at their Langley nursery in 1904. It 'is now fairly well established in alpine collections', noted Prain two years later, and was even listed by an Irish nursery at the time. However, it then apparently died out and, despite Farrer's efforts in 1914, had to wait until the 1930s for its reintroduction from southwest Kansu by the American botanist and explorer Joseph Rock. As Taylor remarked, 'no species has drawn such superlative and almost extravagant epithets.' Farrer, once again, portrays it in his inimitable way, 'with its thick tufts of loose long oval-pointed hairy green leaves, and its abundant uprising single stems, at the top of each of which comes a single large flower of a royal crimson, so floppy and tired in texture that each blossom hangs on its stem like a blood-stained flag hoisted to its pole on a windless dull day in late autumn'. *M. punicea* is about 18 inches in height and produces up to thirty bell-shaped, nodding blooms per plant, of an intense red. However, Clarence Elliott, the outstanding nurseryman and collector, dismissed it as 'curious' rather than beautiful and thought the colour resembled 'slightly stale blood'. But he had not seen it in the wild where it was much more spectacular, according to Farrer, and grew in profusion on grassy slopes. In cultivation it is not an easy plant and seldom sets seed. Like the majority of *Meconopsis* species, it performs better in north and west Britain. It is generally treated as monocarpic, reaching maturity in two years from seed. Taylor advised that it should be grown slowly and that any premature buds should be removed in order to form multiple crowns before it was allowed to flower.

A still greater rarity and one probably not in cultivation is *M. torquata*. It is up to 16 inches high and presents a mass of densely bristly golden leaves, surmounted by thick stems which are crowded with large blue flowers opening from the top downwards. The hairy underside of the petals is unique in the genus. This almost outlandish plant is known as the Lhasa poppy and is restricted to a small area of south central Tibet, where it was originally found in 1904 by an officer on the Younghusband mission. Prain was able to base his description on a single specimen, but subsequent attempts to collect it met with failure. Eventually in 1942 it was rediscovered by Frank Ludlow and large consignments of seed were sent back and distributed. Although germination was good, the young plants suffered and stocks gradually dwindled. It is another monocarpic species and takes several years to flower. Ludlow extolled its colour as 'a very perfect blue, not so pale as "bella" nor so dark as "grandis"'. His sole criticism was that 'the blooms are too closely jammed together.' But as he rightly predicted, 'it will always be the despair of horticulturists.'

In a lighter moment (for he and Sherriff shared a sense of humour, even though they always addressed each other by surnames throughout their long partnership as plant collectors), Ludlow penned a poem on the genus:

> *Concinna*'s mauve, *superba*'s white,
> *Paniculata*'s yellow,
> *Punicea* red – a lovely sight,
> Blue *grandis* – a fine fellow,
> *Sherriff-i-i*, I really think
> 'S the only poppy purely pink.

The discovery of *M. sherriffii*, named in his honour by Taylor, was one of Sherriff's greatest achievements. It happened in July 1936 when he 'came across a nice meconopsis, 2309, which I do not know', growing 15,000 feet up in a mountain pass in southeastern Tibet. A few plants were raised from seeds received in Britain, but none survived from a further batch of seedlings freighted home by air. Thirteen years later Ludlow encountered 'the new pink poppy . . . growing to perfection' in central Bhutan, without initially realising that it was the same species. Here it was prolific and covered the cliffs and boulder scree. This collection of seed germinated well and in 1951 an Award of Merit was given to a plant shown by Mrs Knox Finlay of Keillour Castle. *M. sherriffii* has the typical thick rosette of leaves at the base, pale green and hairy, with more leaves half way up the stem, which ranges from 8 to 30 inches in height. The blooms are borne singly at the top and are cup-shaped before flattening with age. About 4 inches in diameter, they consist of six to nine petals round a cluster of white stamens, of a colour described by Ludlow as 'rose-pink like the first flush of dawn on the snows'. 'The flowers look you straight in the face and do not hold their heads down,' he added. The pink poppy has proved less amenable to cultivation than he hoped and, although perennial, it tends to die after flowering. Unfortunately, it has remained very rare in gardens and could all too easily slip from cultivation, like other *Meconopsis* species, unless efforts are made to maintain it.

Metasequoia *Dawn redwood*

Metasequoia glyptostroboides

The story of the dawn redwood, one of the most momentous discoveries of this century, is a remarkable chain of coincidence. It begins in 1941 when the new genus *Metasequoia* was created. This consisted entirely of fossil plants wrongly assigned over the previous century and contained no living species – so far. That same year a Chinese botanist, T. Kan, was travelling through northeast Szechuan, a remote part which he would probably never have visited had it not been for the evacuation of the government and university to Chungking after the Japanese invasion of China. In a village he noticed a solitary tree, which the locals called water fir and which turned out to be a surviving representative of the newly established genus *Metasequoia*. It was a 'living fossil'.

In 1944 specimens were collected from the tree by T. Wang and three years later an expedition was mounted with a grant from the Arnold Arboretum of Harvard University. This revealed more trees growing in western Hupeh, centred on a valley known as Shui-hsa-pu, *shui-hsa* being the Chinese for water fir. They numbered less than a thousand, covering a small area of the two provinces, and were already dwindling as peasants cut them down to make way for rice fields. The plant was apparently on the verge of extinction in the wild and had been located just in time.

In 1948 it was described and named *Metasequoia glyptostroboides* (Plate 54), referring to its similarity to *Glyptostrobus*, a deciduous conifer of southern China. By then a quantity of seed had been sent back to the Arnold Arboretum, from where it was distributed to botanical institutions throughout the world. As Hui Lin Li, the Chinese-American botanist, wrote, 'probably no plant has ever been accorded such rapid and widespread recognition and dissemination.'

Popularly known as the dawn redwood, it is now firmly established in cultivation in both public and private gardens. Some of the tallest specimens in this country, all from the original seed importation, can be seen at Kew, Wisley, the Savill Garden at Windsor, Nymans in Sussex and Stourhead in Wiltshire. Its rapid growth was a striking feature. One tree in Washington reached 44 feet within ten years and the majority attained at least 60 feet twenty years after introduction. The largest trees observed in China were about 115 feet high and 7 feet in girth, while the maximum possible height has been estimated as 150 feet.

The dawn redwood is tolerant of many situations and soils and is extremely hardy and resistant to pests and diseases. It prefers moist, sheltered, woodland conditions and is sometimes susceptible to spring frosts because growth starts early in the year. Its ornamental merit is unquestioned, with its shapely pyramidal form, delicate fern-like foliage and reddish-brown bark turning dark grey with age. The leaves are a fresh light green in spring and change to pink and brownish-yellow shades before falling in November. Small female cones are often produced, but very rarely male ones, and in only a few cases has the seed been reported as viable. However, it is readily propagated by half-ripe cuttings, taken in late summer and rooted in gentle heat, or by hardwood cuttings placed in a cold frame in winter.

Like the maidenhair tree *Ginkgo biloba*, *M. glyptostroboides* is an immensely precious link with our prehistoric past. It is now secure in cultivation, although it came perilously close to extinction, and remains as the sole representative of a race which was once widely dispersed over the globe.

Muscari *Grape hyacinth*

Grape hyacinths are among the most useful and free-flowering spring bulbs. They often thrive in unpromising situations and increase so prolifically from bulblets or seed that some such as *Muscari neglectum* (*M. racemosum* or *M. atlanticum*) can become invasive. Probably the most popular is the deep-blue *M. botryoides*, with a most attractive white version, which was introduced to Britain at the end of the nineteenth century. However, several of the fifty or so species are much older inhabitants of our gardens, although now unfortunately much less familiar.

The tassel grape hyacinth, *M. comosum*, is widespread throughout the Mediterranean area and is appreciated by the southern Italians and Greeks for the edible bulbs with their bitter onion flavour. It was grown by Gerard in both its purple-blue and white forms, although the latter is today very seldom seen. Parkinson cultivated the variant called 'Monstrosum' or 'Plumosum', in which the normally rather dull, purplish-blue fertile flowers are replaced by sterile,

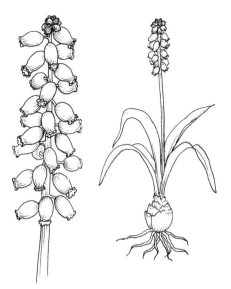

Muscari macrocarpum

thread-like growths of a brighter purple, the whole resembling a miniature feather duster. This attractive plant was at one time offered in vast quantities by the Dutch trade, but has now lost favour and is only occasionally available, possibly owing to virus debilitation of the stocks. Whereas most other species are undemanding in their requirements, *M. comosum* needs a hot, dry site and this may have further contributed to its current scarcity in gardens.

Akin to *M. comosum* in appearance is *M. massayanum*, with greenish or yellow-brown fertile flowers crowned by a topknot of sterile, vivid pink feathers. Described just over fifty years ago, it occurs in southern and eastern Anatolia, Turkey, and is as yet little grown in gardens. It is a charming species to try in a warm, sunny border if it can be obtained.

The sweetly scented *M. macrocarpum* (Plate 55) and *M. muscarimi*, on the other hand, were familiar to the Flemish botanist Clusius in the sixteenth century and were almost certainly grown much earlier. The fragrance of the flowers was thought to resemble musk, hence the generic name *Muscari* from the Persian *mushk*, and has also been compared to the smell of ripe bananas. According to the *Botanical Magazine*, both species were used by ladies of the Turkish harems to pass secret messages to their lovers, though how this was done is not revealed.

One of the loveliest members of the genus, *M. macrocarpum* is distinctive for its bright yellow tubular blooms with flared purplish-brown tips. It was clearly a collector's item in the past. Philip Miller in the 1752 edition of his *Gardener's Dictionary* states that bulbs were being sold at two guineas each in Holland. This price had been halved some seven years later but, as Miller comments, 'until the Price of these Roots is greatly lower'd we can't expect to see this Sort in England; there being few Persons here, who care to give such Prices for

Flowers.' In nature *M. macrocarpum* is distributed through southwest Anatolia and some of the islands off the Turkish coast including Samos and Kos and is also recorded from Crete and Greece. The present stock seems to be derived from bulbs collected by Dr Peter Davis, the taxonomist and authority on eastern Mediterranean plants, in a garden on the Cycladean island of Amorgos, where he also found it in the wild. It has proved quite hardy in the south of England and is grown in gardens in Scotland and no doubt elsewhere in Britain. However, it remains a rarity, if a very desirable one, to most gardeners.

The musk hyacinth, *M. muscarimi*, also known as *M. ambrosiacum* and *M. moschatum*, has the same delightful perfume as its close relative, but is less striking with its bluish-white or greenish flowers turning paler with age. Gerard claimed that it was 'kept and maintained in gardens for the pleasant smell of their flowers, but not for their beautie, for that many stinking field flowers do in beautie far surpass them'. A Turkish endemic from southwest Anatolia, it was widely cultivated for the powerful musk-like scent and as a result has become naturalised in western Italy and Sicily. It too is very infrequently listed by nurseries.

M. macrocarpum and *M. muscarimi* belong to a small group within the genus characterised by thick, irregular, scaly bulbs, large, fleshy roots and broad, strap-shaped leaves. Although not difficult to grow, they are somewhat unusual in their requirements and flower best in sunny, well-drained positions where the bulbs receive a summer baking. They may also be grown successfully in deep pots in an alpine house or cool greenhouse, the sturdy 3- to 4-inch flower spikes filling the air with their fragrance in March or April. Division of the dormant bulbs is an easy method of propagation, as long as care is taken not to damage the fleshy, persistent roots. Seed germinates readily when produced, but the resulting bulbs will not reach flowering size for several years.

Mutisia

'Few plants are more beautiful than this Mutisia – probably the finest of the genus to which it belongs; it ranks even as one of the choicest and best of the Compositae.' The object of such admiration from *The Garden* in 1883 was *Mutisia decurrens* (Plate 56), a remarkable climbing evergreen shrub with brilliantly coloured, large, daisy-like flowers.

The genus *Mutisia* consists of some sixty species native to South America and particularly Chile. It was named in honour of J. C. Mutis, physician, botanist and explorer in the Spanish overseas empire in the eighteenth century. But it is largely to Richard Pearce, who worked for the Exeter firm of Messrs Veitch in South America from 1859 to 1866, that we owe the discovery of the limited number of species grown in gardens. None has ever become common in

Mutisia decurrens

Britain, mainly because of the climate. They tend to be hardy only in milder areas and some need greenhouse protection. As the *Botanical Magazine* pointed out in 1861, 'it is to be feared that the fruticose plants of the high and dry Andes of Chili are difficult of cultivation, and require a very peculiar treatment.'

One of the easiest to grow is *M. clematis*. Climbing to 30 feet or more, it bears rich red blooms throughout the summer and is so rampant as to demand annual pruning. *M. oligodon* has also proved amenable and long-lived. It spreads outwards rather than upwards, with silky pink flowers and partly woolly leaves. In 1928, soon after its introduction by the collector Harold Comber, it won an Award of Merit. As a marvellous informal hedge, it flowered profusely for many years in a garden just outside Porlock in Somerset, which bordered the properties of two outstanding gardeners of this century, E. B. Anderson and Norman Hadden. Both these species are hardy in warm districts, though *M. clematis* is often grown in a cold greenhouse, and both can be increased fairly readily from cuttings.

Comber brought back another species, *M. retusa* or *M. spinosa*, which had been collected by Pearce in 1868. It is a strong rambler up to 30 feet high with pale pink or white flowers. It made an appearance in the 1930 catalogue of the Sussex nursery firm Ingwersen as 'a rare climbing plant from the mountain woodlands in Chile'. The smaller *M. subulata* reached Britain around the same period. It is an awkward plant to collect in the wild, often using a poisonous evergreen as a host. Its flowers, in one form, were described as 'rich and brilliant crimson-scarlet', but it seems to be no longer in cultivation.

Sometimes known as the climbing gazania, *M. decurrens* is perhaps the hardiest and certainly the most striking member of the genus. It is native to Chile and Argentina and was introduced by Pearce in 1859, first flowering in

1861 when it received a First Class Certificate. It scrambles up to about 10 feet in height and clings by means of tendrils at the tips of the narrow, oblong leaves. From June to August it is covered in flowers, 4 to 6 inches across and carried on long individual stalks, of deep orange or bright orange-scarlet with yellow centres. This glorious shrub has tested the skills of several great gardeners and both the Irish gentleman botanist, W. E. Gumbleton, and the celebrated Gloucestershire parson, Canon Ellacombe, had to admit defeat. However, in the 1880s a plant was thriving at Eastnor Castle, Herefordshire, where it was found to do better among the rhododendrons than against a wall. It was vigorous and free-flowering and even ripened seed from which plants were raised. Similar results were obtained at Killerton in Devon, with over 300 flowers one summer, except that here it flourished against a southwest wall. Anderson, who grew this species too in his West Country garden, told how it 'never looked back' after he planted it at the northeast corner of a low wall, with the roots shaded and in a 'super-drained mixture' of soil and sandstone lumps. Most recently, in 1983, *M. decurrens* has been reported growing in a garden on the Isle of Man, clambering up through a jasmine on a southwest wall.

The authorities agree that it does best in a rich, sandy loam with very sharp drainage and should have shade at the roots in the same way as a clematis. It dislikes being trained and prefers to scramble through another plant or over a support. Judging by various accounts, *M. decurrens* is also tolerant of cold and immediately after its introduction it withstood the bitter winter of 1860–61 in the open at Exeter. A century later F. P. Knight, the director of Wisley, had a plant that survived 18°F below freezing.

Perhaps the key to its cultivation lies in understanding the strange structure of the plant. James Comber, as head gardener at Nymans in Sussex, grew several *Mutisia* species collected by his son during the Andean expedition of 1925–7. He explained in the RHS *Journal* of 1949 that *M. decurrens*, when young, possesses only a single thin, wiry stem. Later it branches more freely but is still dependent on the one fragile thread until new shoots emerge from the ground. These suckers, which are tempting to slugs, arise some distance from the original shoot in unexpected places. They are vital to the plant's preservation since the main flowering stem dies down after a few years and has to be replaced.

As Anderson observed, the basal shoot seem 'ideal for propagation, but it has always been stated that to take these is certain death to the plant'. However, cuttings can be obtained from side branches of the stem after flowering and, according to Comber, these root readily in sandy soil and gentle heat – although this is not the experience of many who have tried. From seed, if good seed is available, *M. decurrens* is supposed to germinate freely. Clearly, it can be difficult to increase, but not impossible. As *The Garden* noted in 1883, 'Mr. James O'Brien once had a fine stock of it in Messrs. Henderson's nursery, in the Edgware Road.'

Myosotidium   *New Zealand forget-me-not*

Myosotidium hortensia

The windswept, rain-soaked Chatham Islands in the South Pacific, some 500 miles east of Christchurch, New Zealand, support a unique flora. One of their most outstanding plants is the New Zealand forget-me-not *Myosotidium hortensia* (Plate 51) which, as both its official and popular names imply, resembles a forget-me-not but on a giant scale. Also known as *M. nobile*, it is the sole member of the genus. According to the *Botanical Magazine*, 'it was introduced to Europe through the medium of Mr. Watson, of St. Alban's' and was 'exhibited at a meeting of the Horticultural Society of London, in March, 1858, and attracted much attention'. Joseph Hooker, the much-travelled botanist and later director of Kew, called it 'a most remarkable plant, especially on account of its great size and robust habit'. From its stout, fleshy stem, about 12 to 18 inches high, radiate large, thick leaves which are roughly oval in shape and deeply grooved. The flowers are carried against this glossy green background in dense masses up to 5 inches across and the small, individual blooms are of azure blue often fading to white at the edges with purple centres.

In its native islands, no part of which is further than four miles from the sea, *M. hortensia* is found on the stony shore just above the high tide mark. It grows within reach of the saltwater spray, but beyond that of sheep and pigs, whose grazing threatened it with extinction earlier this century. It is quite widely cultivated in the gardens of New Zealand, where it is also called the Chatham Island lily. In Britain, it has been the despair and the joy of gardeners. For many years after its arrival it was confined to the greenhouse, although it is fairly hardy and once apparently survived a temperature of 22°F in Devon. However, it prefers a mild, damp and preferably maritime climate, such as that of the West Country, much of Ireland and the west coast of Scotland. An article in the *Gardeners' Chronicle* in 1908 recounts how Mr John Enys, of Enys in Cornwall, was the first to grow the New Zealand forget-me-not permanently in the open and achieved far better results than with pot-grown specimens. Some of his plants were 3 feet in height, with leaves nearly as long, and among them was an unusual pure white variant. *M. hortensia*, which is at its best in May, has remained something of a feature of Cornish gardens. It has also prospered in Devon, on the Isle of Wight, in Ireland and in the Scottish Highlands.

Over the years the horticultural columns have offered hints on its cultivation and in the 1950s it was even the subject of a letter to *The Times*, from a sailor who had seen plants growing among rotten seaweed and sharks' carcases. This recipe, or its near equivalent, seems to have been the secret of success at Inverewe in Scotland, where *M. hortensia* flourished after being mulched with a mixture of seaweed and herring fry. In general, it may be said to need a rich, moist, peaty soil, in a sheltered but not too hot situation, and plenty of water during the growing season. It is evergreen and in areas of severe frost should be protected in winter with cloches or dry bracken. Seed germinates irregularly but, if sown as soon as ripe, will usually provide seedlings for planting out the following May and flowering the year after. The young plants either grow or die 'as quickly as cabbages'. When they do live, they often increase to form fine clumps.

M. hortensia is an all or nothing plant, desirable in the extreme but most fastidious as to its requirements in Britain.

Ostrowskia

This spectacular bellflower made its British debut in July 1888, when it was exhibited by Messrs Veitch and immediately won a First Class Certificate, the highest award of the Royal Horticultural Society. A 'remarkable and handsome hardy plant' in William Robinson's words, it soon featured in most of the major catalogues and by the turn of the century was also to be found 'in many Continental gardens', according to the *Botanical Magazine*. More recently in 1953 it has been recorded as growing well in North America. But today, although it has a niche in a few specialist collections, it is almost impossible to obtain commercially.

Ostrowskia magnifica (Plate 57) is native to the mountains of eastern Bukhara in central Asia, where it was discovered by Albert Regel, son of Edward Regel, the celebrated director of the Imperial Botanic Gardens in St Petersburg. It is

Ostrowskia magnifica

the only known species in the genus. The name commemorates M. N. von Ostrowsky, patron of science and Russian minister of imperial domains at the time the plant was described in 1884. In flower it resembles a giant Canterbury bell and is closely related to *Campanula*. Its stout stems up to 5 feet tall are clad in whorled leaves and surmounted by large, bell-shaped blooms, 4 to 6 inches across, in shades of delicate pale purple or lilac with a silvery sheen and darker veining. These appear in June and July and the foliage quickly dies down after setting seed until the following spring. *O. magnifica* requires a hot, sunny position and deep, very well-drained soil to accommodate the long fleshy roots. It dislikes excessive moisture and, although perfectly hardy, its young shoots are vulnerable to early spring frosts – at least in Britain, where a warm spell in winter may encourage precocious growth. A light covering of dry bracken or similar material is a wise precaution.

Reginald Farrer, who grew *O. magnifica* in his garden in Yorkshire, observed that 'it loathes being touched, handled, moved in any way.' Because it so resents disturbance, seed is generally recommended as a better method of propagation than division. It is a slow process, often taking three or four years before flowering size is reached, and some variation in colour is usual. The seed should be sown as soon as ripe in pots of seed compost topped with a thin layer of coarse grit and plunged outside. Immediately germination occurs, the pots are brought into a cool greenhouse and the seedlings grown on until they can be potted individually. They should be transferred to progressively larger pots during the year and, when the leaves die down in late summer, placed in a cold frame over winter. They are then planted out in their permanent quarters in early spring and all further root disturbance is best avoided.

Farrer, of course, claimed that 'there is only one way of dealing with this great high glory. . . . Old specimens must be blasted up in autumn.' His advice was to cut up the huge root into lengths of about 1 foot and replant them, ramming them into holes and covering with sifted soil. Protected with bracken for a winter or two, 'every single section of that Ostrowskia will come shooting up firmly in spring' and after that 'leave him alone for ever and ever.'

'Unique among perennials it is worthy of any care to make it a success', was Robinson's opinion. *O. magnifica* may not be the easiest plant to establish and grow but, given the right situation, soil and drainage conditions, it should be no more trouble to maintain than peonies and other herbaceous plants that hate disturbance. In Farrer's experience, it could be kept 'going gloriously till kingdom come'. Certainly, its performance at Kew and in other gardens demonstrates its superb potential for the gardener.

Paeonia   *Peony*

The thirty or so *Paeonia* species are mainly herbaceous plants, from $1\frac{1}{2}$ to 3 feet high, with a few shrubs in China and Tibet. The genus is spread across the northern hemisphere from California to Europe and North Africa, through Asia Minor to central Asia and on to China and Japan. Except for the two curious outliers in California, *Paeonia brownii* and *P. californica*, which have small, brownish-red flowers, the blooms are large and showy and cover a considerable range of colours. The species are very similar in overall appearance and, together with their numerous hybrid offspring, present few problems of cultivation.

The herbaceous peonies, many of them European natives, have a much longer horticultural history than the shrubby species, which have been known in the West only since the mid-eighteenth century. Pliny, the Roman naturalist, considered the peony the most venerable plant and before him the Greeks had endowed it with magical as well as therapeutic properties. The name, used in the fourth century BC by the Greek philosopher and botanist Theophrastus, comes from Paeon. He, in a rather muddled bit of mythology, was the physician who first employed the plant in medicine; having successfully treated Pluto's wounds, he was then transformed into a peony to save him from the plotting of his jealous teacher; and finally he was translated

Paeonia tenuifolia

to the heavens and worshipped as the god of healing.

Apart from the great curative powers attributed to it, the peony was supposed to ward off devils and evil spirits – a belief perhaps connected with the fact that the black, shiny seeds of some species glow in the dark. On a more practical level, the seeds were valued in the Middle Ages as a seasoning for food and drink, while the roots were cooked and eaten as a vegetable. But such was the aura of superstition surrounding the peony that it could only be uprooted by tying a hungry dog to the plant and luring it with the smell of roast meat. The groan of the peony as it left the ground was said to be fatal to all who heard it, but the loss of the animal was a small sacrifice for such a prize. Gerard scorned this theory as 'most vaine and frivolous for the roots of Peionie as also the Mandrake, may be removed at any time of the yeere, day or hower whatsoever.' However, its medicinal reputation was undiminished. Gerard, followed by the seventeenth-century herbalist Nicholas Culpeper, distinguished the 'Male Peiony' *P. mascula*, from the 'Female Peiony' *P. officinalis*, one or the other being employed against epilepsy and diverse ailments according to the sex of the patient. Hannah Glasse, towards the end of the eighteenth century, included a recipe in her *Complete Confectioner* for 'Compound Piony water', beginning in true Mrs Beeton fashion 'take eighteen piony roots fresh gathered'. Distilled with other herbs and seeds, the mixture was 'exceeding efficacious in all swoonings, weakness of heart, decayed spirits, palsies, apoplexies and both to help and prevent a fit, it will also destroy all heaviness and colness in the liver, restores lost appetite, and fortifies and surprisingly strengthens the stomach.'

Native to southern and central Europe and reputedly Britain, *P. mascula* was almost certainly introduced to the latter, probably by monks for its medicinal value. It is still found on the island of Steep Holme in the Bristol

Channel, close to the site of the twelfth-century priory of St Michael. With its cupped blooms of rich rose-red and neat mounds of dark green foliage, it is seldom seen in gardens today, although it deserves to be.

P. officinalis is widespread in Europe and was brought to this country in the early sixteenth century. It is most familiar in its double red form, 'Rubra Plena', a denizen of cottage gardens. Much less common now are the double pink and double white forms, although these were in most gardens at the beginning of the twentieth century when Gertrude Jekyll was writing. The single dark red, which was well known in the sixteenth and seventeenth centuries, has lost favour and virtually disappeared from general cultivation.

Two equally venerable peonies, which have been grown for at least 300 years, are the fiery scarlet *P. peregrina* from the Balkans and Italy, whose selected clones are sometimes called 'Fire King' or 'Sunbeam' in catalogues, and the beautiful *P. tenuifolia*, with delicately cut ferny leaves and flowers of dark crimson, or pale pink in the form 'Rosea'. These struggle to maintain a hold in nurseries, as does the attractive single red *P. × smouthii*, a hybrid between *P. tenuifolia* and *P. lactiflora*. Single-flowered peonies last a relatively short time in bloom compared to the double-flowered forms and this may account for their gradual decline in popularity. But the double form of *P. tenuifolia*, dating back to the middle of the eighteenth century, has also become exceedingly scarce.

P. lactiflora from Siberia and China, grown for many years as *P. albiflora*, is the chief ancestor of our garden peonies. It produces huge, sweetly fragrant, white blooms with yellow stamens in the centre, set off by handsome, bronze-tinted foliage. 'Whitleyi Major', introduced from Canton by the nurseryman Reginald Whitley of Fulham in 1808, is the nearest representative available of the wild species, whose numerous garden forms have been entwined in the history, legend and poetry of China. In the words of the plantsman A. T. Johnson (cited by Graham Stuart Thomas in his excellent work on perennial garden plants), it was 'a plant adorned with the grace of a thousand years of adoration by the Chinese before it entered our shores'.

The trickle of variants reaching the West in the early nineteenth century soon inspired further improvements and single, double and anemone-flowered forms appeared in shades of white, pink, deep red and red-purple. Notable breeders were Victor Lemoine and Charles Verdier in France, and William Prince and H. A. Terry in the United States, while in Britain the Somerset firm of Kelway became celebrated for their peonies as a result of the work of James Kelway, grandson of the first James who had founded the business in 1850. Many of these Chinese peonies retain their place in gardens. Standards like the incomparable white 'Duchesse de Nemours' (1856), the crimson-flecked white 'Festiva Maxima' (1851), the blush 'Marie Crousse' (1892) and the pink 'Sarah Bernhardt' (1906) are firmly entrenched in the nursery lists and will doubtless be joined by newcomers such as the rich pink, creamy-centred 'Bowl of Beauty' and the dark crimson 'Kelway's Brilliant'. These and others which have stood the test of time and fashion should certainly be secured for the future in the recently established national collections.

But what of the hundreds discarded from the catalogues, lingering anonymously in gardens if they have not been completely extinguished? In any genus where numerous garden forms have been named, it is essential to be selective in deciding on those worthy of conservation. Historically important cultivars, particularly ones which have been influential in breeding, must be kept, as should others showing colour and flower form representative of different periods in the plant's development, with an emphasis on those of sturdy habit and with resistance to disease.

While peony enthusiasts may argue over the cultivars and their credentials for conservation, the species from which they derive attract less attention. Many of these are outstanding garden plants in their own right, but almost unobtainable. Often called Molly-the-witch, *P. mlokosewitschii* was introduced from the Caucasus at the beginning of this century. Reginald Farrer advised that 'this pleasant little assortment of syllables should be practised daily by all who wish to talk familiarly of a sovereign among Paeonias.' Its clear yellow flowers appear in April, usually slightly earlier than the closely related *P. wittmanniana*, another Caucasian which differs in its paler blooms and more robust habit. Hardy and easily grown, both these superb species seed freely but take some years to reach flowering size. One of the fine hybrids of *P. wittmanniana*, 'Avant Garde', has also become a rarity and is known from only one or two gardens. Another equally desirable species, *P. emodi*, from northwest India and Kashmir, bears its pure white perfumed flowers with golden stamens in June on elegantly arching stems about 3 feet high. Few who have seen a clump in bloom can resist trying to acquire it. Yet none of these excellent plants is regularly offered and they call for determined effort if one is to locate a source of supply.

The case of *P. sterniana* illustrates how quickly plants can slip from cultivation, even those as strong as the various species of *Paeonia*. Fruiting specimens of an apparently distinct new species were found in 1938 in the Tsangpo valley of southeastern Tibet by the plant collector Frank Ludlow and Dr (now Sir) George Taylor, the future director of Kew. However, it was not until April 1947 that Ludlow returned to the area, this time with Henry Elliot, to discover an exquisite white-flowered peony in full bloom. Later that year they collected the indigo-blue seeds, from which plants were raised under the number LS & E 14231 and subsequently flourished in several gardens. Since then this fine herbaceous plant, which was described as recently as 1959, has almost departed from cultivation, although one or two specimens are grown in Scotland.

Peonies will perform well on most soils given a well-drained site, but are happiest under alkaline conditions. The herbaceous kinds may be divided by carefully cutting through the fleshy roots to separate the plants into sections, each with two or three growth buds at the apex. This can be done at any time when the plants are dormant, but is best undertaken in early spring when the ground is warming up and before the growth buds have begun to unfold. Of the shrubby peonies, *P. potaninii*, which has a suckering habit, may also be propagated by division, while *P. delavayi* and *P. lutea* are easily raised from seed. Seed of both shrubby and herbaceous types should be sown as soon as ripe in early autumn, since a warm spell is needed to encourage development of the roots, followed by a cold period to break dormancy of the shoot. *P. suffruticosa*, the tree peony, may also be grown from seed, but its many colour variants should be vegetatively propagated by stem or leaf bud cuttings taken from shoots that have flowered. Although much to be preferred on their own roots, tree peonies are usually grafted on to stock of herbaceous peonies.

The one major problem, particularly in a moist, humid atmosphere, is peony wilt, a form of botrytis which quickly kills the young shoots. These should be cut out and burned and further attacks controlled by dusting dry Bordeaux powder on the crowns and applying dichofluanid spray several times at fortnightly intervals.

Of the four main shrubby species of *Paeonia*, the most noble and certainly the most historic is *P. suffruticosa*, the tree peony or moutan (now transliterated mudan), meaning male-red. A native of northern China but scarcely ever recorded from the wild, it has been cultivated since at least the seventh century AD, when in the days of the Tang dynasty it graced the imperial gardens. As a result it acquired the name Hua Wang, king of flowers, and its popularity in China and later Japan, whither it had been brought by the Buddhists, approached cult proportions. A Chinese treatise devoted to the tree peony in 1034 mentions twenty-four cultivars, to which countless others were subsequently added in both countries. It was regarded as a symbol of spring and good fortune in China and was grown not only for ornament but for its ancient medicinal application, the root bark being used to treat blood disorders. It is still planted by the acre in the north of the country for this purpose.

In such domesticated guise, the tree peony reached the West. The form of *P. suffruticosa* first introduced to Britain, through the great scientist Sir Joseph Banks in 1787, was a double-flowered garden variant with white, purplish-red-based blooms. Further introductions during the eighteenth and nineteenth centuries from China and Japan all seem to have been garden selections. Only in 1910 was a possible progenitor discovered, when William Purdom collected a plant near Yennan in the province of Shensi which had large rose-pink, ten-petalled flowers. This became known as var. *spontanea*. His foray to the Moutan-shan in the same region two years later proved unsuccessful, although it had been so covered with wild peonies in the seventeenth century that 'the whole hill appears tinged with red'.

In 1913 Purdom apparently came across a dark magenta crimson form in southern Kansu. It was in this province about forty miles northeast of Wutu that Reginald Farrer, who was travelling with Purdom the next year, caught sight of a wild white peony.

> There, balancing rarely among the brushwood, shone out at me the huge expanded goblets of Paeonia Moutan, refulgent as pure snow and fragrant as heavenly Roses. It grew tall and thin and stately, each plant with two or three thin upstanding wands tipped by the swaying burden of a single upright bloom with heart of gold, each stainless petal flamed at the base with a clean and definite feathered blotch of maroon.

Farrer left his usual memorable record of the occasion, but astonishingly did not take any specimens. However, in 1925 the celebrated American plant collector Joseph Rock was staying at the Choni lamasery in southwest Kansu, where he found a moutan very similar to Farrer's growing in the garden. Dr Rock later explained in a letter to Sir Frederick Stern, the distinguished plantsman and authority on the genus, 'that it looked to me like a wild species. The Lamas told me it came from Kansu but from which locality they did not know. . . . The Lamasery has been entirely destroyed and the Lamas all killed by Mohammedans, so the plant in all probability does not exist any more.' Seed was sent back to the Arnold Arboretum in the USA and distributed from there, although the exact date of introduction is unclear. Stern received a young plant from Canada in 1936, which bloomed two years later. Seeds from this peony, fittingly enough, were then despatched to Dr Rock in China to replace the plants at Choni, but with what success is not recorded.

Rock's peony (Plate 58) still flourishes in Sir Frederick's garden at Highdown in Sussex and is being grown in several other parts of the country. It is a well-clothed shrub some 6 to 8 feet tall and as much across and its enormous 8-inch flowers, white with a crimson-purple base and intensely perfumed, are produced in abundance during May. It is a magnificent spectacle in full bloom and quickly forms a relatively compact plant, unlike many of the named forms of tree peony grown today which tend to be rather gawky and thin-branched. It is also more resilient to late spring frosts, which often damage the young growth and flowers of tree peonies. But unfortunately 'Rock's Variety' is extremely difficult to propagate, since seed is only occasionally set and vegetative means often fail. Despite the accolade of a First Class Certificate in 1943, when it was 'thought to be the true wild ancestor of the garden tree peony', this outstanding plant has never become common in cultivation. At one time it was sold by Notcutts, the tree and shrub specialists of Woodbridge in Suffolk, who did not actually list it in their catalogue because demand outstripped supply. Now it is very rarely available, although plants with single pink, purple-centred flowers are sometimes offered as Rock's peony. There is some controversy over this, but the specimen originally grown by Stern was definitely described by him as white-flowered. Until science can supply more reliable methods of propagation, its survival will depend on the devotion of individual gardeners. It is therefore encouraging to learn, in a recent report from China, that tree peonies have been successfully propagated by tissue culture techniques.

A familiar inhabitant of gardens, by contrast, is *P. lutea* var. *ludlowii*, which has largely displaced the typical form of *P. lutea*. The latter was introduced from Yunnan, southwest China, by the French missionary and botanist J. M. Delavay in 1887. It is a dwarf shrub up to 3 feet in height, with golden yellow blooms sometimes stained carmine at the base and finely cut foliage. It is rare in gardens, although easily grown from seed, as is the taller and more vigorous var. *ludlowii*. Both hybridise with *P. suffruticosa* and with the rich blood-red *P. delavayi*, another of the missionary's Chinese discoveries which reached Britain in 1908 and is now firmly established in cultivation.

Many hybrids were raised between *P. lutea* and *P. suffruticosa* by the French firm Lemoine of Nancy, while in the United States Professor A. P. Saunders also used *P. delavayi* in his breeding programme. Some excellent garden plants were evolved, with sumptuous 6- to 8-inch blooms borne in May and June. But where are they now? Some of Lemoine's hybrids persist tenuously in gardens but hardly at all in the European trade, like the heavily scented double sulphur-yellow 'Chromatella', the similar 'Souvenir de Maxime Cornu', yellow flushed reddish-brown, and 'L'Espérance', with pale yellow flowers blotched crimson at the base and the recipient of an FCC in 1931. 'Argosy', a compact shrub up to 4 feet high, with semi-double, 7-inch primrose flowers stained carmine at the base, gained an FCC in 1956 and is just extant. Others from the Saunders stable seem to have been casualties, such as the velvety dark red 'Black Pirate' (FCC 1959), the blackish-maroon 'Black Douglas' (AM 1957), both semi-doubles with contrasting yellow stamens, and 'Roman Gold' (AM 1957), sulphur-yellow with red basal markings. 'Sybil Stern' (FCC 1962), a huge, rich scarlet-flowered shrub raised by Sir Frederick Stern, is still grown in one or two gardens but no longer features in catalogues.

The same fate has overtaken a large number of the European and Japanese selections of *P. suffruticosa*, which were widely grown earlier this century. Except for the very occasionally listed 'Bijou de Chusan', a double white, and double pinks such as 'Elizabeth', they have faded from the garden scene in Europe. In the USA a few nurseries maintain stocks and it would be well worth reintroducing these fine garden plants from there if they could be traced.

The last of the four major shrubby species of *Paeonia* is *P. potaninii*, from western Szechwan and northwest Yunnan in China. About 2 to 3 feet high, it varies in colour from deep crimson to white and, in var. *trollioides*, yellow, flowering in late May and early June. It should be easily obtainable, since it increases freely from suckers. But it is not often offered by nurseries.

Pamianthe

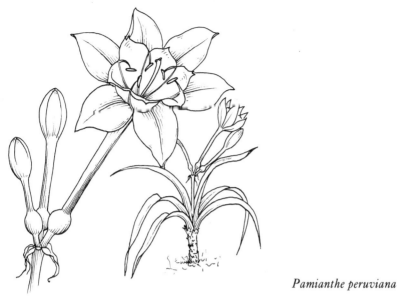

Pamianthe peruviana

South America is the home of many beautiful and desirable bulbous plants of the *Amaryllidaceae*, the family to which the daffodil and snowdrop also belong. Numerous species of *Hymenocallis*, *Hippeastrum*, *Eucharis*, *Zephyranthes* and similar genera were introduced from there during the nineteenth and early twentieth centuries and warmly received by European gardeners ever keen to fill their greenhouses with novelties.

The advent in 1930 of a new member of the family and one of exceptional horticultural merit therefore aroused great interest. That noted enthusiast, Major Albert Pam of Wormley Bury in Hertfordshire, had received some bulbs from Peru two years before. They were found in the warm temperate zone of the central north at an altitude of about 6,000 feet, growing in sandy conditions 'with some evaporation water not far off'. Initially thought to be a species of *Ismene*, a genus now absorbed into *Hymenocallis*, they first bloomed in Major Pam's greenhouse in February 1930. When flowering specimens were shown before the scientific committee of the Royal Horticultural Society the next month, it was evident that they represented a hitherto unrecognised genus and not merely a species new to science. Although Pam's plant was clearly related to the familiar *Hymenocallis* and *Pancratium*, it was immediately distinguished by its 2-foot-long false stems formed from the tightly folded leaf bases, a character unknown in either genus. Further differences later emerged in the structure of the ovary and the winged seeds.

This magnificent plant was named *Pamianthe peruviana* (Plate 59) to honour its introducer, in the *Botanical Magazine* for 1933. The general arrangement of the blooms resembles that of *Pancratium maritimum*, the summer-flowing sea lily which inhabits sand dunes along the Mediterranean coast. But the growth habit is distinctive with its false stem, while the curving, strap-shaped, evergreen leaves reach up to 2½ feet in length. From the centrally placed erect flower stem arise in early spring five or six enormous blooms, often measuring over 5 inches across at the mouth and 9 inches long. White tinted with cream and exquisitely scented, their open bell-like coronas are flanked by six spreading segments and carried on a long, slender, green tube.

P. peruviana is undemanding in its requirements and will thrive and flower regularly in a cool greenhouse, given well-drained, reasonably fertile compost. It is slightly stoloniferous and makes fresh growths a short way from the main bulb, which may be carefully separated when developed to the stage of forming a new bulb. Seed is freely and frequently produced and, if sown immediately after being shed from the capsule, will germinate within about three weeks in a propagating frame. Plants raised from seed sown one April by Major Pam and maintained in active growth (without being allowed a dormant period) had grown false stems 5 to 6 inches long just over a year later – an extremely fast growth rate for any bulbous plant and indicative of its rapid acclimatisation to cultivation.

Such was its impact on the horticultural scene that *P. peruviana* gained a First Class Certificate in February 1933. On this occasion it was exhibited by Sir William Lawrence of Dorking, who was renowned like Pam as one of the finest plantsmen of the period. Easily grown and propagated, *P. peruviana* is a superb flowering pot plant for the cool greenhouse. It is also an excellent cut flower, the lovely fragrant blooms lasting well in water, and should have potential for commercial florists. It was listed as recently as the 1960s by Messrs Van Tubergen, the Dutch bulb firm, but has become unaccountably rare and is now only occasionally to be seen in botanic gardens. Unless steps are taken to increase stock from these few plants, *P. peruviana* will have departed from cultivation after a sojourn of little more than fifty years.

Papaver *Poppy*

The word *Papaver*, the ancient Latin name for the poppy, is said to be derived from the sound made when chewing poppy seeds. An alternative theory is that it has the same root as the old Celtic word *papa*, pap, because poppy juice used to be mixed with the food given to fractious infants to make them sleep. Such explanations, however implausible, point to the antiquity of the poppy and its association with man. The annual *Papaver somniferum* has been cultivated for thousands of years, both as a source of opium and for the edible seed, which 'is good to season bread with', as Gerard noted, and which also yields oil. The

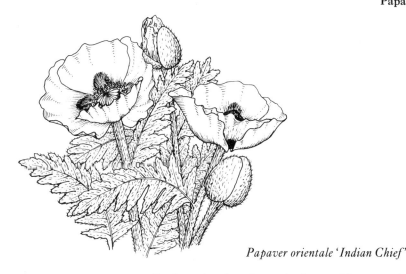

Papaver orientale 'Indian Chief'

common or corn poppy *P. rhoeas* has long been the bane of farmers, defying all attempts to eradicate it including the use of modern weedkillers. Its powers of reproduction made it a symbol of fertility to the Romans and an emblem of remembrance in more recent times So resilient are its seeds that, when they were disturbed by the digging of the trenches in the First World War, they germinated after years of dormancy to cover the fields of Flanders with red poppies.

Growing wild throughout Britain, Europe and beyond, the common poppy has been a much loved garden annual since at least the eighteenth century. The most famous selection, the Shirley poppy, was developed by the Reverend William Wilks, vicar of Shirley near Croydon. As secretary to the Royal Horticultural Society, he did much to revive its flagging fortunes and membership and was also a pioneer of the wild flower garden. He told how 'in the summer of (I think) 1879 or 1880 I noticed in a wilderness corner of my garden, among a patch of field poppies, one bloom with a narrow white edge.' After careful selection of its seedling descendants and the removal of any rogues showing a trace of black, he raised a race of poppies with a 'wonderfully light, bright, tissue-paper like appearance', ranging in colour from white to pink to red. For cut flowers Wilks advised that they should be picked early in the morning with a jug of water in one hand, and plunged straight into this to prevent the milky sap escaping.

Annuals and biennials predominate in the genus and with one notable exception it offers few worthwhile perennials from its fifty or more species. 'The most showy of all poppies', in William Robinson's opinion, and 'among the noblest of hardy plants' is the perennial *P. orientale* (Plate 60). It is native to Armenia, where it was discovered by the seventeenth-century French botanist J. P. de Tournefort, and was first grown in this country by the royal gardener and nurseryman George London, which dates its arrival to pre-1714. Its bristly stem grows to 2 or 3 feet from a clump of long, coarsely cut, hairy leaves at the base and is topped with huge flowers, 4 to 6 inches across and consisting of the characteristic four, or sometimes six, petals. These are a spectacular scarlet, with or without a central blotch of dark violet, and are produced in May and June.

The oriental poppy was cultivated and appreciated in its own right for nearly two centuries, although it is no longer particularly common in gardens. It was only in 1906 that the first 'improvement' took place – and then by accident. Amos Perry was inspecting a batch of seedlings at his nursery one day when he noticed one with pink flowers. He named it 'Mrs Perry' after his wife and set to work on an even paler form, but without success. However, in 1913 he received an irate letter from a customer complaining that the effect of his pink-and-red border had been ruined by a single white poppy. Perry managed to exchange this culprit for a few *Montbretia* corms, to the owner's satisfaction and his own, and the result was 'Perry's White'. Both these fortuitous cultivars are still available today.

Perry's Hardy Plant Farm at Enfield in Middlesex now began to specialise in this 'gorgeous set of garden plants'. 'Mrs Stobart' won an Award of Merit in 1924, when it was described as 'a large flowered bright cerise variety tinted with rose and having black blotches at the base of the petals' and slightly fringed margins. 'Indian Chief', also $2\frac{1}{2}$ to 3 feet high, has blooms of deep mahogany red. 'One of the most delicately coloured', according to a Perry catalogue of the 1920s, was 'E. A. Bowles', which was called after his illustrious gardening neighbour and friend and has 'medium sized flowers, prettily crimped, charming shade of apricot changing to shell pink'. A little less tall, 'May Queen' is a brilliant scarlet with double blooms. The dwarf 'Peter Pan' has large and abundant flowers of bright crimson. Almost certainly, some of these cultivars are hybrids of *P. orientale* and the closely related *P. bracteatum*, from Turkey and Iran. All were listed regularly in the inter-war years, by Perry and other firms.

Poppies generally prefer dry, light soil and a position in full sun. They should be planted in autumn or spring and may need staking as the heavy flower heads develop. While the species itself is readily increased from seed, the cultivars should be propagated by root cuttings taken from dormant plants in mid-winter. It is not a difficult operation but, like so many other excellent garden plants which require only a little extra trouble to propagate, these named forms have fallen victim to the times and are now seldom offered in the trade or seen in gardens.

Passiflora *Passion flower*

Passiflora antioquiensis

When the passion flower was introduced to Europe at the beginning of the seventeenth century, it was already known by this fanciful name. Spanish priests who first encountered it in South America had identified its curious construction with the sufferings of Christ: the five sepals and five petals (collectively tepals) represented the ten Apostles, Peter and Judas being absent; the corona inside these, a ring of coloured filaments, was the crown of thorns; the five stamens on a prominent central column were the five wounds and the three stigmas at the top of the three nails; and the lobes of the leaves and curling tendrils were the hands and whips of Christ's persecutors.

Parkinson vented his Protestant wrath at such superstition, but this did not prevent him from growing the first species to reach this country, *Passiflora incarnata*. The common passion flower, *P. caerulea*, followed at the end of the century and was recorded in the duchess of Beaufort's garden in 1699. With its capacity for rapid climbing, its glorious flowers, predominantly of blue, or in a later variant of white, and its decorative orange fruits, it is still widely grown today. In Victorian times it was especially popular in the London suburbs. It is the only species that is nearly hardy in Britain and survives outside against a sheltered wall in many areas.

The genus *Passiflora* now embraces the long-tubed species formerly separated as *Tacsonia* and contains more than 500 species, mostly climbers concentrated in central and south America. They are remarkable for their flowers and ornamental, often edible, fruits. Several, including the granadillas *P. edulis* and *P. quadrangularis*, are cultivated commercially for this reason. All are vigorous, free-flowering plants of easy culture. They can be grown in ordinary, well-drained soil in large tubs or a greenhouse border and will be more floriferous if the mixture is not too rich and the roots are slightly restricted. Plentiful watering is required during the growing season and the rampant growths should be thinned if necessary after flowering. Propagation is straightforward, by cuttings of the young shoots taken in spring and rooted in gentle heat, or from seed. Some of the passion flowers are definitely hothouse plants, but others can survive a temperature of 45°F in winter. A very few, notably *P. antioquiensis* (Plate 61) and *P. umbilicata*, may approach *P. caerulea* in hardiness and have been known to prosper out of doors in the mild west. The former 'according to its discoverer ... resists a temperature of the freezing-point in its own country'.

Once known as *Tacsonia vanvolxemii*, *P. antioquiensis* is native to the province of Antioquia in Colombia. It was found in a garden in Bogotá by the traveller and 'zealous amateur', van Volxem, and was brought back to Belgium in 1858. The *Botanical Magazine* greeted it as 'one of the most striking and beautiful plants hitherto introduced into Europe'. It seems first to have been cultivated in Britain by the nurserymen Lucombe & Pince of Exeter and quickly covered the roof of their show house with its numerous branching stems. The leaves are more delicate than in some species and are either narrow and unlobed or deeply divided into three points, dark green on top and downy beneath. From their axils the flowers hang on long, thread like stalks, almost 6 inches across and of rich carmine-crimson, with a white mouth to the slender tube surrounded by a dark violet ring. Robert Pince, writing in the *Gardeners' Chronicle* of 1866, compared the blooms to 'brilliantly-coloured parachutes suspended in the air'. Because of their pendulous habit, he advised training the plant on rafters or a roof. His plant apparently flowered all through the summer and even in January and had withstood a winter temperature of 40°F. He thought that it could be tried outside in warm districts, as had been done at his nursery against an east wall though admittedly only in the summer and autumn.

The Victorian gardening writer Shirley Hibberd mentioned a good example of 'this magnificent beauty' in the great conservatory at Eastnor Castle, Herefordshire, where 'the plant clothes the whole of the roof structure'. But unfortunately the owners of spacious plant houses to whom he recommended the culture of passion flowers are today very few – which probably explains the scarcity in general cultivation of one of the finest species, *P. antioquiensis*.

Picrasma

Picrasma quassioides

This attractive tree was first described in 1825 (in the genus *Simaba*), but did not reach Britain until 1890 when it was introduced to Kew from Japan,. It is a member of the family *Simaroubaceae*, to which the very much taller *Ailanthus altissima*, popularly known as the tree of heaven, belongs. The generic name is derived from the Greek word for bitterness, a reference to the exceedingly bitter taste pervading the whole plant. The specific epithet *quassioides* gives further emphasis to this quality. It refers to its similarity to *Quassia amara*, a related tree from Surinam which is the source of the quassia of commerce, used as a bitter tonic and in medicine. From *Picrasma quassioides* (Plate 62) itself various concoctions are brewed in the Far East as a cure for fever and in India, according to the *Botanical Magazine*, the leaves are applied to relieve itch.

P. *quassioides* has a wide distribution in nature, growing in many areas of the temperate belt of the Himalaya through China to Korea and Japan. The main populations occur at an altitude of 5,000 to 6,000 feet and introductions from Japan have proved hardy in Britain. It is sometimes recorded as a scrambling shrub in the wild where it may attain a height of 40 feet or so, but in cultivation it forms a graceful small tree some 15 to 30 feet high. The bark of the young shoots is reddish-brown, conspicuously flecked with yellow spots, and the neat, pinnately divided, alternate leaves are about 15 inches long and composed of dark green leaflets which contrast pleasantly with the crimson leaf stalks. In autumn the foliage turns orange and scarlet before falling. As seen at the Westonbirt Arboretum, Gloucestershire, the University Botanic Garden,

Cambridge, and Wakehurst Place, Sussex, it is one of the finest of trees for autumn effect. The short-branched flower clusters are also tinted red and the small flowers, yellowish-green flushed with purple, appear in May and are followed by sprays of red pea-shaped fruits.

In spite of its horticultural appeal, *P. quassioides* remains rare in gardens, perhaps because it does not flower or fruit regularly in Britain. Seed affords a ready means of propagation when produced. Like many other members of the *Simaroubaceae*, it can also be increased by root cuttings, which should be taken during December or early January when the plants are fully dormant. As a specimen tree for small gardens where the impact of its handsome foliage and brilliant autumn colours can be appreciated, *P. quassioides* has everything to recommend it. Easily grown and increased, it surely deserves to be better known.

Pleione

Pleione forrestii

Pleiones are among the most delightful and approachable members of the orchid family. About fourteen species have so far been named, all native to China, India and surrounding regions. At least two have still to be introduced to cultivation, although they have been sighted in the wild and even collected on several occasions. In Greek mythology Pleione was the mother of the seven Pleiades, who were courted by various gods before being transformed into stars. The name Indian crocus is sometimes applied to these diminutive orchids, with their single large flower (occasionally two or three) emerging from the pseudobulb or swollen stem. The flowers may be white, pink, mauve or yellow and, with the exception of the two autumn-flowering species *Pleione praecox* and *P. maculata*, are produced between February and May and last for about a fortnight. The distinctive tubular lip of the bloom, framed with spreading tepals, is fringed or crinkled and splashed with a darker colour. The flowers are followed by leaves of bright or dull green, roughly spear-shaped and usually pleated.

As the only yellow-flowered species, *P. forrestii* is especially valuable. It was discovered, but not introduced, by George Forrest in 1906 in western Yunnan, China, where it grew on moss-covered boulders and cliffs in a shady valley at about 10,000 feet. He described it as having 'orange yellow blooms laced and marked deep brown' with 'the precocious flowers arising from the deep green moss having all the appearance of our yellow crocus'. Living plants were eventually introduced under this name in 1924, but their number dwindled until only one representative in cultivation was left at the Royal Botanic Garden, Edinburgh. From this, stock was built up in the 1950s and made commercially available, becoming much sought-after by gardeners. However, this so-called *P. forrestii*, with its fragrant, red-veined flowers of creamy yellow to light orange, has since turned out to be an imposter, with no right to the name. It is now known as *P. × confusa* (Plate 63) and is a natural hybrid, probably between the true *P. forrestii* and the rare white *P. albiflora*.

The true *P. forrestii* was finally and successfully introduced to cultivation from Yunnan in 1981 by the Sino-British expedition. It seems to be variable in colour for, unlike Forrest's original account, the flowers of recent importations are described as canary yellow with dark red stripes or blotches on the fringed wavy lip. They are slightly smaller than *P. × confusa* and faintly scented. Supplies of two other species, *P. delavayi* and *P. yunnanensis*, were replenished at the same time.

Pleiones are much easier to grow than many orchids. They are probably best in a cool greenhouse or alpine house, although the most commonly cultivated species *P. formosana* will survive outside in a sheltered rock garden. The pseudobulbs should be potted into shallow containers in January or February before growth begins, using a bark-based compost which is free-draining but moist. They should be watered sparingly when the buds appear and then liberally after flowering, keeping the atmosphere humid and giving a weekly liquid feed. Once the leaves have become yellow and the plants are dormant, no water is required until the following spring. The pseudobulbs last for a year, but each one generally produces two or three new pseudobulbs which can be potted up in early spring. Tiny bulbils are also formed and can be grown in the same way, reaching flowering size in two or three years. The procedure is similar with the autumn-flowering species, which bloom just before dormancy.

P. forrestii is unfortunately slower to increase than many other species, since it produces only one pseudobulb at a time and fewer bulbils. It is also of fairly limited distribution in the wild. For these reasons alone, it is essential that it should be maintained in cultivation and that stocks should be accumulated and distributed. Even more important, perhaps, is the fact that the species is unique to the genus in terms of colour. It has already shown its potential and been used to introduce yellow into recent hybrids. *P. forrestii* received an Award of Merit at Chelsea in 1985 and hopefully such horticultural recognition will secure it a firmer place in cultivation.

Podophyllum

Podophyllum pleianthum

Podophyllum is a genus of some ten or eleven perennials from eastern Asia and eastern North America. It takes its name from *podos*, foot, and *phyllon*, wing, since the large, lobed leaves are supposed to resemble the webbed foot of a duck. Botanically it wavers on the edge of the *Berberis* family and the *Ranunculaceae*, but is now usually accorded a family of its own, the *Podophyllaceae*. This includes a number of woodland plants such as *Ranzania* and *Jeffersonia* which are sought after by enthusiasts but still unfamiliar to many gardeners.

'Plants of lush opulent beauty, all for easy culture in deep rich soil in a rather cool place', wrote Reginald Farrer of *Podophyllum peltatum*. It is the sole North American species and inhabits moist woodland areas where the horizontal rhizomes spread freely through the leafy soil, producing its delicate, nodding, white 2-inch cups on 12-inch stems under umbrella-like foliage as it unfurls in late May. The blooms are succeeded by edible apple- or plum-type fruits of yellow or occasionally red, which are temptingly succulent but sadly insipid. These have given rise to one of its common names, May apple. The other, wild mandrake, probably derives from the similarity of the fruits and their properties to those of the true European mandrake, although the two plants are unrelated. Podophyllum, a purgative drug, is extracted from the dried rhizomes and roots of *P. peltatum*, which like the leaves are said to be poisonous.

The May apple was introduced to Britain as long ago as 1664. However, the most commonly grown species today is the clump-forming, fleshy-rooted *P. hexandrum* (*P. emodi*) from the Himalaya. Its white or sometimes pink flowers, cup-shaped and generally upright, appear after the bronze-marbled, deeply cleft leaves have expanded. They are followed by hanging fruits, compared in the usual Farrerian style to 'an oblong Persimmon, of brilliant scarlet and orange, beloved by birds, but of rich effect if these can be induced to permit'. Seed from the fruit pulp, washed clean of sticky fluid and sown in autumn, germinates readily in spring and is a simple method of increase.

Even more striking is the Formosan *P. pleianthum* (Plate 64), sometimes placed with a few other species in the genus *Dysosma*. This is a stately woodlander with creeping rhizomes from which ascend foot-high stems, overtopped by sunshade-like leaves sheltering the clusters of large, pendulous, dark red-purple bells. The flowers unfortunately emit an unpleasant smell, as do those of the closely allied *P. versipelle*, which is similar in hue but rather smaller in bloom. This was discovered in ravines in the Lofau mountains of Kwantung and has since been collected in other Chinese provinces such as Szechuan and Hupeh. Both species were in cultivation at Kew earlier this century. *P. pleianthum* arrived via Hong Kong in 1885, while *P. versipelle* reached the Royal Gardens in 1903, from a collection by E. H. Wilson on behalf of the renowned Chelsea nursery of Veitch. Today the Edinburgh Royal Botanic Garden is one of the few places where it may be seen. Both have virtually disappeared from gardens, although they were grown without difficulty at Kew and apparently easily raised from seed. Such handsome and unusual plants would be valuable additions to the woodland garden and are certainly worthy of reintroduction and wider distribution.

Poliothyrsis

Poliothyrsis sinensis (Plate 66) was one of the discoveries made in the Chinese province of Hupeh by the Irish doctor Augustine Henry, in about 1889. However, it was nearly twenty years before its introduction to the Western world, when seeds collected by E. H. Wilson were sent to the Arnold Arboretum in the USA and distributed from there in 1908. For a long time it was believed to be the only member of the genus, but this is now thought to contain two additional species about which little is known. The name comes from the Greek *polios*, greyish-white, and *thyrsos*, panicle.

Poliothyrsis sinensis

A small deciduous tree, it eventually grows to 30 to 40 feet in height. Its scented flowers, of creamy white turning to yellow, are produced in loose clusters up to 6 inches long in August and September. The narrow, oval leaves are a shiny dark green, attractively tinted and downy on the underside at the beginning of the year. It is a native of central China, where it is found in forests at an altitude of about 8,000 feet. In Britain it is perfectly hardy and demands no special attention from the gardener. Some young seedlings at Kew were casualties of an exceptionally harsh winter in 1908–9, but the rest survived and went on to flourish growing in ordinary soil.

Despite its attributes and the bestowal of an Award of Merit in 1960, *P. sinensis* has never become common in Britain. It has been grown at Glasnevin in Ireland and at Caerhays in Cornwall, where it had reached a height of 49 feet in 1971 according to W. J. Bean. But it takes time to achieve such dimensions and is a tree eminently suitable for small gardens. As Bean remarked, 'it deserves to be more widely grown for its fragrant flowers, which are borne late in the season.'

Polygonatum *Solomon's seal*

The common Solomon's seal, also known as David's harp or ladder to heaven, is *Polygonatum multiflorum*. It is found locally in England and Wales and is widespread in Europe and part of Asia. Although some fifty-five species are recognised, it is one of the few members of this attractive liliaceous genus of woodland plants to be cultivated. None can be considered spectacular, but they

Polygonatum punctatum

are often elegant in growth and accommodating in their cultural requirements and thrive in leaf-rich soil and light shade. Thrusting their graceful, lily-like shoots rapidly aloft as spring arrives and flowering from April to June, they creep about by means of horizontal, nobbly rhizomes, whence the generic name, from *poly*, many, and *gonu*, knee joint.

The popular name Solomon's seal may derive from the fact that the roots when cut reveal marks suggestive of Hebrew characters. Gerard gives an alternative explanation and attributes it to the 'singular vertue that it hath in sealing or healing up wounds, broken bones and such like', a property which the Greek physician Dioscorides had referred to in the first century. According to Gerard, 'the roote stamped while it is freshe taketh away in one night, or two at the most, any bruse, blacke or blew spots gotten by fals or women's wilfulness, in stumbling upon their hastie husbands fists.' The later herbalist Nicholas Culpeper recommends a distillation of the plant as a facewash to clear the complexion. The roots have been used as a flour substitute in times of food shortage and in Sikkim and Nepal the young shoots of various species are eaten as a vegetable.

P. multiflorum and the scented *P. odoratum* or angled Solomon's seal, together with the hybrid between them called *P. × hybridum*, are all familiar to gardeners. But the double form of *P. odoratum*, with its neatly overlapping green and white bells, is seldom available and the variegated form seems equally elusive, though it is occasionally offered. Closely related is the dwarf *P. humile* from China, Japan and Korea, which is usually no more than 6 inches tall and is very easy to grow. This too is rarely seen outside the gardens of collectors.

A slender species 4 to 5 feet high, *P. verticillatum* has dense whorls of narrow leaves, pointed and slightly curled at the tips, and clusters of small, greenish-white flowers in the leaf axils. It is distributed throughout northern Europe and Asia and varies considerably, one variant from the Himalaya having purple-tinged blooms. The red berries are a distinctive feature of *P. verticillatum* and its allies. These include *P. cirrhifolium*, a robust version with curved leaf tips whose young foliage is often bronze-tinted; the purplish-pink *P. roseum* from China and Soviet central Asia; and the Chinese *P. stewartianum*, which bears greenish-white flowers heavily suffused purplish-pink and translucent, red-dotted fruits. Sometimes seen in botanic gardens, none of these species has made much impact on commercial lists.

The delightful little *P. geminiflorum* (Plate 65), 18 inches tall at the most, is native to the western Himalaya and, as recently recorded, Sikkim. Its delicate purplish stems are clothed with faintly greyish-green, normally bronze-tinged leaves, opposite or grouped in threes, and pairs of waisted, drooping flowers, white tipped with green. It certainly deserves wider cultivation and, although known only from one or two introductions, it appears to be hardy and perfectly amenable.

The diminutive *P. hookeri*, unlike the majority of Solomon's seals, occurs in short turf or semi-scree conditions in alpine zones of the Himalaya and China. Generally under 2 inches in height, its tufts of leaves are crowded in the upper part of the short stem and carry singly in their axils the upright flowers of bright purple-pink. This charming plant, hardy, easily grown and readily increased by division of the rhizomes, remains inexplicably the province of the enthusiast.

Potentilla

The best known of the potentillas today is *Potentilla fruticosa*. It, or rather the numerous varieties, forms and hybrids which have displaced the species itself, has become one of our most popular shrubs and is an ideal candidate for the small garden with its neat habit and long flowering season. It occurs wild throughout the northern hemisphere, including the British Isles. It was originally recorded in the Lake District and Teeside, but is now a great rarity restricted to Yorkshire and the west of Ireland. There are several other natives of Britain, with charming names like cinquefoil, silverweed, tormentil and barren strawberry. Many had their medicinal uses, for the treatment of such diverse ailments as the ague, diarrhoea, ulcers and sore feet. The generic name, from the Latin *potens*, powerful, may allude to these supposed properties or, as a diminutive of *potentia*, it could mean the opposite, plant of little power. The name cinquefoil refers to the typically hand-shaped leaf with five divisions,

Potentilla atrosanguinea

which was adopted as a symbol of the five senses of man particularly in heraldry.

A shrubby species as the epithet indicates, *P. fruticosa* is in this respect the least representative of *Potentilla* as a whole. Of the few shrubs in the genus, most are its close allies. One, however, is quite distinct, both botanically and in its striking appearance. *P. salesoviana* belongs to the *Comarum* section, which is sometimes classified separately, and is akin to the marsh cinquefoil *P. palustris*. Its scarcely branched, erect, reddish-brown stems are 3 to 4 feet high and clad in large, sharply toothed leaves of a shiny dark green with greyish undersides. At their tips they bear clusters of creamy white blooms, often tinged with pink and up to $1\frac{1}{2}$ inches across, in June and July.

It is an inhabitant of central Asia, from Mongolia to the Himalaya to Siberia, and is 'confined to river shingles and suchlike barren hungry places', according to Reginald Farrer. His advice to gardeners was 'to immediately learn its true character by putting it on hunger-strike'. Farrer himself never saw it, but his friend William Purdom did, on their trip to the Chinese province of Kansu in 1914. In Farrer's words, 'the bloom is free, and its effect of remarkable beauty', an opinion later endorsed by the naturalist and collector Oleg Polunin, who came across it during an expedition in 1960. Despite its obvious promise and its early introduction to Britain in 1823, *P. salesoviana* has remained rare in cultivation. It was listed by Messrs Hillier of Winchester in the past as an 'unusual dwarf shrub' and grown at Nymans in Sussex before the First World War. But today it is very seldom seen.

Distributed across the northern hemisphere, the 350 or so members of the genus are mostly herbaceous perennials. Pre-eminent among them is *P. atrosanguinea*, which furnished Victorian flower beds in the same way as

P. fruticosa supplies our own shrub borders today. It was discovered in Nepal by Nathaniel Wallich, superintendent of the Calcutta Botanic Garden, and the nursery firm Loddiges of Hackney 'received seeds of it in 1821, from Mr. Broeager, of Hooghly, in Bengal'. It has sprays of dark velvety red flowers set off by green and silver strawberry-like foliage and is a 'charming plant', in the words of the *Botanical Magazine*. But it has not often been grown in its own right. Breeders were quick to spot the potential of it and two other Himalayan species which arrived at that period, *P. argyrophylla*, a near relative with clear yellow flowers, and the purplish *P. nepalensis*. The results were on the market within twenty years and were soon taken up by the public. They were to continue to be an established feature of gardens for the next half century.

The range of cultivars in the past was enormous, with single, semi-double or fully double blooms in shades across the spectrum from mahogany brown to brilliant scarlet, dark orange to canary yellow. William Robinson preferred the double sorts as being 'most showy, lasting in perfection both on the plants and when cut'. Of these, there were 'about 3 dozen distinct named kinds, all to be obtained from any of the large hardy plant nurseries'. Robinson gave 'a good selection' of over twenty, including 'Louis van Houtte', a large deep crimson with yellow markings; 'Phoebus', reddish-orange; 'Etna', maroon; 'Volcan' or 'Vulcan', bright red; 'Vase d'Or', clear lemon yellow; and 'Le Vésuve' or 'Vesuvius', so much admired by E. A. Bowles for 'its deep scarlet and buff double flowers, which always remind me ... of newly made strawberry jam'. Some of these survived into the twentieth century and a few are still to be seen occasionally. But only two from Robinson's list are definitely in commerce, 'William Rollison', vermilion and yellow, and 'Monsieur Rouillard' (Plate 68), blood-red with yellow, though neither is particularly common. Others like the wonderfully named 'Belzebuth', 'Escarboucle' and 'Dr Andry' have disappeared without trace.

The reign of *P. atrosanguinea* in all its glorious variety was already drawing to a close by the 1920s. From a high point in the 1880s and 1890s, the number of forms offered in catalogues had generally dwindled to about half a dozen. Some old favourites lingered on, such as the double lemon and scarlet 'Arc en Ciel', and the deep crimson-maroon 'Glasell's Crimson' which Messrs Bloom of Bressingham, Norfolk described as 'rare and beautiful' in the 1960s. The most widely available now are the single-flowered 'Gibson's Scarlet', a veteran from the 1900s (which should, apparently, have been credited to a Captain Pinwill of Cornwall), and the brilliant red 'Flamenco', the semi-double 'Gloire de Nancy' (or 'Glory of Nancy') in orange and copper and the bright 'Yellow Queen', together with the short-lived selection of *P. nepalensis*, 'Miss Willmott' and the hybrid 'Roxana'. It is a poor showing compared to the wealth of forms from which our predecessors could choose.

Mostly about 2 feet in height, free-flowering throughout the summer and long-lived, the *P. atrosanguinea* cultivars make excellent garden plants. They thrive in ordinary soil and full sun, but will tolerate slight shade as well as drought and frost, and they are readily increased by division of the roots. As Alan Bloom, founder of the famous Bressingham nursery, wrote in 1977, 'it is surprising that so few herbaceous potentillas are seen in gardens' and 'sad to think that ... some should have become Cinderellas'.

Primula *Primrose, Polyanthus, Auricula*

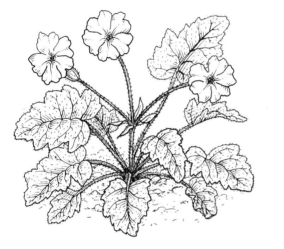

Primula rockii

The word primrose is said to be derived, through its older variants primerole, prymerose and prime-rose, from the Latin *prima rosa*, first or earliest rose. It was apparently used indiscriminately for several plants before Shakespeare's time and also in a figurative sense, denoting the best or finest. The generic name *Primula*, on the other hand, was supplied by the cowslip, *Primula veris*, literally firstling of spring. Its English name, meaning cow dung, may refer to the fact that it flourishes in fields grazed by cattle.

Like the cowslip, the primrose *P. vulgaris* (*P. acaulis*), is native to Britain and Europe. It has been cultivated for hundreds of years, originally as a salad or vegetable, and was recommended by Thomas Tusser, author of *Five Hundred Pointes of Good Husbandrie*, in 1573 among his 'seeds and herbs for the kitchen'. It had the usual medicinal qualities, as a dressing for wounds, a cure for headaches, an emetic and a remedy 'for Palsie and pains in the ioynts'. Its ornamental value was equally appreciated, not only in the normal guise of the single yellow primrose, but in white, in doubles of both shades, and in such quaint aberrations as the hose-in-hose, jack-in-the-green and green-flowered primrose to which the Elizabethans were partial. Pink, purple and red were added to the colour range with the arrival in the 1630s of 'Tradescant's Turkie purple Primrose', a subspecies *sibthorpii* of *P. vulgaris*. But, despite the continued popularity of the primrose in its various manifestations, it was little developed beyond this and there were few named forms before the nineteenth century. Never elevated to the distinction of the auricula or polyanthus, it was a cherished but humble garden plant and as such increasingly vulnerable to the inroads of others.

The double primrose 'of all the rest is of the greatest beautie' wrote Gerard. But even this was taken for granted and, as John Rea remarked in his *Flora, Ceres and Pomona* of 1665, 'were it not so common in every Country-woman's garden, it would be more respected.' In the 1730s Philip Miller's assortment of doubles in the Apothecaries' Garden at Chelsea was 'accidentally obtained'. Thomas Hogg of Paddington Green, in his book on florists' flowers a century later, listed those available merely as six 'different coloured sorts' – the venerable yellow or sulphur and, Gerard's favourite, the white 'Alba Plena' (Plate 67), along with pink, lilac, purple and crimson.

Towards the end of the nineteenth century these were still the 'best-known', according to William Robinson. The double primrose had suffered something of an eclipse in the interim, when it was 'cast aside to make way for gaudier things', but it was then enjoying a revival. Many of the choicest kinds were grown in the pre-1914 period, especially in Ireland where they flourished in the damp climate. 'Prince Silverwings', crimson-violet laced with silver and tinged gold in the centre, was the most famous of the double polyanthus-type primroses. It seems to have been rediscovered by Tom Smith of the Daisy Hill nursery in Newry, Northern Ireland, who was also responsible for one of the current survivors, which he called 'Our Pat' after his daughter. Like 'Prince Silverwings', the deep violet 'Arthur de Moulin' had the unusual attribute of yielding pollen. It was supposedly connected with the Irish peer Lord Ventry through the family name de Moleyns, but it may have originated on the Continent. From Europe came other celebrated forms such as 'Arthur de Smit', rich purple fringed with yellow; 'Marie Crousse II', lavender splashed with white and scented, which received an Award of Merit in 1882; 'Madame Pompadour' or 'Crimson Velvet', notable for its great ruby-red flowers and for being extremely difficult to grow; and its more amenable relative 'Rose du Barri'.

By 1939, when Sacheverell Sitwell in his book *Old-Fashioned Flowers* drew attention to the scarcity of double primroses, a number of these were already on the verge of the extinction to which they and many more have since been consigned. However, about twenty-five sorts were still in commerce if in short supply. They included some of uncertain age like 'Burgundy', 'Carnea Plena', 'Curiosity' or 'Golden Pheasant', 'French Grey' or 'Dingy', 'Harlequin', 'Irish Sulphur', 'Ladies' Delight', 'Marine Blue' and 'Salmonea'. Several were more recent finds from old gardens, such as 'Chevithorne Pink' and 'Chevithorne Purple' from Devon, 'Tyrian Purple' from Cornwall, and the Glazeley primroses located by Major C. H. Taylor of Bridgnorth. Others, whose subsequent loss is the more reprehensible, date from the early part of this century. Among them were 'Downshill Ensign', the last representative of a group raised by Murray Thomson whose finest product was 'Bluebird', which won an AM in 1930 before it disappeared; 'William Chalmers' and 'Crathes Crimson' from Scotland; 'Castlederg', a chance seedling from Co. Tyrone; and 'Buxton's Blue', a sport from a single primrose found in E. C. Buxton's garden in Wales, which his great gardening neighbour A. T. Johnson described as 'doubtless the best double-blue primrose ... ever produced'. The Bon Accord race, herald of the renewed interest in double primroses, was similarly short-lived. Named after the motto of Aberdeen, it was the creation of the Scottish firm of Cocker & Sons, the specialist rose nursery, in the late nineteenth century. The plants were often of polyanthus habit, with flat, regular blooms in different shades. The eminent nurseryman Amos Perry, of Enfield in Middlesex, had 'every confidence in offering them' in the 1920s. But within a decade he retained only three of the fifteen or so Bon Accords in his catalogue.

Double primroses 'will grow in almost any earth provided they have a shady situation' asserted Miller in his *Gardeners' Dictionary* of 1731. Clearly our forebears had no trouble with them. However, they are more delicate than single primroses and can only be propagated by division, which should be carried out every two or three years. Reginald Farrer agreed with Robinson, for once, that the double primroses were 'apt to prove of less easy and perennial cultivation in the well-prepared gardens of the rich and mighty than in the immemorial cottage-borders of the humble and meek'. At the beginning of this century the resilient double white and double lilac could still be seen in 'many a village, especially in the Midland counties'. But like so many other cottage garden flowers, the double primroses seem to have relied largely on neighbourly interchange for their preservation and, as that tradition has faded, so have they.

'From the days of Parkinson', noted Farrer in *The English Rock Garden*, 'freaks, reduplications and virescent forms have been frequent, and particularly valued among gardeners. ... Nowadays, however, the passion for Hose-in-hose, Jacks-in-the-green and Galligaskins, has passed away.' The galligaskins were so called from their resemblance to the wide breeches worn by Tudor and Stuart gentlemen. Together with the jackanapes-on-horseback and other curiosities they did not long outlast the age whose fashions they charmingly reflected. But the hose-in-hose or cup-and-saucer, with its double-decker flowers, and the jack-in-the-green or jack-in-the-pulpit, with a ruff of leaves framing the petals, were familiar to later generations in several named forms. Many of them again were Irish in origin. Of the hose-in-hose, 'Irish Sparkler', 'Lady Molly', 'Lady Dora', the delightful 'Lady Lettice', and 'Erin's Gem', which has been identified with the Elizabethan 'Pantaloon', were to be found in Ireland in the 1930s. Also widely grown in the past were 'Ashfort', 'Brimstone', 'Canary Bird', 'Castle Howard' from the Yorkshire stately home, 'Dark Beauty', 'Old Vivid', 'Gold-laced Hose' and, among the jack-in-the-greens, 'Donegal Danny', 'Eldorado' and 'Feathers'. None is easily traced today and some have entirely vanished.

The single primrose, of course, has been cultivated for centuries. There was little deliberate alteration and named forms were relatively sparse. 'Miss Massey', however, 'a single glowing Pompadour' enhanced by vivid green leaves, was a common inhabitant of gardens at the beginning of the century. It and its fellows like 'Belle des Jardins', 'John Hammond', 'McWatt's Claret' and the white 'Harbinger', which gained a First Class Certificate in 1866, are now largely forgotten. A new species with bright purple, yellow-centred flowers, which was introduced from the Caucasus in 1912, hastened the decline of these garden forms. 'P. juliae has taken the plunge into civilisation amid cries of general applause', wrote Farrer. It was soon to transform the single primrose with the countless hybrids derived from it, although many of them in their turn enjoyed only a fleeting existence. Supreme examples of this P. × juliana group were 'Buckland Scarlet' and 'Buckland Belle', a luminous blue with pale yellow eye, raised at Buckland Monachorum in Devon. They were still obtainable in the 1950s, but like most of the others apart from 'Wanda' are seldom encountered today.

Just as popular and just as transient were the Garryarde cultivars, a race of primroses with striking bronze foliage. The first one seems to have arisen in the garden of James Whiteside Dane, of Garryarde in Co. Kildare, and was being distributed from Glasnevin in the 1920s as 'Dane's Primrose'. From Dane the Dublin actor Cecil Monson acquired 'Appleblossom', with clustered pink and white blooms on red stems. It is now extinct and so, it is feared, are its progeny, the brilliant red 'The Grail', 'Sir Galahad' and several more. Others with the Garryarde label probably had a different ancestry involving P. juliae and one of them, the soft pink 'Guinevere', remains quite plentiful in commerce.

The polyanthus, P. × variabilis, has always been more comfortable as a garden plant than its parents, the primrose and the cowslip. The two species frequently cross in the wild to produce the oxlip (the false one, as opposed to the true oxlip, P. elatior), which was presumably known to gardeners of old. However, the polyanthus did not emerge as a distinct entity until about the mid-seventeenth century, when one Edward Morgan is recorded as having transferred plants of Primula veris polyanthos from a Warwickshire wood to his London garden. It was grown by Sir Thomas Hanmer, author of the useful Garden Book of 1659, whose friend John Rea called it 'the red cowslip or oxlip', being 'of several sorts, all bearing many flowers on one stalk'. Some twenty years later, both John Evelyn, the diarist and horticulturist, and the Reverend Samuel Gilbert, Rea's son-in-law and author of The Florist's Vade-Mecum, referred to it by the name polyanthus, from the Greek polyanthos, many-flowered.

Despite its belated début, the polyanthus quickly became an established feature of the cottage garden like its relatives. But unlike them it was the object of improvement from an early stage. By 1770 the Reverend William Hanbury, in his *A Complete Body of Planting and Gardening*, could boast of 'more than a thousand varieties ... at once in blow in a single bed'. By the end of the eighteenth century, it had captured the imagination of florists, especially the artisans of the Midlands, the north of England and parts of Scotland. Their efforts were concentrated exclusively on the laced polyanthus, a dark crimson or black with the petals outlined in white or preferably yellow and repeated in the central eye. It was grown in pots and judged by the same rigid criteria as the tulip, carnation and other florists' flowers. At its peak in the mid-nineteenth century it almost outdid the auricula. But its subsequent downfall was swift and total and the vast majority of these gold- and silver-laced kinds are now defunct. Only a few such as 'Cheshire Favourite', 'Duke of Wellington' and 'Lancashire Hero' persisted into the 1930s, their names recalling the time and the place of the show polyanthus in its prime.

In the twentieth century the polyanthus has returned triumphant to the garden with the development by seedsmen of vigorous, large-flowered breeds. The modern seed-raised polyanthus provides a colourful and long-lasting display and is one of our most dependable border plants. In the face of such progress, the number of old named forms of garden polyanthus has inevitably dwindled. Division is the only method of propagation in their case, but they are otherwise simple to grow in moist soil and partial shade. In the 1930s Sitwell mentioned a number of casualties, mainly of Irish origin. Others which apparently fared better included 'Bartimeus', velvety dark crimson and lacking a central eye; 'Beltany Red', with a green centre and thin yellow lacing; 'Hunter's Moon', apricot with a yellow eye and perfumed; 'Fair Maid', deep orange-scarlet with a gold patch; and 'Barrowby Gem', rich yellow and deliciously scented. The latter, described as 'a newcomer and a great favourite' in one catalogue of the inter-war period, was then regularly listed. Needless to say, all are now rare.

From the time when Gerard admired 'this beautifull and brave plant' to the present day when shows and societies flourish in its honour, the auricula has elicited more constant devotion than any other primula. The sixteenth-century Flemish botanist Clusius made the first reference to *Auricula ursi* in cultivation. Following him, Gerard called it bear's ears in allusion to the shape of the leaves and also mountain cowslip. *P. auricula* occurs wild in the European Alps, where local people used to take the roots to prevent vertigo 'before they ascend the rocks or other high places'. But the species itself, which was well-known to the ancients, played a less dominant role in the creation of the cultivated auricula than *P. × pubescens*, a hybrid between *P. auricula* and *P. hirsuta*. From this the alpine, show and border auriculas are principally descended.

The auricula is traditionally said to have been brought by Huguenot refugees and reached Britain shortly before the publication of Gerard's herbal in 1597. The three kinds specified there had risen to twenty-one when Parkinson in 1629 so lyrically praised their flowers, 'every one ... a Nosegay alone of itself ... with a pretty sweete sent, which doth add an encrease of pleasure in those that make them an ornament for their wearing'. Within thirty years Hanmer was stating that 'the sorts of this flower are not to be numbered nor the colours of all of them bee fitly named or described', though he managed to list some forty. A double and 'two rare striped Auriculas' were much esteemed at the period and commanded high prices, but these are long since lost.

Growers were already exercising their skills on the auricula. Rea gave several named forms in his *Flora, Ceres and Pomona*, including 'Mistris Buggs her fine purple ... raised by her in Battersey, near London'. By the early eighteenth century it was launched as a florists' flower and in that capacity was destined to be the most enduring of them all. *The Distinguishing Properties of a Fine Auricula* in 1757 was the first of many treatises to define the standards of excellence required. It ushered in the most important class, the edged auricula, with a green or white border to the petals, a ring of distinct colour inside it and in the middle a circular eye covered with pure white meal, the characteristic paste. The show or stage auricula was grown in pots or on staging housed under a wooden canopy in order to protect its floury blooms from rain. Various fantastic recipes were proposed for the growing medium, with ingredients ranging from goose dung to 'juicy pieces of meat', and these contributed to the mystique of the auricula as well as to the weakening of individual plants. As Hogg observed, 'the florists who grow this flower are numerous, and the different composts recommended by them are equally numerous as the florists themselves. Persons often take extraordinary pains, and incur unnecessary expense, to injure, if not destroy, their flowers.'

During the first half of the nineteenth century when the craze was at its height, the cloth workers and miners of Lancashire and Cheshire vied for the perfect auricula and also for the ideal gold-laced polyanthus and the heaviest gooseberry. In the south enthusiasm waned a little earlier. By the 1850s, according to George Glenny, that voluble expert on floristry, the auricula fanciers had been 'hunted out of their gardens to make way for the enlargement of our London Babel'. But the foundation of the National Auricula Society twenty years later marked a renaissance for the show auricula. Together with the smooth-leaved alpine auricula, it has continued to prosper both in Britain and the USA.

The border auriculas, which conform to neither class, have been less fortunate. These delightful plants, generally powdered on the blooms and foliage and often very fragrant, flower freely from April to midsummer. In a sunny or slightly shady position they form clumps and demand little attention apart from division every few years. They graced many a cottage garden in the past and like other primulas were widely grown in Ireland. The earl of Meath, for example, collected several hundred named forms in the early eighteenth century. Numerous cultivars were of Irish origin, among them 'Old Irish Blue', 'Queen Alexandra', and the lemon yellow 'Celtic King', which appeared in an Irish catalogue as late as the 1950s, but has now sunk into obscurity.

The same fate has overtaken most of these border auriculas. Especially regrettable is the disappearance of 'Adam Lord', navy blue with a creamy centre; 'Blue Mist'; 'Linnet', green, brown and mustard; 'Mrs Nicholls', pale yellow with a white ring; and 'McWatt's Blue', raised in Scotland by Dr McWatt, an authority on primulas 'Broadwell Gold' was found by Joe Elliott in a Cotswolds garden and is still available. In the 1930s his father, Clarence Elliott, stocked several kinds at his Six Hills nursery, Stevenage, including 'Old Red Dusty Miller' with 'deep, wallflower red blossoms'. But it was then 'very rare', as was 'Old Purple Dusty Miller'. It seems that 'Old Yellow Dusty Miller' alone is left to represent this antique race.

'A cold awe sweeps across the gardener as he comes at last into the shadow of this grim and glorious name.' Thus Farrer in *The English Rock Garden*, obviously feeling the same emotion, embarked on his entry for *Primula*, the longest in the book. It is a vast genus comprising at least 500 species and is widely distributed over Europe, Asia and North America. Taxing not only gardeners but botanists too, it has been divided into thirty main sections. Some are of scant horticultural merit, others such as the Nivales group contain species which are highly desirable but notoriously stubborn in cultivation. Farrer was anxious to dispel the primula's bad reputation, but he had to admit the existence of 'both miffs and mimps, especially among the Asiatics, now come into a too-kindly and cosseting exile'.

The first oriental species to reach Britain was the drumstick primula *P. denticulata*, an early introduction in about 1837. It is easily grown and is still one of the most popular of the Asiatics, with *P. sikkimensis*, *P. japonica*, *P. pulverulenta* and *P. florindae*. But the beginning of the twentieth century, when Farrer was writing, saw a flood of introductions from the Far East (requiring a special appendix to his classic) which has continued ever since. Bereft of their natural conditions, many of these were to prove a challenge in the West.

Farrer was one of several who encountered but failed to secure *P. kingii*. It was discovered in eastern Sikkim in 1878 by Dungboo, collecting for Sir George King, the director of the Calcutta Botanic Garden, and was later found in neighbouring Himalayan states. Normally growing in wet pasture and bog at an altitude of about 14,000 feet, this diminutive but striking plant, 4 to 8 inches high, carries above its neat tuft of leaves a head of 'rich claret-purple bells, so sombre as almost to be satiny black'. It first flowered in cultivation at Edinburgh in 1936 and gained an AM, but then died without setting seed. It belongs to another section of the genus, Amethystina, with a poor horticultural record. However, it has been grown successfully in Scotland, notably by the plant collector and explorer of the Himalaya, George Sherriff, and his wife in whose garden it flourished by the edge of a stream.

The rarity in cultivation of *P. pycnoloba* is less understandable. It responds readily to alpine treatment and may be propagated by detaching and replanting the small root buds. It was described from specimens gathered by Prince Henri d'Orléans in 1890 in western Szechuan, China, and introduced in 1906 when E. H. Wilson sent seeds home to James Veitch & Sons of Chelsea. In Farrer's words, it is 'one of the oddest freaks in the race' and since it is not closely related to any other species it is of some botanical significance. It is up to 8 inches high, scattered all over with white hairs, and has clusters of narrow, funnel-shaped flowers, white edged with dark pink, which are virtually hidden by the surrounding leafy green calyx and resemble 'eccentric shaggy little five-segmented Daffodils'.

From the same Chinese province, *P. rockii* is confined to the mountains of the southwest and occurs on limestone cliffs and boulders. It was first collected by the American naturalist and traveller Joseph Rock in 1928 and made its entrance six years later, winning an AM the following year. It is classified in the Bullatae section and is a tiny plant with flowers made up of rich yellow, deeply toothed petals. It performs well in an alpine house, but is not completely hardy and seldom sets seed in cultivation. Propagation by division of the woody rootstock is slow and difficult. Although it has been exhibited at a few shows and attracted commendations, it has never become common and is 'probably in the hands of only one or two enthusiasts', according to the *Botanical Magazine* in 1970.

The collectors Frank Ludlow and George Sherriff located a number of primula species in Tibet and sent them back to the Royal Botanic Garden, Edinburgh, in 1947. Among them was *P. tayloriana*, named in honour of Dr (now Sir) George Taylor who had been their companion on an earlier Himalayan expedition. Seeds were distributed and several plants brought to flowering stage, one of which received an AM in 1949. This delightful primula belongs to the extensive Farinosae section and is about 4 inches high, producing up to eight blooms per stalk, violet with a white or pale yellow eye. It too has failed to secure a firm place in cultivation.

Given the huge size of the genus, it is hardly surprising that many other species besides these Asiatics have been neglected. But in the case of *P.* × *bowlesii* perhaps oblivion was deserved. Certainly its discoverer, E. A. Bowles, did little to promote this 'ugly duckling hybrid' between two inhabitants of the Italian Alps. He wondered whether foreigners would pronounce the name 'Bovvleaysii'. 'In spite of its lovely parents, rosy pedemontana and the true viscosa of imperial purple, it is a mawkish magenta in all the specimens we have found save one, which was a cheery crimson-purple.' It is, however, very scarce in the wild and Bowles 'was glad to be the first to flower my Primrose'.

Pulsatilla *Pasque flower*

Pulsatilla vulgaris

If not already native to Britain, the pasque flower was a very early introduction from the Continent and may have been brought by the Romans. It was said to grow wild where the Danes once shed their blood and was so plentiful in the Middle Ages that the petals were used to dye Easter eggs green. Today *Pulsatilla vulgaris* is a rare inhabitant of chalk downs and pastures in central England. By the end of the sixteenth century, however, it was secure in cultivation and Gerard noted that it served 'for the adorning of gardens and garlands'. He also claimed credit for changing its name from passe flower, or surpassing flower, to pasque flower, since it blooms at Easter time.

Formerly known as *Anemone pulsatilla*, *P. vulgaris* is now placed in a separate but closely related genus of some twelve species which are native mainly to Europe. Their cup-shaped flowers appear in spring, often before the leaves have opened, and are followed by long, feathery seed heads, the chief distinguishing feature from the genus *Anemone*. The derivation of the Italian name *Pulsatilla* is explained by 'the downy seed being beaten about by the wind', according to Philip Miller. From this prolific output of seed, sown fresh in the summer, pulsatillas can be increased easily. They are long-lived when established and thrive in well-drained, fairly dry soil and a sunny situation.

The pasque flower varies in the colour of its blooms, which normally range from pale to deep purple but sometimes occur in white or red. The form 'Mrs Van der Elst' was 'by far its loveliest development' in Reginald Farrer's opinion, despite 'the barbarous and intolerable name'. It had 'chalices ... of a soft rosy shell-pink, absolutely clean and true, without the slightest taint of mauve or magenta'. Originally raised in 1904, it was always scarce and may have been less vigorous than the more usually grown purple-flowered plant. It was listed in a catalogue as recently as the 1950s, but by then was 'very rare indeed' and it seems subsequently to have vanished.

In 1936, a plant with large flowers 'of a beautiful, satiny lavender colour' was exhibited and won an Award of Merit as *Anemone pulsatilla* 'Budapest Variety' (Plate 69). Its provenance was vague, but four years later Dorothy Gorton wrote that she had first come across it in 1920 on the streets of Budapest, where it was being sold as a cut flower by a peasant woman. She had eventually located some plants growing in rough grass on the golf course outside the city, from which seed was obtained and sent home. However, it remained something of a mystery as well as a rarity. In 1963 it was shown as *P. vulgaris* 'Budapest' and gained a First Class Certificate, although the committee thought 'the name *Pulsatilla vulgaris* var. *grandis* was sufficient'. Since it was first described in 1831, this plant has been variously assigned by botanists to *P. vulgaris*, *P. grandis* and *P. halleri*. It appears to belong to the eastern European group of the *P. vulgaris* complex and is perhaps best separated under the name *P. halleri*, since it is distinguished particularly by the blooms developing well before the leaves.

Distributed in eastern Europe, this magnificent pulsatilla is one of the earliest to flower. It is normally about 5 to 6 inches high, occasionally taller, and covered in silky, golden hairs. It produces upright flowers up to 3 inches across, with broad, rounded petals framing a central boss of yellow stamens. As in the common pasque flower, the colour is variable, from a pale lavender-blue to ice-blue 'like shot-silk taffeta' and occasionally white. The tufted leaves which follow, bringing the final height to about 18 inches, are much dissected and sharply lobed. It is a hardy and vigorous plant and as many as sixty blooms have been recorded on a single specimen. But nearly half a century after its début in Britain, it is still not cultivated as widely as it deserves. Only by careful selection of colour forms raised from seed of *P. halleri* are plants with the ice-blue blooms of 'Budapest' likely to become available again.

Quercus   *Oak*

Steeped in folklore and redolent of history, the oak is perhaps the best known and most loved of all trees. It has been of supreme economic importance to man, chiefly because of the excellence of its timber which is particularly valuable in shipbuilding and house construction. Its bark too was once much used in the leather tanning industry and in one species it still supplies the cork of commerce, while even its acorns had a purpose in the past as the staple diet of pigs.

Among the 450 or more species recognised botanically in this vast genus, the common or pedunculate oak, *Quercus robur*, is in its own right almost unrivalled in majesty and longevity. It has in addition produced numerous variants of horticultural merit. One of the most ornamental is the golden oak 'Concordia' (Plate 70), which originated in the famous Belgian nursery of A.

Quercus alnifolia

van Geert around 1843 and received a First Class Certificate as long ago as 1868. It was introduced to Britain by the celebrated firm Lee of Hammersmith who, apart from their remarkable range of oaks, carried an extensive stock of trees, shrubs, herbaceous and greenhouse plants, vegetables and seeds during their 150 years' tenure of ground that was once a vineyard and is now the site of Olympia.

'Concordia' is less vigorous in constitution than its green-leaved brethren, but it forms a fine, rounded tree in time, about 40 feet high and clothed in spring and summer with foliage of a bright yellow, which gradually turns pale green. Its counterpart in purple is forma *purpurascens*, of which several clones have been described and were regularly offered in the nineteenth century. In the slow-growing 'Atropurpurea' the leaves and young shoots develop a rich purple colouring in spring, changing to brownish-purple as the foliage matures. The deep purple 'Nigra' is similar, but has a slight plum-like bloom to the leaves and keeps its colour for most of the season. Neither, regrettably, seems to be available in the trade, although efforts are being made to propagate these and other variants when authentic examples can be traced. Since they do not come true from seed, this can only be achieved by grafting on to seedlings – an operation of some skill which few nurserymen today are willing to undertake for the low and slow financial returns involved. The same problem besets many oak species as well, which often turn out to be hybrids when raised from seed of cultivated plants. 'Concordia' at least, is now obtainable from one firm and with patience other attractive forms of the native English oak may reappear in specialist catalogues.

The Turkey oak, *Q. cerris*, from southern and central Europe, is one of the hardiest and handsomest of oaks, with its whiskered buds and acorn cups. It is of relatively quick growth and may reach over 100 feet. Useful for maritime conditions and on alkaline soils, it is familiar in various forms which differ widely in leaf size and shape. However, the superb 'Variegata' with leaves banded creamy white at the margins is seldom seen or offered. There is a broad-spreading specimen at Wisley, planted over a century ago, which shows how effective and decorative this variegated Turkey oak can be. It is now being propagated for eventual distribution.

Much more robust are the hybrids of *Q. cerris* with the cork oak, the evergreen *Q. suber*. Grouped as *Q.* × *hispanica*, they are magnificent trees with their thick, fissured bark and glossy, almost evergreen leaves. They are perfectly adapted to chalky soils but equally happy under more acid regimes. The original hybrid, famous as the Lucombe oak ('Lucombeana'), was raised in about 1763 by the nurseryman William Lucombe, founder of the family business in Exeter, who propagated and sold it in great quantity. J. C. Loudon tells how Lucombe, as an old man, felled one of his own oaks for his coffin, but found he had miscalculated and lived on. A few years later he cut down a second tree for the same purpose and this time correctly anticipated his death, at the age of ninety-eight.

The Lucombe oak, up to 100 feet high, the Fulham oak ('Fulhamensis'), a clone of slightly later date from the nursery of Whitley & Osborne in Fulham, and the smaller 'Ambrozyana', from Czechoslovakia, are represented in a number of British gardens but rarely offered in the trade. This is a great pity, for all are long-lived, easily adaptable trees of noble aspect and not too difficult to propagate by grafting on to stocks of *Q. cerris*, which comes readily from seed.

The golden oak of Cyprus, *Q. alnifolia*, is known in the wild only from the Troodos range on that island, where it carpets the mountain slopes 6,000 feet above sea level. An evergreen shrub or small tree, it is similar in general appearance to the familiar holm oak *Q. ilex* and in cultivation may eventually reach a height of twenty to thirty feet. The yellow, felted undersurface of the leaves, which gives rise to its common name, contrasts pleasantly with the dark green upper surface. In the moister conditions of Britain it tends to be yellowish-grey rather than yellow, but in dry climates the colouring is more pronounced. Although slow growing, *Q. alnifolia* is easily suited in a well-drained, sunny site and is hardy in most parts of Britain. However, it is seldom seen and only a handful of specimens of any size are recorded. It should certainly be more widely grown, both for its own merits and to secure it more firmly in cultivation in view of its restricted distribution in nature.

Scanning those two bibles of the tree and shrub enthusiast – Bean's *Trees and Shrubs Hardy in the British Isles* and Hilliers' *Manual* – one can read descriptions of well over a hundred species of oak and their variants in cultivation in botanic and private gardens and arboreta. A search through current catalogues give a much more dismal picture of what is available and the majority of nurseries (with two notable exceptions) list two or three different oaks at the most. 'For some reason the planting of oaks in parks and gardens has fallen into desuetude in recent times', remarks Bean. As with so many genera which have slipped from public favour, it is only by extolling their undoubted worth that an interest will be created in the many striking oak species and clones deserving of cultivation. Demand from gardeners is essential in order to persuade the horticultural trade to acquire, propagate and supply such plants. But nurserymen in turn must advertise their wares, so that gardeners seeking the more unusual are stimulated to buy.

Ranunculus   *Buttercup*

Ranunculus insignis

'Mountain, meadow, and marsh herbs', as William Robinson defined them, the 300 or more species of *Ranunculus* are widely distributed across the globe. The Latin name, used by Pliny in the first century, is a diminutive of *rana*, frog, and suggests their normally moisture-loving disposition. Some, such as the wild water crowfoot *Ranunculus aquatilis*, and the spearworts *R. lingua* and *R. flammula*, are plants of pond and bog. Britain has several native species in addition to these, including the two common buttercups, *R. acris*, whose flowers rubbed on a cow's udder were thought to improve the milk, and *R. bulbosus*; *R. ficaria*, the lesser celandine or pilewort as it was known, from the curative effect of its tubers; and the creeping buttercup *R. repens*, an invasive spreader. All produce double forms, which were loosely termed bachelor's buttons by Gerard. These were appreciated by gardeners of his period and after, but are now inexplicably scarce.

More lamentable is the virtual disappearance of the lovely white bachelor's buttons, *R. aconitifolius*. Introduced from Europe by 1596, it soon became an established favourite of cottage gardens and was still widely available from the nursery trade before 1914. Its double variety, fair maids of France, or of Kent, is supposed to have been brought over by Huguenot refugees at the end of the sixteenth century. It was equally familiar to gardeners of the past. Both today are 'as difficult to find as bachelor's buttons themselves'.

Most species of *Ranunculus* are hardy and easily suited in ordinary, preferably damp soil, and sun or shade. However, the garden ranunculus, *R. asiaticus* (Plate 72), has always demanded and merited exceptional treatment. Ideally a bed should be specially prepared of rich, free-draining soil, reduced to a fine tilth for the small, claw-like roots. These are planted in early spring and lifted again in the autumn. It 'is a flower very generally, but at the same time very unsuccessfully cultivated' observed Thomas Hogg in his *Treatise* on florists' flowers of 1812 – with a trace of relief, one suspects. He was an authority on the carnation, the florist's flower par excellence, whose supremacy was then under threat from *R. asiaticus*. It was oriental in origin like its other rivals, the tulip and the pink, and had been imported from Turkey at the end of the sixteenth century. A hundred years later, after the florists had set to work, the garden ranunculus boasted perhaps more varieties than any other flower. These were broadly divided into two sections, the compact Persian and the slightly coarser Turban. One catalogue in 1792 named nearly 800 forms. It was still at the peak of popularity when Hogg tried to describe the range:

> Here yellow globular blossoms present themselves in all shades, from the pale straw to the golden crocus; red of all tints – pink, rose, and flame colour; purple and crimson of every dye; black, brown, olive, and violet, of every hue. Besides these, there are yellow-spotted flowers, brown-spotted, and white-spotted, red and purple streaked, red and white striped, red and yellow striped, besides mottled and brindled in countless varieties.

Within thirty years the garden ranunculus was in decline, probably because of its cultural requirements. Mackintosh's *Flower Garden* of 1838 could still speak of its 'most innumerable diversities', but by the end of the century the number of different kinds obtainable had dwindled to about a dozen. From the lists of modern nurserymen where *R. asiaticus*, or rather the semi-double selection usually offered, seldom occupies more than a single entry, it is hard to believe that it once so engaged the art of the florist and the imagination of the public.

Some of the most dramatic buttercups come from New Zealand. Sir Joseph Hooker, the celebrated director of Kew and an authority on the New Zealand flora, considered them 'the finest known', but few unfortunately are amenable to cultivation. The magnificent *R. lyallii* 'is always ardently talked of', noted Reginald Farrer. It grows up to 4 feet high from its huge rhizomes and has large, scalloped leaves and 'a wide shower of many-petalled white flowers'. It forms great colonies in high glacial areas of the New Zealand alps, but is almost impossible to grow even in the gardens of its homeland.

More tractable among its relatives is *R. insignis*. This too occurs in the mountains of the interior at altitudes of 4,000 to 5,000 feet and was discovered on the North Island by the Reverend William Colenso, who assisted Hooker in his study of the local flora. It is a variable plant, usually 2 to 3 feet high, with thick, hairy leaves, round or kidney-shaped, and branching stems which bear blooms up to 2 inches in diameter of deep glistening gold. Exactly when *R. insignis* first reached Britain is not recorded, although it was exhibited in 1974 by Messrs Ingwersen of East Grinstead, Sussex, and received a Certificate of Preliminary Commendation. Flowering here in the early summer, it does better in the cool, damp climate of the northwest and Scotland and is not easy to grow in the south.

The genus also contains several excellent rock garden plants, some of them fairly recently introduced. Two of the oldest, however, are *R. amplexicaulis* and *R. parnassifolius*, dating from 1633 and 1769 and both European. In 1957 Mr C. H. Hammer showed a hybrid between the two that had arisen spontaneously in his Essex garden. It was named 'Essex', but was then apparently lost until in 1978 the director of Kew won an Award of Merit for the same plant. It is about 8 inches high and forms a clump of oval, reddish-green leaves at the base. Above these the slender, sparsely hairy stems carry cup-shaped flowers an inch or more across, with rounded overlapping petals of white veined with pink. This delightful dwarf buttercup has inherited the best features of its parents and certainly deserves to be more widely grown.

Rosa *Rose*

The recent history of the rose is an encouraging example of just what can be achieved in the conservation of plants. Largely through the enterprise of one individual, Graham Stuart Thomas, the author and gardens consultant to the National Trust, many of the roses grown by our forebears have been rescued from oblivion since the Second World War. It is now possible to admire them in collections such as those at Mottisfont, Sissinghurst, Castle Howard, Hidcote and Wisley. They can also be purchased from specialist firms and, such is the current vogue for 'old' roses, from many general nurseries as well.

Broadly defined, the old roses embrace those in cultivation up to the end of the nineteenth century, before the advent of the modern hybrid teas and floribundas which so thoroughly supplanted them. They fall into two main sections according to their age. First, there are the truly old ones, the five main ancestral roses. These comprise the French rose *Rosa gallica*, the ancient and principal species; the white rose *R. × alba*; the damask rose *R. damascena*; the

Rosa centifolia 'Muscosa'

musk rose *R. moschata*; and the cabbage rose *R. centifolia*, together with its offspring the moss rose *R. centifolia* 'Muscosa'. From the sixteenth century until about the 1830s, these and their derivatives reigned supreme in European gardens. The eighteenth century saw an enormous proliferation of cultivars, particularly on the Continent. Loddiges of Hackney, who were renowned for their range of trees and shrubs, listed nearly 1,500 different roses in their 1826 catalogue, mostly of French origin. Up to the end of the nineteenth century France continued to be the source of some of the finest roses raised from the original five.

Second, there are the more recent roses of the last century which resulted from the infusion of oriental blood with the existing European stock. The four Chinese roses introduced around 1800 brought with them the novel attribute of continuous flowering. This was a great advance on the single burst of bloom characteristic of *R. gallica* and its relatives – all, that is, except the autumn damask, which had been prized for its ability to flower in the summer and again in the autumn. From the China roses were developed, accidentally at first, new selections including the Bourbons, the Noisettes, the teas and later the hybrid perpetuals. Their arrival marked the first major upheaval in the rose world, although the older roses managed to cling on until at least the middle of the century in the face of new competition. The 1848 edition of William Paul's *The Rose Garden* still contained almost 800 Gallicas, Albas, mosses and their fellows. But by the 1903 edition this figure had shrunk to 87.

No sooner had the really old roses surrendered to the more modern breeds, especially the popular hybrid perpetuals, than these in their turn were ousted by the hybrid teas and floribundas. The old roses of both kinds had their champions, even in eclipse. William Robinson, Canon Ellacombe, Ellen

Willmott and Gertrude Jekyll all defended the historic and the species roses against the brash onslaught of the bedding types. Lord Penzance, himself a noted rose-grower, in 1889 drew attention to the disappearance of the Bourbons, Portlands and Albas. He was reassured some years later by George Paul, one of the celebrated rose-breeding brothers, that the Bourbon roses were being retrieved and that the common moss rose was in demand again. But the losses were still dramatic. Most of the Bourbons were eventually forgotten, as the learned epicure E. A. Bunyard, another campaigner for old roses, observed in 1936. With them went the Noisettes (apart from the original which survives), the bulk of the early tea roses and the later hybrid perpetuals, practically the entire Boursault group and others like it, together with the countless older cultivars produced before 1800, particularly among the Albas. The musk rose itself, *R. moschata*, was feared to be extinct in Britain until it was located by Mr Thomas in E. A. Bowles's garden at Myddelton House, Enfield.

Many other roses have been saved and restored to gardens, sometimes like the musk rose from a single remaining plant. Notable examples are 'Félicité Parmentier', a compact Alba with flat, blush-pink blooms, and 'Desprez à Fleur Jaune', a climbing Noisette with double orange-yellow and buff flowers, which both date from the 1830s. They are a tribute to the outstanding success of the rescue operation on the old roses. As a result gardeners can once more enjoy the major historic roses and a fair sample of the nineteenth-century roses, even though, regrettably, it has been possible to salvage only a tiny proportion from the past.

The genus *Rosa* consists almost exclusively of deciduous bushy or climbing shrubs and is distributed throughout the northern hemisphere, with a preponderance in eastern Asia. Some 3,000 specific names have been assigned over the years, a figure which has now been reduced by general consent to about 250 'good species'. Much of the confusion has arisen because of the natural tendency of roses to vary and hybridise. Thus the white rose, the damask and the cabbage are all ancient hybrids, with *R. gallica* as a common parent. One of the most remarkable spontaneous variants is the common moss rose *R. centifolia* 'Muscosa'. It is a sport or mutant of the cabbage rose and is covered in a soft, mossy growth on the flower stalks and sepals. According to Miss Jekyll, this 'has a special and delicious scent, of a cordial quality which mingles with, and much enhances, the excellent sweetness of the flower'. In every other respect it is a replica of *R. centifolia*, 3 to 5 feet in height, with the same limp leaves and goblet-shaped double blooms, densely packed with petals of rich pink and heavily fragrant.

Apart from a Norman legend attributing the creation of the moss rose to an angel, its origin remains uncertain. However, C. C. Hurst, the pioneering Cambridge geneticist who researched the heredity of the garden rose, helped to clarify the matter in 1922. It seems first to have occurred in Europe some time before 1720, when it was growing at the Leiden botanic garden, and to have reached this country by the 1730s if not before. According to the nurseryman H. Shailer of Battersea, who was involved in its subsequent development, 'it was sent over with some orange trees from the Italian States . . . in or about the year 1735', but then escaped notice for a further twenty years. The original moss rose proceeded to sport a series of variants parallel to those of R. *centifolia* – the white moss in 1788, sold as 'Shailer's White Moss' and from which was propagated a striped moss; 'Moss de Meaux', which appeared in the West Country in 1801 or may perhaps have been introduced from France in 1814; the single red moss appearing in 1807 and again in 1814 and 1852, a fertile form which became an ancestor of the modern moss roses; and the sage-leaf moss, discovered by Shailer in 1813.

'The Victorian age', wrote Bunyard in his book *Old Garden Roses*, 'would have seemed incomplete without the moss rose, so firmly did it entwine the hearts of those amiable days.' Worn in buttonholes and endlessly painted and versified, it outlasted the other old roses into the 1900s. As Miss Jekyll observed, it was still 'so well known that one need say no more' except, prophetically, that it 'should never be lost or forgotten'. Today there is a wide choice of hybrid moss roses, dating from the second half of the nineteenth century. They are derived from the single moss and from the moss form of the autumn damask, which had also produced a mossy sport, in this case repeat flowering. However, apart from the advantage of several flushes of bloom, they do not compare with the quality of R. *centifolia* 'Muscosa' and its early progeny. The first common pink moss and the common white are still available. But the sage-leaf moss, 'a delicate shell-like form, and . . . a beautiful blush', was 'nearly extinct' even when Shailer was writing. The old striped moss was equally transient. Most lamentable is the demise of 'Moss de Meaux', which was mentioned by Miss Jekyll but was already missing by Bunyard's time in the 1930s. 'This curious variety', he explained, 'was found in a garden belonging to a Mr. Perry, of Taunton, in 1801', where it had sprung as a sucker from the miniature cabbage rose, 'Rose de Meaux', which was growing next to a moss. Only about 9 inches high, it had a reddish tinge to the stems and flowers of pale rose opening flat. It became a speciality of the nurserymen Lee & Kennedy of Hammersmith and was illustrated by the artist P. J. Redouté in his magnificent *Les Roses*, published between 1817 and 1824.

It is sad to think that of the four China roses imported around 1800, two should have sunk into obscurity. Cultivated by generations of Chinese, they were hybrids between the wild species R. *chinensis* and R. *gigantea*. All were destined to play a significant role in the future of the garden rose. Following the introduction of 'Slater's Crimson China' and 'Parson's Pink China' in the 1790s, the first tea rose arrived probably in 1809. It had been purchased the previous year from a nursery near Canton by an agent of the East India Company and was sent home to Sir Abraham Hume of Hertfordshire, after whom it was called 'Hume's Blush Tea-scented China'. Such was its novelty that in 1810, at the height of the Napoleonic wars, a special truce was negotiated in the Channel to allow free passage to a ship taking specimens to that great rose lover, the Empress Josephine.

The second tea rose, 'Parks's Yellow China', was acquired from the same nursery in 1824 by John Damper Parks, collector for the Horticultural Society in London. Both were known initially as *R. odorata* because of their strong perfume, which is supposed to resemble the scent of a freshly opened packet of China tea. With their clusters of large-petalled flowers, smooth, bright green leaves and, like the other Chinas, 'perpetual' flowering habit, they were the principal ancestors of the modern hybrid teas. 'Parks's Yellow China' was also a valuable addition to the colour range, until *R. foetida* was used in breeding towards the end of the century.

In the West, the two original tea roses proved tender. 'Hume's Blush Tea-scented China' is now thought to be extinct here, although there is a suggestion that it may be among some old roses recently located by Mr Thomas in Bermuda. However, 'Parks's Yellow China' has resurfaced after a long absence in the catalogue of one British rose grower, having probably been imported from Australia or New Zealand. It is to be hoped that this delightful and historic rose, with its pale yellow, tightly packed flowers, will soon regain its rightful place in European gardens.

Most of the early tea roses descended from them have also vanished. Unfortunately they inherited not only the delicious tea scent but the lack of hardiness. They had their day on the Riviera, where Lord Brougham was celebrated for his collection at Cannes, and in the great conservatories of England. Their languid blooms of soft pink, coppery yellow or creamy white somehow epitomise the faded glamour of the late Victorian and Edwardian age.

R. gigantea itself, one of the progenitors of the China roses, is a species of impressive proportions, as the name implies. It is a rampant climber which has been known to reach a height of 80 feet, and the fragrant white or cream flowers are the largest in the genus, at up to $5\frac{1}{2}$ inches across. It is native to the Chinese province of Yunnan, northeast India and Burma, where it was discovered in 1882 and subsequently collected, apparently having been sighted two miles away through field glasses. It first flowered in the West in 1898, at Lord Brougham's garden in Cannes, eventually growing to nearly 5 foot in diameter at the base of the trunk. It took less kindly to the British climate and at Kew was confined to the Temperate House, although in several parts of southern England it has performed moderately well outside against a wall. It was even recorded as surviving a severe frost in Suffolk earlier this century, but is clearly more suitable for milder districts. As far as can be ascertained, this remarkable species is now represented in Britain by a solitary plant at Mount Stewart, Co. Down, a recent replacement of one which flourished there for many years.

Closely akin to *R. gigantea* is 'Fortune's Double Yellow' (Plate 74), also known as 'Beauty of Glazenwood', which was introduced in 1845. Like the earlier China roses and of similar lineage, it had probably long been in cultivation before Robert Fortune, collecting for the Horticultural Society, first caught sight of it in the garden of a wealthy Mandarin at Ningpo on the southeastern coast of China. Fortune described how 'on entering one of the gardens on a fine morning in May I was struck by a mass of yellow flowers which completely covered a distant part of the wall; the colour was not a common yellow but had something of buff in it which gave the flower a striking and uncommon appearance. I immediately ran up to the place and to my surprise and delight found that I had discovered a most beautiful new yellow climbing Rose.' Scrambling or climbing to a maximum of 20 feet, it bears in midsummer small clusters of perfumed semi-double blooms about 3 to 4 inches across, of yellow flushed coppery red. Sadly, this unusual and charming rose is again rather tender in this country, although 'it is one of the best of roses for cold-house treatment' in Miss Jekyll's words. Always a rarity, it has recently been traced in southern Ireland and is obtainable, just, in the trade.

In contrast to the China roses introduced at the same period, *R. clinophylla* has a very small place in the history of the genus. It is a near ally of the Macartney rose, *R. bracteata*, a parent of the familiar 'Mermaid', but it has produced few hybrids and has itself been neglected. It is a rambler, with dense foliage and soft down on the branches and undersides of the leaves. Its large flowers, of creamy white flushed pink in the centre and faintly scented, emerge on very short stalks from a collar of bracts and are followed by woolly hips. A native of northern India and neighbouring countries, it was collected in Nepal in about 1803 by Francis Buchanan-Hamilton, director of the Calcutta Botanic Garden, and brought to England some time before 1818, whence it found its way to France and the garden of Monsieur Boursault, whose name is perpetuated in the Boursault roses. His plant, flowering in July, was figured in the first volume of Redouté's *Les Roses*, as *R. clinophylla* or 'rosier à feuilles penchées', both names referring to the drooping leaves. John Lindley, the influential botanist and later secretary of the Horticultural Society, declared it 'a highly desirable addition' in the *Botanical Register* of 1823 and, a few years later, J. C. Loudon admired it at Loddiges' nursery in Hackney, where it had climbed to 11 feet against a wall and was blooming profusely. Yet 'the species seems to have dropped out of cultivation', according to W. J. Bean. Unusually for a rose, it is evergreen and also rather tender, which may well be one reason. Miss Jekyll perhaps hinted at another when she recommended it as 'scarcely suitable for a garden, but good for a wild place'.

Another species which has stood outside the mainstream is *R. roxburghii*, though it has been crossed with other roses and was responsible for two fine hybrids, 'Triomphe de la Guillotière' and 'Jardin de la Croix', which seem to have perished. This striking plant with its peeling bark, straight thorns and small, shiny, upstanding leaves, makes a compact bush 5 to 7 feet or more in height and bears fragrant flowers about 2 inches across in June. These are succeeded by big, prickly, green fruits, hence the name burr or chestnut rose. Its vigorous single-flowered form, with wide blooms of light to dark rose, was introduced from Japan before 1880 and from China in 1908 by E. H. Wilson.

The double form of *R. roxburghii* which is so sought after today was the first to reach Europe and flowered at James Colvill's Chelsea nursery in 1824. It is less robust in constitution and has larger, very full flowers of pale pink deepening to crimson in the centre. The *Botanical Register* considered it 'the most elegant of all the roses we are acquainted with'. Long cultivated in China, it was noticed in a collection of Chinese drawings by Lindley, who described it as *R. microphylla*. It was then located in the Calcutta Botanic Garden, whose director, Dr W. Roxburgh, had obtained it from Canton. Some ten years after its arrival it was flourishing at an Essex nursery, but was said to be vulnerable to severe frost. The wealthy Ellen Willmott grew it in her garden at Tresserve in the French Savoy, where it bloomed from May to December, with the flowers often 5 inches in diameter. But as she rightly remarked in her classic account of *The Genus Rosa*, issued from 1910 to 1914, 'it is still comparatively rare in English gardens.'

The resources of the Far East, which is particularly rich in fine roses, were untapped until the coming of the China roses. However, several of the native European species have played a part in the evolution of the garden rose. In Britain, the wild *R. arvensis* was the progenitor of the Ayrshire rose in the 1760s. This was one of the few ramblers available to gardeners at the time and was extensively grown, but it is now presumed lost. From the sweet brier or eglantine, *R. eglanteria*, Lord Penzance developed the race of Penzance briers at the end of the nineteenth century. Even the dog rose *R. canina* has performed a humble but vital service as the stock most frequently used for garden roses and as a parent.

The burnet or Scotch rose *R. pimpinellifolia*, also known as *R. spinosissima*, secured a niche in the Victorian garden after hundreds of cultivars were raised by a Scottish nurseryman in the late eighteenth century. Long lived and easily propagated, a number of these are extant. It was later crossed with hybrid teas to produce some excellent shrub roses. The species is widespread throughout Europe, including Britain, and central Asia and is variable in the wild. Var. *myriacantha* is very similar in height, about 2 to 3 feet, and in its flowers, of white, cream or pale pink. But it is totally distinctive in having numerous glands on the leaves, flower stalks and sepals, and in the long, slender spines on the stems. Redouté portrayed it as the 'rosier à mille épines'. It is an inhabitant of Europe from Spain and the south of France to Armenia, but as Miss Willmott correctly concluded again it is 'rare in cultivation in England'.

An outstanding form of *R. pimpinellifolia* and in Bean's view 'one of the most lovely of single roses' is 'Hispida'. Its history is obscure, although it is probably a native of Siberia and was in cultivation in Britain by 1781. A sturdy shrub up to 6 feet high, its stems are thickly clad in brown bristles and the large flowers, turning from yellow to creamy white, appear at the end of May. In this century it was a great favourite of the plantsman and writer A. T. Johnson, one of the very few people to have grown it.

In addition to its cultivated hybrids, *R. pimpinellifolia* has often crossed spontaneously with other species. A natural hybrid with the dog rose was discovered in about 1795 a few miles from Belfast by John Templeton, a prominent Irish gardener. He propagated it from cuttings and sent plants to two London nurserymen. A few years later the Dublin Society awarded him a prize of five guineas for finding a new Irish plant and the rose was presented to the Irish National Botanic Gardens, Glasnevin, where it prospered for many years. It was described and illustrated with a wood engraving by Templeton and given the appropriate name of *R. × hibernica*. A strong-growing shrub about 10 feet high or more, it is scattered with curved prickles and carries small clusters of clear pink blooms and subsequently round red hips. It has a very long flowering season and was once reported as lasting in bloom from the end of May to the beginning of November.

R. × hibernica has since been found in other parts of the British Isles, but it is a rarity both in the wild and in gardens. By the early twentieth century its original site near Belfast was threatened by the building of a new road and railway. The sole surviving bush was saved from there in the 1960s by the Queen's University of Belfast and is now being propagated for distribution.

There is a vast literature on roses which the reader may easily consult and this is hardly the place to give advice on their culture. There are plants to suit a wide range of situations and they are generally undemanding in their requirements. Most roses are readily increased by budding scions on to stocks of *R. canina* or *R. laxa* selections during the summer. Many cultivars may also be propagated by hardwood cuttings taken in October. The second method is straightforward and often preferable since no suckering occurs from plants grown on their own roots. On the other hand some roses are invasive when grown in this way and can be as great a nuisance in the garden as a suckering rootstock.

Scabiosa *Scabious*

The blue perennial scabious *Scabiosa columbaria*, is a native of Britain and a common sight on chalk downs and pastures. In the Middle Ages and before, it was valued as a cure for scabies or the itch and was even cultivated for that purpose, whence the name *Scabiosa*. The genus contains perhaps 100 species, inhabitants of Europe, Africa and Asia, although only a minority have found their way into gardens. Of the annuals the most familiar is probably

Scabiosa caucasica 'Constancy'

S. atropurpurea, known as the sweet scabious or mourning widow. It comes from southern Europe and its fragrant, deep crimson flowers are often used for funeral wreaths in Mediterranean countries.

Some other species certainly deserve wider recognition. The perennial *S. fischeri*, for instance, was one of the plants championed by Thomas Hay, who supervised the royal parks in London. It was described in 1839 and grown at the Luxembourg botanic garden, but did not reach Britain until a century later after seeds had been collected in Manchuria, winning an Award of Merit in 1935. It is like a slightly smaller version of *S. caucasica*, if tidier in habit and more reliable, and has blooms of dense violet-blue.

With its round pincushions carried on stems about 2 feet high, *S. caucasica* and its cultivars are well known as garden plants and commercial cut flowers. The species, with blooms of light blue, was introduced from the Caucasus in 1803 and made its début at George Loddiges's nursery in Hackney. Despite its obvious attributes and its very long flowering season, from early summer well into the autumn, it was grown unaltered for over a hundred years before anyone attempted to improve it. Today the species itself has been largely superseded by cultivars offering a range of shades from white to pale lilac to rich purple, sometimes with semi-double flowers. Among those available are 'Moreheim Blue', 'Bressingham White', 'Moonstone' and, the most popular, 'Clive Greaves' and 'Miss Willmott' dating from the 1930s. All are easily grown in ordinary, well-drained, preferably limy soil and a sunny position. They tend to be short-lived especially in acid conditions, but may be propagated by division in spring.

These cultivars in their turn have supplanted the many earlier garden forms such as 'Penhill Blue' and its kin (Plate 71). J. C. House of Bristol was the pioneering nurseryman who first exploited the potential of *S. caucasica*. 'Diamond' received an Award of Merit in 1920, when it was praised for 'the great depth of the charming lavender-blue colour of the flowers, which measure about $3\frac{1}{4}$ inches across'. 'Constancy' was a powder blue and 'Mrs Isaac House' was considered one of the finest whites. 'Isaac House' was the 'darkest violet purple scabious ever raised, but a weakly plant', with a profusion of flowers on tall stems.

Messrs House exhibited their novelties at the Shrewsbury show in 1920. One visitor thought the display 'most exquisite' and worthy of far more attention than it had received. But the next year the House stand at the RHS show drew only a brief comment from *The Garden*, alone of the gardening press. The new cultivars were not cheap, at one guinea each, and after their ineffectual launch on the scene they remained scarce. Although they were submitted to the Wisley trials in 1938, very few nurseries listed them in the inter-war period. One of those that did, a Gloucestershire firm, grew considerable stocks in the 1930s. However, the plants were ploughed in during the war when the land was taken over by a farmer.

Lack of publicity, expense and probably their frail constitution all seem to have contributed to the failure of these beautiful cultivars to make the horticultural grade. Always rare in the trade and in gardens, they have now apparently been lost for ever. The unfortunate Mr House had merely pointed the way for others to follow more profitably.

Stuartia

Stuartia pteropetiolata

There are few small trees to match the stuartias in decorative value, with their beautiful bloom in high summer, their attractively tinted leaves in autumn and, in the case of several species, their ornamental bark in winter. They are native to the southeastern United States, Japan, Korea and China and belong to the same section of the tea family as *Camellia*. But, unlike their much more familiar relatives, they have been sadly neglected by gardeners and have never achieved the popularity they deserve.

'For this elegant plant I am obliged to my good friend, Mr. Clayton, who sent it to me from Virginia, and three months after its arrival it blossomed in my garden at Fulham in May, 1742.' The owner of the garden was Mark Catesby, the Suffolk-born naturalist and plant collector, and he was referring to *Stuartia malacodendron*, the species on which Linnaeus was to base his new genus. Within a year or two it was also growing at Kenwood near London, then the residence of John Stuart, earl of Bute, prime minister in 1762–3 and a noted amateur botanist, who was instrumental in establishing the botanic garden at Kew. An illustration of the plant was dedicated to the earl but with his name wrongly spelt and, as a result of this misunderstanding, Linnaeus published the generic name as *Stewartia* in 1746, which was subsequently corrected to *Stuartia*.

S. malacodendron is a small deciduous tree or large shrub of some 12 to 15 feet. Its handsome white flowers with fringed margins, gently cupped and 3 inches across, are set off by the central boss of purple-filamented, blue-anthered stamens. They are displayed along the slightly arching branchlets during July and August, at a time when most shrubs have finished flowering. As with the other cultivated species, it prefers a moist acid or neutral soil rich in humus and, although perfectly hardy, is best grown in a warm, sunny position in open woodland. Partly perhaps because of its relatively slow growth and partly because it often finds the British summers too cool to bloom freely, it has never been common in gardens. Less than a century after its introduction only a few specimens were known and 'it is now one of the rarest of American shrubs' according to W. J. Bean.

The other American species, *S. ovata*, is equally rare in gardens but equally lovely. A small tree of about 15 feet, which occurs wild in the mountainous areas of the southeastern USA, its flowers in July and August are 'almost translucent in their purity', in William Robinson's words. Creamy-white, occasionally flushed red, and finely scalloped at the edges, they are 3 to 4 inches in diameter. The highly desirable var. *grandiflora*, with larger blooms and purple instead of whitish stamens, seems to be even scarcer in gardens than the species itself. Both are worth every effort to obtain and grow.

The species from eastern Asia are just as beautiful and somewhat easier to grow. The superb *S. pseudocamellia* (Plate 73) from Japan won a First Class Certificate in 1888 when exhibited by Messrs Veitch of Chelsea soon after its arrival. It is now secured in several large gardens and is sometimes available from the nursery trade in limited numbers. Usually a small tree 25 to 30 feet high, it may eventually reach 50 feet or more. The creamy-white, cup-shaped flowers, a little smaller than those of its American cousins, are borne in abundance and its merits are enhanced by the yellow and red autumn foliage and flaking bark. Var. *koreana* is distinguished by having rather flatter blooms and broader leaves. It was introduced to Britain in 1931 and in Bean's opinion is 'perhaps the best of the genus for small gardens'.

Four related species, all with white flowers and about 35 feet high, are *S. monadelpha* and *S. serrata* from Japan and *S. sinensis* and *S. rostrata* from China. Three were introduced at the beginning of this century but are seldom seen outside collections. The small-flowered *S. monadelpha* is a pleasant, medium-sized tree with slightly peeling, smooth, reddish-brown bark. Its near ally *S. serrata* is superior for garden purposes with its larger, creamy-white blooms stained red on the outside, which are plentifully produced throughout June and July. The bark of *S. sinensis*, introduced by E. H. Wilson from Hupeh in 1901, is particularly striking. In summer it is as 'smooth as alabaster and the colour of weathered sandstone', as Bean expressed it, turning purple in autumn and then brown and peeling in irregular flakes to reveal the fresh bark beneath.

Previously confused with *S. sinensis*, *S. rostrata* differs most obviously in its greyish-brown, shallowly fissured bark. Although introduced to the USA in 1936, it was only named in 1974 and until recently was believed not to be grown in Britain. A few examples have now been located but it has remained extremely elusive and the rarest of the stuartias in cultivation.

A number of evergreen species from China which were formerly included in the genus *Hartia* have been transferred to *Stuartia*. However, only one, *S. pteropetiolata* from Yunnan, is cultivated and then very infrequently as a glasshouse plant or in sheltered gardens in the mild southwestern counties of England. It had been discovered by Dr Augustine Henry and was later collected by George Forrest, who observed that the Chinese used the leaves for making tea. A graceful shrub or tree, it has dark, glossy green, toothed leaves on red-winged stalks, carried on spreading, semi-pendent branches, and is bedecked in June with neat, white, salver-shaped flowers. In Cornwall it has been recorded as reaching heights of over 50 feet.

Stuartias do not relish dry or chalky conditions, but in humus-rich, moist soils they present few problems. Propagation is also fairly easy, either from seed, which is amply produced in some species, or from semi-ripe cuttings of the current year's growth. There can be no doubt about their virtues and it is hard to understand why they have never caught on with the gardening public. As Robinson wrote in *The English Flower Garden*, 'though these beautiful shrubs flower at a time when the shrub-garden is past its best, they are seldom planted.' Unfortunately, his comment is as true today as a hundred years ago. The stuartias have yet to earn the recognition from gardeners that is their due.

Tecophilaea *Chilean crocus*

Tecophilaea cyanocrocus

'No, no. Let salesmen say what they will, this glorious Gentian-blue Crocus from Chili is quite impossible of general cultivation in England.' Undeterred by Reginald Farrer, the nursery catalogues have listed *Tecophilaea cyanocrocus* (Plate 79) quite regularly since its introduction over a hundred years ago and it is still available, at a price, from a few firms such as Messrs Van Tubergen of Holland. However, it has remained a rarity both in and out of cultivation.

The genus was named in the early nineteenth century by the Italian physician C. G. Bertero, who practised in Chile, and commemorates Tecofila, a botanical artist and daughter of his friend Luigi Colla of Turin. It is native to Chile and consists of two species with crocus-like corms and flowers. The other species, *T. violiflora*, has purplish flowers and is inferior from a garden standpoint, although much more widely distributed in its natural habitat. The exquisite *T. cyanocrocus* itself is (or perhaps was) found very locally around Santiago in the Andes, at altitudes of about 10,000 feet. It occurs in damp volcanic soil, which is covered with snow in winter and is dry and parched in summer. After a burst of rapid growth, it flowers from October to November – late spring in the southern hemisphere. It is tempting fodder for cattle, which adds to its scarcity, and it is difficult to detect when not in bloom. Largely as a result of over-collection by humans, it may already be extinct in the wild.

The Chilean crocus, as it was soon to be known, was discovered in 1862 and collected a few years later by the English zoologist Dr Edwyn Reed. The first imported plants flowered at Messrs Haage & Schmidt of Erfurt, Germany, in 1872. The new arrival was much publicised and greatly admired, but could seldom be persuaded to bloom. Gardeners across the Channel apparently met with more success. It was reported from near Paris that *T. cyanocrocus* had withstood the extremely severe winter of 1879–80 outside, buried under the snow, and had flowered freely the next March. In 1892, it won a First Class Certificate in Britain and was later grown successfully at Bodnant in north Wales and on the east coast of Ireland. It can be seen today at the Cambridge Botanic Garden where it is a feature of the alpine house in spring. Its large, bell-shaped blooms, with gracefully curving petals opening wide, in light or deep or violet blue, are produced on short stems amid a few slender sheathing leaves about 4 inches in length. The finest variety is *leichtlinii*, named after the German nurseryman Max Leichtlin of Baden-Baden, who played some part in its introduction and that of many other plants at the time. It is sky blue with a conspicuous white centre and sweetly scented. Patrick Synge, the author, botanist and gardener, knew 'of no other flower outside the gentians with this colour'. Another variant, *violacea*, is also grown, but is less striking in colour.

Writing in *The Garden* of 1881, Leichtlin forecast 'a first-rate position for this desirable bulb from "the Valley of Paradise"'. Unhappily, few have solved the problem of how best to grow it. In cultivation *T. cyanocrocus* lacks two of the key factors that nature supplies – a long period of dry heat to ripen the corms and an equally long period of dormancy before a brief growing season. Cold storage to retard growth has been suggested as one method of treatment. It is usually recommended for the cool greenhouse, where the corms should be planted in the autumn, about 3 inches deep, in pots containing a compost of rich, sandy loam. Water is withheld until the leaves appear and then given frequently. After flowering in early spring, the foliage dies down and the plants should be allowed to dry out for the summer. *T. cyanocrocus* may be propagated with relative ease, either by detaching the cormlets from the main corm and potting them separately in the autumn, or by sowing seed at the same time of year.

Vulnerable in the wild or possibly already lost and only precariously in cultivation because of its capriciousness, the Chilean crocus is an obvious candidate for horticultural conservation. The gardener with the determination to grow it will be doubly rewarded – by the knowledge that he is contributing to its survival and by its natural beauty.

Tulipa *Tulip*

Few plants can match the extravagant and unpredictable history of the tulip. It was a curiously late arrival to the West in the mid-sixteenth century, but had swept the Continent within decades and attracted an almost fanatical following, inciting men to crime and causing them to lose fortunes. From previous obscurity it emerged in a myriad of garden forms and simultaneously

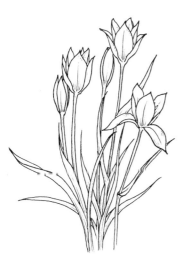

Tulipa sprengeri

in the shape of several native species which no one seems to have noticed before. Further 'species' mysteriously appeared in Europe after some two hundred years, to the consternation of botanists. The modern garden tulip was launched at the end of the nineteenth century, but again it came from undisclosed origins. Only then, from about the 1870s, were the true dimensions of the genus and its home belatedly revealed by the exploration of central Asia and the discovery of new species.

Although the tulip was mentioned in Persian and Russian literature of the twelfth century and had long been grown in Turkish gardens, it was apparently unheard of in Europe before 1554. That year, the imperial ambassador Augerius de Busbequius, on his way to the sultan's court, saw flowers 'which the Turks call "tulipam"'. In fact they used the Persian name *lalé* and the word *Tulipa* arose out of a misunderstanding, when his hosts compared the bloom to a turban or *tuliband* in their language. Through Busbequius bulbs and seeds reached Vienna and were subsequently acquired by the Flemish botanist Clusius. Tulips were reported shortly afterwards from two other cities and in 1570 from Antwerp. A merchant there had been sent some bulbs in a consignment of cloth from Constantinople and, mistaking them for a kind of onion, he ate a few of them, but luckily not all. From this date the tulip advanced rapidly in the West, entering England in about 1578, probably via Clusius. He was also responsible for its establishment in Holland. He took the priceless bulbs with him to Leiden in 1593, on his appointment as professor of botany, and these were soon stolen and widely distributed.

The new plants were known misleadingly as *T. gesneriana*, after the immensely learned Swiss naturalist Conrad von Gesner, who illustrated one of the first introductions, at Augsburg in 1561. However, the Turkish tulips were the product of lengthy cultivation, a garden race of uncertain ancestry and astonishing diversity. Apart from the parrot tulips, all the main groups of the future could be distinguished even at this period. 'Broken' tulips, variously streaked with colour on a white or yellow background, were already much sought after. The vogue for tulips spread quickly through western Europe and culminated in the famous Dutch tulip mania of 1634–7, when bulbs exchanged hands at ridiculous prices amid a mounting fever of speculation until inevitably the market collapsed. In Turkey, where the popularity of the tulip was undiminished and its varieties numbered over a thousand, a similar rage was experienced a century later.

In England the tulip fashion proceeded more sedately, although by 1629 according to Parkinson, 'there is no Lady or Gentlewoman of any worth, that is not caught with this delight.' Unable 'to tell you of all the sorts of Tulipas', he refers to more than a hundred, a figure which had risen to nearly two hundred in John Rea's *Flora, Ceres and Pomona* of 1665. Rea extolled their attractions in verse and singled out one, striped in pale purple, deep scarlet and white, as being so exquisite 'that all the others are disgraced'. Its owner was his friend Sir Thomas Hanmer, a royalist, who had managed to deliver a bulb of this prize plant to his fellow keen gardener John Lambert, the parliamentarian general (dubbed by his enemies 'Knight of ye Golden Tulip') – a pleasant instance of horticultural harmony across the lines of civil war.

> Then comes the tulip-race, where beauty plays
> Her idle freaks; from family diffused
> To family, as flies the father-dust,
> The varied colours run; and while they break
> On the charmed eye, the exulting florist marks
> With secret pride the wonders of his hand.

By the time the poet James Thomson penned these lines in *The Seasons* of 1746, the tulip had moved into the sphere of the florists. They concentrated their skills on inducing 'broken' forms from plain tulips called 'breeders', which were grown exclusively for the purpose, and offered weird recipes for achieving the parti-coloured effect, since it was not then understood to result from a virus. Like other florists' flowers the tulip gathered its own mystique and terminology. Its desirable properties were first defined by Philip Miller in 1732, then reiterated by James Maddock of Walworth, author of *The Florists' Directory* and nurseryman, whose catalogue of 1796 contained 665 kinds of tulip, and finally laid down in the 1830s by George Glenny, the 'flower dictator'. The ideal was a bloom with all six petals symmetrically marked and 'perfectly uniform', expanding to a full bowl shape without 'exhibiting any vacancy between'. The broken forms were assigned to three main colour categories, rose, bybloemen and bizarre, and were also divided into feathered, with fine lines round the border of the petals, and flamed, with an additional blaze down the centre.

These choice tulips were extremely expensive. As the florist Thomas Hogg of Paddington Green noted in 1823, 'a moderate collection ... could not be purchased for a sum much less than one thousand pounds'. Later he maintained that the high prices were 'so deterring and repulsive of the fancy, that persons with a taste and fondness for this flower are afraid to indulge and enter into it'. Initially the tulip was beyond the means of the artisan florists who adopted so many other flowers. But to them it owed its last great surge of popularity in the middle of the nineteenth century. The founding of the Wakefield and North of England Tulip Society in 1836 and of the Royal National Tulip Society in 1849 signalled this revival, which was expressed in tulip shows up and down the country and a 'tulip war' between northern and southern fanciers over the standards required for their exhibits. However, the end was swift, as James Douglas recalled in his book *Hardy Florists' Flowers* in 1880. Up to 1854 the nurseryman Groom, of Clapham Rise in London, had advertised some of his named varieties at 100 guineas each. 'The following year the whole of Mr Groom's roots were sold by auction as they stood in rows, at very low prices, and from this time the tulip declined in the public favour at a rapid rate.'

The English florists' tulip never recovered, for the scene was radically transformed by the first of the new garden breeds to emanate from Holland in 1889. The Darwin tulips were pioneered by the Haarlem firm E. H. Krelage, from Flemish stock but otherwise undivulged origins. With their formal blooms on tall, sturdy stems, they soon became an obligatory feature of public flower schemes. One of them was chosen for planting in Hyde Park to match the uniform of the guards. The Darwins in turn contributed to races such as the Mendel tulips, Rembrandts and Darwin hybrids, which are equally common in gardens today.

The flamed and feathered tulips of the past were already in retreat and now sank into oblivion. They were dropped by all the bulb merchants except for the imaginative Barr & Sons of Covent Garden and were kept up only by a 'noble little band' to which E. A. Bowles belonged. The new tulips were more to the public taste and also exposed the defects of the old – their more exacting cultural needs, their lack of vigour and of resilience to the weather and, most important perhaps, the absence of any guarantee that their bulbs would produce the expected striped flower. According to Sir Daniel Hall, the foremost authority on the genus and also a distinguished agriculturalist, just under thirty forms of the English florists' tulip were still available by 1929. Among them were the historic 'Talisman', 'Samuel Barlow' and, Bowles's favourite 'Sir Joseph Paxton'. The last two have survived, in the *Classified List* of 1981, with a mere handful of companions. Casualties from the prolific ranks of the old tulips were unavoidable over the years, but not their wholesale abandonment. Many proved remarkably enduring, as their few relics demonstrate. They are grown today on a tiny scale and no longer offered in the trade, which makes it the more essential to retain them as representatives of a vanished class. Bowles's belief that 'the love for the English tulip will some day revive' has not yet been realised, but perhaps the setting up of the collection at Chatsworth in Derbyshire will be a step in the right direction.

'It is much the rage to obtain new plants and neglect old ones' wrote Glenny in 1848 – a sentiment which applies not only to the tulip at various points in its career but to many other flowers. In the late nineteenth century a large number of tulips were rescued, often from old gardens, by two nurserymen more usually associated with daffodils, Peter Barr and W. B. Hartland of Cork. These cottage tulips, as they are called, had been discarded by the florists for some deficiency in shape or colour or as worthless 'breeders' and they came in a mixed assortment of forms with flared, pointed or rounded petals. Individual naming caused great confusion when plants were rediscovered and re-christened and, as the bulb enthusiast and author the Reverend Joseph Jacob put it, 'the aliases that some flowers have to support would do credit to a hardened criminal.'

The cottage tulips were publicised by Hartland with an exhibition in 1896 and in a book which he wrote about them. They received a warm welcome and Jacob predicted in 1912 that they would be the tulips of the twentieth century, together with the Darwins. But today they have been virtually ousted by the modern breeds, apart from a few entrenched stalwarts. Among these are the venerable 'Zomerschoon', rose flaked with white, which has been traced back to 1620; the well-known red and yellow 'Keizerskroon', from the eighteenth century or earlier; and the golden yellow 'Mrs Moon', commemorating the wife of the illustrator H. G. Moon, an associate of William Robinson. A notable gem was the fragrant primrose yellow 'Ellen Willmott' from 1900, but this and many of its fellows now seem impossible to locate. Sadly, the eclipse of the cottage tulip, along with the demise of the florists' tulip, means the weakening of a link with the original garden race from Turkey.

The Turkish tulips had persisted, however, in another surprising guise which came to light in the early nineteenth century. The first of nearly thirty Continental 'species' was discovered near Florence in 1822, and the rest surfaced at regular intervals over the next seventy years, mainly in northern Italy, Savoy and eastern France. These were duly named as species, though not without endless botanical debate. They were actually garden refugees descended from the Turkish introductions and, like them, are members of the Gesnerian section of the genus. The so-called *T. didieri*, found in 1846 at St Jean-de-Maurienne in the present French Savoy, bears a solitary, bell-shaped flower of pointed segments, scarlet with a small, dark blotch faintly edged in pale yellow, on a stem up to 12 inches high. It is typical of the neo-tulips and, according to Hall in his classic study of 1940, the commonest. But it is now labelled rare in catalogues if featured at all. The same applies to *T. mauritiana*, also from St Jean, which won an Award of Merit in 1901. Perhaps the last of these extraordinary remnants, *T. grengiolensis*, usually having a pale yellow bloom with a red margin, appeared in Switzerland in 1946. It too is only occasionally offered and the neo-tulips as such are very infrequently seen today.

Strangely enough, it was not until the advent of the tulip from Turkey that Europeans recognised the existence of wild species, although not all were truly indigenous or entitled to specific rank. Parkinson describes among others 'the red Bolonia Tulipa', *T. oculus-solis*, probably a form from Asia Minor which had become naturalised in northern Italy; and 'this rare Tulipa, wherewith we have been but lately acquainted', *T. clusiana*, which occurs wild in the south of France but is also of eastern origin, as its old name of Persian tulip implies. The European tulips were often garden strays and some had a long record of cultivation. But all continued in relative obscurity, overshadowed by the Turkish tulips.

One of the first to be identified in 1563 was *T. sylvestris*, which is thought to have been introduced to Britain by the Romans if it was not already native. It is distributed in the southern USSR, northwest Iran, North Africa and southern Europe and is naturalised further north and west as far as Britain. It was known as the yellow tulip of Bologna, 'near which city it is still abundant' in Hall's words, and is 'essentially a weed of vineyards'. Its scented, clear yellow flowers, with petals reddening and curved at the pointed tips, are carried generally in pairs on stems up to 12 inches high in April and May. Their greenish exterior, larger size and unhappily their greater reluctance to materialise in the British climate are the chief characteristics distinguishing it from the closely allied *T. australis* (which is sometimes treated as a subspecies).

A form of *T. sylvestris* which Hall recommended as 'preferable for gardens' was encountered at Tabriz in northwest Iran by B. Gilliat-Smith. In a letter of 1928 he reported that it 'is sold in ungainly bunches in the streets . . . and is wild in these orchards'. More upright in habit and notably in the slender leaves, its blooms are of lemon yellow. Like other variants of *T. sylvestris*, it is easily grown in a warm, sunny position and well-drained soil and spreads freely by means of stolons. To encourage bloom Hall advised restricting the bulbs with an edging of slates. The Tabriz form was marketed in the past by Messrs Van Tubergen, but is seldom available now. It is certainly worth seeking out for the brilliance of its flowers and their delicious perfume when they open in the sun.

Indisputably native to Europe, more particularly to the island of Crete, *T. saxatilis* (Plate 75) has always been a horticultural rarity. Despite its early recognition and Parkinson's full account of the 'Tulipa of Candie', it did not gain a firm hold in cultivation until the 1870s after stock was renewed by the great gardener and explorer, H. J. Elwes. It achieved an AM in 1896. 'One of the most beautiful tulips' in Hall's opinion, its long, flat, broad leaves emerge in December, followed in April and May by cup-shaped blooms of pale purplish-pink with a sharply defined yellow patch at the base and deep purple or brown anthers, on stems 10 to 12 inches tall. Parkinson remarked that he had 'not yet heard that it hath very often flowered in our Country'. It too is reticent about blooming and instead multiplies with abandon from the long, horizontal stolons. However, given conditions similar to those for *T. sylvestris* and the same confinement of the bulbs, it is capable of a fine display in Britain – a small effort for the reward of its exquisite and unusual flowers.

While the species were largely ignored in favour of the garden tulips, knowledge of the genus as a whole barely advanced, apart from the misleading detour into neo-tulips which occupied nineteenth-century botanists. A lingering notion of the tulip as a Turkish flower was only undermined with the Russian penetration of central Asia in the 1870s, when the real extent and focus of the genus began to be appreciated. Some of the most magnificent new species were described by Edward Regel, director of the Imperial Botanic Gardens at St Petersburg, among them *T. greigii* and *T. kaufmanniana* which were destined for such an important role in the modern evolution of the tulip. A number of them had been supplied by his son Albert, who was stationed as a physician at Turkestan in southern Russia and collected many other plants in the region. These riches were brought to the public by the Dutch bulb merchants Messrs C. G. Van Tubergen, founded in Haarlem in the 1850s, and helped to make them internationally famous. They also employed their own collectors in the early twentieth century and through their enterprise many more new species were added, including the influential *T. fosteriana* with its huge flowers of vivid scarlet, first sent in a consignment from Samarkand by a hotel proprietor in 1904.

These introductions changed the tulip world as dramatically as the new garden breeds being raised in Holland at the time, with which they also mingled. The garden variants and hybrids derived from *T. kaufmanniana*, *T. greigii* and *T. fosteriana* constitute three major sections in the current classification of tulips, and species such as *T. eichleri*, *T. praestans*, *T. hoogiana* and *T. linifolia* are widely grown in their own right. Despite initial doubts, the species often proved quite amenable to cultivation and have the advantage over garden forms in apparently being resistant to virus disease. However, several of Regel's discoveries from middle Asia have remained unaccountably scarce. For instance, *T. lanata* was described in 1884 and collected for Van Tubergen in Bukhara and later in northwest Persia. It was also found planted on the roofs of mosques in Kashmir, having probably been imported by the Moghuls in the sixteenth century. Up to 20 inches high, its large open cup-like flower is matt scarlet with a deep olive blotch broadly edged in yellow. 'One of the very finest and most brilliant tulips' as Hall commented, it received an A M in 1935. It is hardy, easily grown and readily propagated from the stolons.

The elusiveness of *T. ingens* is more understandable, since it must be 'persevered with in a warm soil and with some overhead shelter'. It was collected in the early twentieth century by Graeber, another Van Tubergen contact living in Tashkent. It sports a loosely bell-shaped bloom of bright, glossy scarlet, buff on the reverse and with a long black stain, on a stem up to 10 inches tall but usually shorter. Although sometimes listed by specialist nurseries, it 'has mostly disappeared from English gardens' as Hall observed.

By the time Hall published his monograph on the genus in 1940, it was clear that its focal point lay in central Asia. This has been substantiated by the fact that over 60 per cent of species have since been located in the Tien Shan and Pamir-Alai region. Next in importance, with just a few outliers further west in Europe and North Africa, is the area covering the Caucasus, Iran and Asia Minor. Van Tubergen were active here as well and one of their agents in northern Turkey, an Armenian schoolmaster, furnished them with local irises, snowdrops and tulips. These included *T. sprengeri*, described in 1894. It is a distinctive species both botanically and because of its very late flowering in May. To Bowles, it was 'always rather sad to see the first one open, for it means the close of the Tulip season'. It is about 10 to 12 inches high, with erect, shiny green leaves and a starry flower composed of well-spaced narrow segments, pointed and curling at the edges, intense tomato-red on the inner surfaces and buff-tinted on the back of the outer segments. Long-lived, free-flowering, adaptable, tolerant of shade, increasing rapidly from self-sown seed and blooming in three to four years, it is 'an excellent garden tulip', in Hall's view. It won an A M in 1948. *T. sprengeri* is offered fairly regularly in commerce, but for some reason remains very expensive and is unfamiliar to most gardeners. It deserves to be much more extensively grown, not only for its own charms, but to ensure its place in cultivation since it has not been sighted recently in the wild.

Although better established in gardens, several other species have not been located for some time in their natural habitats. Among them are the easily-grown dwarf *T. aucheriana*, with pinkish blooms, and the more temperamental *T. urumiensis*, a diminutive relative of *T. australis*, both from Iran. *T. montana* was introduced from the same country in 1826, but retained merely a foothold in cultivation until its re-collection under the misnomer *T. wilsoniana* at the beginning of this century and on subsequent occasions. This superb tulip has a flat, circular flower with pointed tips to the spoon-shaped petals, of intense scarlet with a small black blotch at the base. It is quite readily obtainable in the trade, but its numbers are said to be dwindling in the wild because of soil erosion and grazing cattle.

The resources of the genus *Tulipa* are doubtless still untapped. There may be some species awaiting discovery and there are certainly others which are known but not yet secured in cultivation. Hall had to append to his book a long list of 'species not seen in a living state'. One of these was the lovely *T. willmottiae*, which has a large lemon-yellow flower with a blue-black centre. It was named in honour of Ellen Willmott, the celebrated gardener of Warley Place in Essex, who was a devotee of tulips as well as of roses. It had been collected in 1899 in Turkish Armenia by A. Kronenburg, travelling for Van

Tubergen, and sent to them in large quantities together with *T. eichleri* and many unusual bulbs. It would be a most desirable addition to our gardens if only it could be reintroduced.

Vinca *Periwinkle*

Vinca major 'Multiplex'

The long serpentine shoots of the periwinkle inspired the word *Vinca*, from the Latin *vincula*, band, or *Pervinca* in Pliny's version, which in turn gave rise to the English common name. These supple growths and the slightly astringent flavour of the foliage fostered a belief that the plant possessed spiritual and physical binding powers. As reported by the herbalist Nicholas Culpeper, 'Venus owns this herb and saith that the leaves eaten by man and wife together cause love between them.' Other authorities suggested chewing the leaves to staunch nosebleeds and cure toothache, or tying the stems round the calf of the leg to relieve cramp. Also known as band plant, cut finger and joy of the ground, the periwinkle had more sinister connotations, which are reflected in such colloquial names as the French *violette des sorciers*. It was used to garland criminals on their way to execution and in Italy, where it was called *fiore di morte*, to adorn dead infants.

The genus consists of six or seven evergreen or deciduous subshrubs and herbaceous perennials, distributed from southern and central Europe and North Africa across to southwestern and central Asia. Most inhabit shady woodland, wandering freely through the surrounding vegetation and forming dense mats of groundcover. The familiar greater and lesser periwinkles, *V. major* and *V. minor*, are often found wild in Britain but have almost certainly strayed from cultivation and become naturalised. Cultivated for nearly two thousand years, both species now occur throughout much of

Europe. With its characteristic large, purple-blue flowers, *V. major* does not vary greatly, although several forms with variegated foliage are common, together with white-flowered clones and the narrow-petalled, deep violet 'Oxyloba'. However, the double blue 'Multiplex' (Plate 76), dating from before 1831, is rarely if ever seen now.

The smaller-flowered and smaller-leafed *V. minor* is much more variable. In 1623 Caspar Bauhin, one of the earliest classifiers of plants, noted blue, white, reddish and purplish forms, both single and double. Parkinson, on the other hand, mentions only pale blue and white singles and a dark red purple in both single and double-flowered forms. Almost all the older colour variants, single and double, and the clones with variegated foliage have been located and propagated in recent years – with two unfortunate exceptions. The double white 'Plena Alba', described by the botanist Richard Weston in 1770, cannot currently be traced; and 'Rosea Plena', a double violet-rose from before 1889, appears to have been lost, although it was recorded as lately as 1949 in Holland. However, some are sceptical about whether the double white and double pink forms of the lesser periwinkle ever existed at all.

'The supremely beautiful Periwinkle of the family, worthy of the choicest garden, is the too seldom seen *V. herbacea* … bearing in spring and again all through the summer most lovely clear delicate stars of blue that sometimes on cool or grassy banks make the whole expanse a shimmering galaxy.' The object of Reginald Farrer's admiration is the most variable and broadly dispersed member of the genus, native to much of central and eastern Europe and western Asia. Unlike its evergreen relatives, it dies back during winter to a perennial rootstock and sends forth its long trails each spring, spangled with inch-wide, blue-violet flowers for several weeks. The shoots root down at the tips to form plantlets, before retreating at winter's approach. In the wild *V. herbacea* grows in open, sunny situations on rocky slopes or at the edges of fields. It prefers an equivalent garden position, where it will happily colonise its allotted area without ever becoming invasive. Curiously enough, although it is so common in nature and so easy to maintain, this delightful periwinkle is rarely grown in gardens.

Widespread in the western Mediterranean region is *V. difformis*, which is similar in general habit to *V. major* but winter-flowering. Its blooms are grey-blue to deep blue with a white centre. In Italy, according to E. A. Bowles, it used to be grown massed as a bedding plant and in Canon Ellacombe's famous garden at Bitton in Gloucestershire 'under a spreading pine it is a charming sight all winter.' It is tender in most parts of Britain, but makes an excellent plant for pots and hanging baskets, blooming profusely throughout the winter. The selected forms 'Dubia', in deep blue, and the blue and white 'Bicolor' are particularly fine. *V. difformis* is seldom found today and deserves to be much more generally grown. Like all these periwinkles, it is readily propagated from natural layers or soft cuttings of the young shoots.

Viola   *Pansy, Violet*

Viola gracilis

'No race is more fertile of more exquisite beauty, but no race is also more fertile in dull and dowdy species,' wrote Reginald Farrer. The genus *Viola*, in which over a thousand species have been named, is now believed to contain about half that number distributed throughout the temperate world. A mere handful of these have had any horticultural significance, while two in particular, *V. tricolor* and *V. odorata*, have played a role out of all proportion to the rest. Both native to the British Isles and both adapted relatively recently for gardens, they have provided us with some of our best-loved flowering plants.

By the reign of Elizabeth I *V. tricolor* had acquired a string of endearing names, among them love-in-idleness, three-faces-in-a-hood, herb trinity, heart's-ease and pansy, from the French *pensée*, thought. It was admired, so Gerard said, for 'the beautie and bravery' of its colours, 'purple, yellow, and white or blew', and was grown unchanged for generations until the early nineteenth century when, coincidentally it would seem, its garden potential was first realised. In about 1812 Lady Mary Bennet had an assortment of pansies in a heart-shaped bed at Walton-on-Thames. These inspired the nurseryman James Lee, son of the founder of the leading Hammersmith firm, to develop some twenty cultivars in partnership with her gardener. A year or so later T. Thompson was cultivating wild pansies which had been gathered in the grounds at Iver, Buckinghamshire, by his master Lord Gambier. He 'found that they improved far beyond my most sanguine expectations' and 'in consequence thereof, I collected all the varieties that could be obtained.' The break came in about 1830 in the shape of a chance seedling noticed by Thompson which had a small dark patch in the centre. This, the hallmark of the modern pansy, was to launch it on its successful career. By the end of the decade at least 400 named kinds were in existence. Societies devoted to the pansy were set up and it quickly joined the ranks of the florists' flowers.

Growers of the show pansy, as it had become, aimed to transform the 'native deformity' of the heart's-ease into 'a bold, circular, velvety, rich flower', an ideal which is charmingly depicted in the *Florist* of 1848.

Our present-day pansies are more recognisable in another class, the Belgian or fancy pansies. These were bred from English stock on the Continent, untrammelled by florists' rules, and had larger, less formal blooms with a much expanded blotch in the middle. They returned to Britain around 1850 and like the show pansies were taken up as florists' flowers by miners in the Midlands and north of England. But in gardens the fancy pansies swiftly replaced the show pansies and in public parks, from the 1870s onwards, they became a standard feature of mass bedding, as their descendants are today.

Pansies are now grouped botanically as *V.* × *wittrockiana* and are generally grown as annuals or biennials from breeds selected by seedsmen. The old show pansies have almost entirely died out. So too have the majority of named forms of *V. tricolor*, which were a regular item in catalogues until the beginning of this century. A fortunate exception is 'E. A. Bowles' or 'Bowles' Black'. According to the nurseryman Amos Perry, of Enfield, Middlesex, it arose as a seedling of *V. tricolor nigra* in a friend's garden, whereupon Perry, as was his wont, dedicated it to his great gardening neighbour in 1901. Farrer considered it 'one of the quaintest things of all . . . a little bushy plant . . . with abundant small pansies of dense black-violet velvet throughout the season, thriving anywhere, and sowing itself freely'. Unlike most named forms, which can only be propagated by cuttings, it comes almost true from seed if isolated from others. This has no doubt helped to prolong its existence.

Since the late nineteenth century, the pansies have had to compete for attention with the violas and violettas. The violas are classified as *V.* × *williamsii* and date from the 1860s when the Scotsman James Grieve, famous for the apple which bears his name, started to experiment. They were mainly derived from crossing the show pansies with the mountain pansy *V. lutea*, another British species, and possibly with *V. cornuta* from the Pyrenees. Compact, free-flowering and perennial, they had obvious advantages over the floppy exhibition pansies and were quickly appreciated by gardeners. The violettas also claim *V. cornuta* as a parent and are like miniature violas, distinguished by the absence of markings or rays on the petals and by their strong vanilla scent. They were the creation of Dr Charles Stuart of Berwickshire in the 1880s, whose work was later continued by D. B. Crane.

Both have fared better over the years than the pansies and many of their old cultivars are available, especially of the violas. These include the unusual khaki-yellow 'Irish Molly'; the white 'Lady Tennyson'; 'King of the Blues' and 'Pickering Blue'; and probably the oldest, from the 1860s, the deep yellow 'Bullion'. The lovely 'Moseley Perfection', a uniform golden-yellow, had been feared lost but is once more on the market. 'Jackanapes' (Plate 77), which was called after her pet monkey by Gertrude Jekyll, is also enjoying a welcome revival with its chocolate-brown and yellow flowers. However, the light mauve 'Maggie Mott' has become scarce recently and should be earmarked before it is too late as a plant that needs to be kept in circulation.

The pansies and their ilk will continue to flower from March to November with regular deadheading. They prefer a cool, moist, but well-drained, fertile soil in a sunny position. Seed may be sown in September for plant-ing in early spring, or in June for planting in the autumn when they may need some protection through the winter. However, the plants will vary unless raised from cuttings. For these, non-flowered shoots are removed from the middle of the plant and rooted in a cold frame in late summer or early autumn to grow on before planting out the following spring.

The second dominant member of the genus, *V. odorata*, is a familiar inhabitant of the countryside and widespread throughout Europe, north Africa and Asia. The sweet violet was the emblem of ancient Athens and also of the supporters of Napoleon Bonaparte. It is one of the oldest flowers to be cultivated commercially and had many attributes apart from the decorative and odoriferous. The Greeks valued it for a purple dye and medicinally, as did the medieval herbalists; the Arabs used it to make sherbet, their national drink; its candied blooms have been a sweetmeat since the Middle Ages, and the leaves were often eaten; it yields a syrup which is a chemical indicator like litmus paper; and it is a source of perfume, although violet scent was actually extracted from the orris root, *Iris florentina*, until the nineteenth century.

The sweet violet like the heart's-ease was grown unaltered in English gardens for centuries. However, it showed greater variation, with single and double sorts in purple and white, which Gerard grew, as well as lilac and rose. It was only with the introduction of several species from Europe in the early nineteenth century that new forms were evolved. The Russian violets, from *V. suavis* (then known as *V. cyanea*), were in the vanguard, but their celebrity was fairly brief and all have since disappeared. The large single-flowered cultivars, on the other hand, were still popular in the 1930s. 'Czar', the first of these, almost true purple and fragrant, gained an Award of Merit in 1865. From it were descended many more over the next sixty years, characterised by bigger, rounded flowers on long, thick stems and in different shades, although occasionally without scent.

'Kaiser Wilhelm II', with heavily perfumed deep blue blooms up to 2 inches across, arrived from Germany in 1895 and won an AM in 1913. During the First World War its name was changed for patriotic reasons to 'King of the Belgians'. F. E. Dillistone then appropriated this name for his own selection of 'Kaiser Wilhelm II', claiming that it had better resistance to red spider mite and that the king himself had given permission. It was not the only instance of a copyright dispute among violet growers. This fine cultivar became an important commercial crop, especially in Devon, and was recommended to growers by the Ministry of Agriculture. But like countless violets of the

Victorian and Edwardian era it has departed from the scene. Only the stalwart 'Czar', 'Princess of Wales' and 'Coeur d'Alsace' are left to represent the single forms which were once so familiar to gardeners.

Scented double violets also progressed from the 1820s onwards. The major introductions to Britain took place in the 1860s with the advent of 'Queen of Violets', purple opening to white, and 'King of Violets', deep indigo blue. These were joined by 'Patrie', which was said to be almost perpetual flowering, 'Chamber's Victoria', 'Brandyana' and others. 'Brandyana' was widely grown at the period. Its flowers were described in one catalogue as 'intense dark purple, with a well-defined rosy pink stripe down each petal which makes it a gem and a cultivar not to be easily forgotten'. This, alas, has been its fate, along with most of the doubles.

Semi-double violets were prized for their long stout stems and very fragrant blooms, which were of violet blue with a distinctive inner rosette of smaller petals sometimes in a lighter colour. They originated in France in the 1900s and became a speciality of J. J. Kettle of Dorset. 'Countess of Shaftesbury', 'Mrs Lloyd George', also identified with 'Cyclops', and 'Princess Mary' occurred on his farm as seedlings of the single 'Princess of Wales'. They found favour with gardeners and in the trade and the last two were approved by the Ministry of Agriculture as commercial cut flowers until the 1960s. None is readily available now.

Given the peak of fashion which the violet in all its guises achieved, the losses are dramatic. It was a favourite of Queen Victoria and Queen Alexandra, whose royal approval must have enhanced its attraction for the masses. The *Gardeners' Chronicle* in 1897 reported that 'thousands of city clerks appear at the office every morning with a fresh bunch of violets in their buttonholes.' In 1910, 'this charming and sweet flower is more extensively grown each year' and in the 1930s, as Dillistone observed, there was 'scarcely a private garden of any pretension that does not cultivate violets'. Dillistone & Woodthorpe of Suffolk were one of the leading violet farms. In the mid-nineteenth century when they already stocked over twenty kinds, the industry was established around London and in the West Country. Violets were also imported in quantity from France up to 1914. While the growing of violets declined near the capital, partly because of their need for clean air, it prospered in the southwest. Kettle of Corfe Mullen listed more than seventy cultivars in the 1920s and Devon became the chief market centre in the 1930s. Even after the Second World War, Grace Zambra of Dawlish carried a remarkable range.

Hardy and easily grown in ordinary garden soil which has been well worked and enriched, violets bloom from September until the frosts and again in early spring. Frame culture is designed simply to prolong flowering through the winter and is otherwise unnecessary. They may be planted in spring or autumn. Propagation from seed is straightforward and can lead to interesting variation. To increase named forms, old plants should be divided after flowering and separated into pieces with two or three crowns for replanting. Alternatively, runners may be taken off and planted in April, or cuttings detached with a few rootlets on them and rooted in a cold frame in March.

Most lamentable perhaps is the virtual demise of the Parma violet. No nineteenth-century gardening book was complete without instructions on its culture, just as no lady of style would be seen without a bunch pinned to her corsage, particularly when in the hunting field. It is reputed to have been brought from the eastern Mediterranean by Genoese and Venetian merchants and from Italy it reached Britain by 1820. It is possibly derived from *V. alba* and differs from *V. odorata* in its compact habit, lacking the long runners, and narrow, glossy leaves, in its tenderness and in the hint of wallflower mingled with its violet perfume. In Britain Parma violets require the protection of a cold frame and will produce their large double flowers on tall stems from autumn to May. Propagation of named forms is similar to that described for sweet violets.

The first and only Parma violet until the middle of the last century was called the Neapolitan violet or, in French, 'la violette de Parme' or 'de Naples'. It had flowers of pale lavender on thin, wiry stems. By the 1860s when the term Parma violet was gradually coming into use, there were at least four cultivars. Among them was 'Marie-Louise', a rich violet-mauve with red splashes, which rapidly became one of the most popular. 'De Parme', probably the same as 'Duchesse de Parme', appeared in about 1873, having been imported from Florence. It was a more vigorous version of the original 'Neapolitan' and of a deeper shade. It was followed by the mauve 'Lady Hume Campbell', which had been discovered by its namesake near Milan, and 'Madame Millet' from France, the closest approach to red. A unique white Parma violet was purchased from the Italian Comte Brazza di Savorgnin by the Swanley nursery of Henry Cannell, who dubbed it 'Swanley White'. Other nurserymen contested their monopoly, however, and sold it as 'Comte Brazza'. Under this name it was awarded a First Class Certificate in 1883.

The rage for violets was not confined to Europe. A thriving industry in the USA was the source of many new cultivars – to Farrer's irritation: 'unfortunately in these later years, the enormous multitudes of American violets have taken (no less than American heiresses) to overflowing into our continent undescribed.' A striking rosy lilac with a penetrating scent, 'Mrs John J. Astor' won an AM in 1899 and was soon widely cultivated despite its delicate constitution. Much hardier and also easier to propagate than many Parma violets was 'Mrs Arthur', a deep blue with a white eye. It was put on the market in about 1902 and remained common until the late 1930s.

The two world wars hastened the end of the Parma violets. In the 1920s they were still offered by most nurseries and universally grown, although they were already something of a luxury. By the next decade many had been dropped from the lists and the steady output of new forms had slowed to a trickle. 'President Poincaré', with almost navy blue flowers, was one of the last. After the Second World War about a dozen kinds of Parma violet were still to be found. But some twenty years later only four were commercially obtainable – 'Duchesse de Parme', 'Marie-Louise', 'Mrs John J. Astor' and 'Swanley White' – and now it is doubtful whether any have survived, except perhaps 'Duchesse de Parme'. The old 'Neapolitan' lingered until a short time ago, but that too is feared to be extinct.

It is not surprising that a number of the species in this immense genus have been overlooked. Mrs Zambra collected several treasures, including *V. jooi*, which 'has delightful pinkish-lilac flowers on stiff stalks of three to four inches, seeds itself most freely and blooms at any time it feels disposed'. The taller *V. glabella*, with flowers that are 'really apricot', she thought 'the best of the so-called yellow violets'. Both do well in a rock garden like many *Viola* species, but are very seldom seen.

Most elusive of all is *V. gracilis*. The true species comes from Mount Olympus, near Bursa in Turkey, 'the plants of South Italy and Greece being imposters' in Farrer's words. 'No garden introduction of the last century has been more lovely and delightful than this violet,' he continued, 'in the habit and vigour of *V. cornuta*, much neater in the dense upstanding armies of its blossom, and with its rather nobler and profuse great violet-pansies of the most shimmering imperial purple velvet, with a tweak to the petals that gives each flower an inimitable butterfly grace.' It grows happily in any light soil, but is variable from seed and must be increased by cuttings. However, it is a great rarity in cultivation and has been superseded by coarser hybrids or 'mules ... under pompous names', as Farrer put it, which lack 'the freakish elfin loveliness' and 'its intensity of dark and velvety violence'.

Worsleya   *Blue amaryllis*

High in the Organ mountains of Brazil near Rio de Janeiro grows the famed blue amaryllis, which is generally considered to be one of the most difficult members of the family *Amaryllidaceae* to flower in cultivation. Placed on past occasions in *Amaryllis* and *Hippeastrum*, it has finally been accorded its own genus *Worsleya*, after Arthington Worsley, a mining engineer who travelled extensively in South America and became a specialist in bulbous plants on his retirement to Middlesex. It was introduced to Europe in about 1863, initially described as *Amaryllis procera*. In the *Botanical Magazine* it is depicted under yet another name, *Amaryllis rayneri*, from specimens flowered by a Dr Rayner of Uxbridge in 1870. The bulbs had been sent to him by W. D. Christie, a British diplomat in Brazil, and had been collected in 1862 on a mountain near Petropolis, where the plant was known locally as lily of the empress.

Each flower head consists of up to six trumpet-like blooms, similar in shape

Worsleya procera

to those of *Amaryllis belladonna* and with a wavy edge to the segments. The colour is deep blue-mauve or blue-violet, fading almost to white in the centre and often copiously flecked red-purple. *Worsleya procera* (Plate 78) is distinguished from the closely related genera *Amaryllis* and *Hippeastrum* not only by the colour of the flowers but by the long false stems, some 2 to 5 feet in length on mature plants. These are made up of the tightly folded bases of the leathery evergreen leaves, scimitar-shaped and pendent, which may themselves be up to 3 feet long. The black angled seeds also lack the wings of *Hippeastrum* and *Amaryllis* seeds and are thicker. Botanically, therefore, *Worsleya* seems sufficiently distinct to merit separate generic status, particularly since attempts to cross it with *Hippeastrum* species, many of which hybridise readily, have all failed.

In its natural habitat *W. procera* is found at an altitude of about 3,000 feet where it grows in exposed positions in full sun. The bulbs are anchored to the soft, porous, granite-like rock by fleshy, thong-like roots. These penetrate deeply into crevices filled with black leafmould, from which the fine feeding roots gain nourishment. In the *Gardeners' Chronicle* in 1929, Worsley gave a fascinating account of his journey to Brazil a few years previously to study what was then called *Hippeastrum procerum*.

Growing on ledges, often but a foot wide, on the face of the cliffs, and with little foot-hold but the rock, heavy storms often fling hundreds of great bulbs down the precipices. But they obtain some support from a species of rambling and twining *Philodendron* which intertwines itself among the bulbs and their roots and forms a kind of rope to hold them in their places.

With normal minimum temperatures at night of about 40 to 45°F during the dry winter months, it is subject to occasional ground frosts. In summer the temperature seldom exceeds 80°F and the air is saturated by the brief evening thunderstorms that constantly occur in the mountains.

In the wild the blue amaryllis normally flowers in January or February, but in cultivation it blooms in late July and August. Worsley flowered freshly imported bulbs in March, which then settled down to bloom in August, grown in 'nine inch drainpipes filled with rock, charcoal and chippings of stone covered with a little Oak-leaf and bits of live moss (not Sphagnum)'. Despite his detailed hints, others have been less successful than Worsley in persuading it to bloom. Even such a skilled cultivator of bulbs as Major Albert Pam, of Wormley Bury in Hertfordshire, had to wait fourteen years for any results. Newly imported bulbs have been recorded as flowering the year after they were received, no doubt because the rudiments of the flower had already been formed, but then remaining stubbornly unproductive. However, in Major Pam's case his recipe for a sharply drained compost (mixing fibrous loam with the soil shaken out with *Osmunda* fibre and adding plenty of charcoal) eventually proved acceptable. Growing in a warm pit in the glasshouse in full sun, with frequent overhead syringing and watering to keep the compost continually moist, it flowered regularly each August in subsequent years. *W. procera* achieved an Award of Merit in 1949 and the accolade of a First Class Certificate in 1954, exhibited on both occasions by Pam.

This remarkable plant is a great challenge to the grower and is still very uncommon in cultivation. But it is one of the most beautiful of all flowering bulbs and worth every effort to acquire.

Xanthoceras

The lovely but neglected *Xanthoceras sorbifolium* (Plate 80) belongs to the *Sapindaceae* and is one of the very few members of this predominantly tropical family which may be grown by gardeners in temperate zones. It is native to northern China and was introduced to Europe by J. P. Armand David, the first of the great Jesuit missionaries to explore this still dangerous region, who gave his name to the delightful handkerchief tree *Davidia involucrata* and also to Père David's deer. A seedling of *X. sorbifolium* which he sent back to the Paris Museum in 1866 was successfully established and reached flowering size some seven years later.

A deciduous shrub or occasionally small tree up to 20 feet, *X. sorbifolium* is of stiff upright growth. It produces erect 6- to 8-inch sprays of bloom at the ends of the previous year's shoots in May. The individual salver-shaped flowers are over 1 inch across, with white petals stained carmine at the base and

Xanthoceras sorbifolium

horn-like yellow appendages rising from the disk bearing the flower parts. These account for the generic name, from the Greek *xanthos*, yellow, and *ceras*, horn. Like many plants from habitats subject to extremes of temperature in winter and summer, it needs a position where the rather pithy wood can be well ripened and flower bud set. It is very effective loosely trained against a south or west wall whose reflected heat serves this purpose. The alternate pinnate leaves, with up to 17 toothed leaflets, unfold with the flowers in May and are prone to damage from late frosts. Although perfectly hardy, it is therefore best planted in a site away from frost pockets and requires no more than a good, well-drained loam to thrive. Large fruits similar to those of the horse chestnut are freely borne and seed is the easiest method of propagation. It can also be raised from cuttings.

It is difficult to understand why this charming and unusual shrub is so seldom seen in gardens. It is a welcome change from the ever popular rhododendrons and azaleas flowering at the same period and a foil for their brilliant colours, while in its own right it is a plant of great character which merits much more attention from nurserymen and gardeners.

Biographical Notes

William Jackson Bean (1863–1947) joined the Royal Botanic Gardens, Kew, as a student in 1883 and later became curator, remaining there for forty-six years. His *Trees and Shrubs Hardy in the British Isles* was first published in 1914 and ran to a seventh edition in 1950, which had been prepared by him before his death. The eighth edition in 1970, with further amendments in 1976, was a thorough revision carried out by Desmond Clarke under the general editorship of Sir George Taylor. 'Bean', as it is usually known, is the standard reference book on the subject, a mine of botanical and horticultural information enhanced by the author's personal experience and lucid style. He also wrote a history of Kew and a number of other works.

Edward Augustus Bowles (1865–1954) was one of the most distinguished amateur gardeners of recent times, as well as being a knowledgeable plantsman, a fine botanist and illustrator and a successful author on both a popular and serious level. A trilogy of books, *My Garden in Spring*, *My Garden in Summer*, and *My Garden in Autumn and Winter*, which appeared between 1914 and 1915, communicated his delight in gardening. His *Handbook of Crocus and Colchicum* of 1924 is still regarded as the classic account of the genera and was followed by the *Handbook of Narcissus* in 1934. Bowles enjoyed a long association with the Royal Horticultural Society and was a familiar and welcome figure at shows and meetings. His garden at Myddelton House in Enfield, north of London, reflected his wide interests, not only in bulbs but in plants of all kinds, with a particular emphasis on the new and the rare. It soon became famous for its choice plants and its unusual features, such as the 'lunatic asylum' containing oddities like the corkscrew hazel. The garden fell into neglect after his death but is now being restored through the efforts of the National Council for the Conservation of Plants and Gardens.

Reginald John Farrer (1880–1920) is commemorated in the names of several plants which he introduced or reintroduced to cultivation, notably the beautiful but elusive *Gentiana farreri* and (although the credit really belongs to William Purdom) *Viburnum farreri*, the popular winter-flowering shrub commonly known as *V. fragrans*. These and a number of lilies, primulas and other plants resulted from a trip to the province of Kansu in northern China with Purdom in 1914–15. It was followed in 1919 by a visit to Upper Burma with E. H. M. Cox, on which Farrer died from an illness. Compared to many of his contemporaries, however, Farrer's achievements as a plant collector were insignificant. He is chiefly remembered as an author, with the gift of portraying his adventures and his plants in rich and imaginative prose. Among his many books were *My Rock Garden*, 1907, *In a Yorkshire Garden*, 1909, *On the Eaves of the World*, 1917, *The Rainbow Bridge*, 1921, and the most enduring of all *The English Rock Garden*, published in 1919 and subsequently reprinted many times. All were written in an individual style that can only be described as Farrerian. He was a Yorkshireman of outspoken opinions and also of strong enthusiasms, particularly for alpine and rock garden plants which he did so much to popularise.

George Forrest (1873–1932) ranks with E. H. Wilson among the most outstanding plant collectors of this century. A Scotsman and a fine botanist, he made seven expeditions to western China between 1904 and 1932, working mainly in the province of Yunnan, and died there of heart failure. On his first journey he narrowly escaped a gang of murderous Tibetans. Forrest was financed by the Royal Horticultural Society, the Rhododendron Society and private individuals, especially J. C. Williams of Caerhays Castle, Cornwall. He rewarded them with the discovery of some 300 reputed new species of rhododendron, of which the best known is probably *R. griersonianum*. His immense haul also included numerous lilies, magnolias and over a hundred primulas, together with such familiar plants as *Gentiana sino-ornata*, *Pieris forrestii* and *Camellia saluenensis*, which first flowered at Caerhays and became a parent of *C. × williamsii*.

John Gerard (1545–1612) was the author of the immortal and oft-quoted *Herball, or generall Historie of Plantes*, first published in 1597 and revised by Thomas Johnson in 1633. It is one of the earliest botanical books to be written in English, not Latin, and charmingly describes some 200 plants with their 'vertues' for health or for food. It was far from original, being largely an adaptation and translation of the work of the Flemish physician Rembert Dodoens. Even the illustrations were mostly borrowed from another herbal. Gerard dedicated his magnum opus to Lord Burghley, minister to Queen Elizabeth I, in whose gardens he had been employed. In his own garden in Holborn he grew more than a thousand 'fine and rare' plants, which he listed in his *Catalogus* of 1596. For this reason, the date of introduction of many of the plants first mentioned there or in his herbal is given as 1596 or 1597.

Gertrude Jekyll (1843–1932) was undoubtedly the pre-eminent lady gardener of this century and a potent influence on all who have followed. A talented painter and craftswoman, she began by contributing articles to William Robinson's magazine the *Garden*, of which she was joint editor for a period, and later wrote for *Country Life* and the *Journal* of the Royal Horticultural Society. Most of her books appeared between 1899 and 1912, including *Wood and Garden*, *Home and Garden*, *Gardens for Small Country Houses* and *Colour Schemes for the Flower Garden*. Meanwhile she was laying out gardens in the 'natural' style, as espoused by Robinson. She drew her inspiration from the countryside and was a champion of cottage gardens and old-fashioned flowers. But her special contribution was the artistic flair for colour and effect which imbued her planting and the straightforward but perceptive way in which she expressed it in print. She lived at Munstead Wood near Godalming in Surrey, a house designed for her by the architect Edwin Lutyens, with whom she collaborated on several projects.

Linnaeus or Carl von Linné (1707–78) was a Swedish naturalist, brilliant teacher and indefatigable author of more than 180 published titles, who shaped the scientific world by establishing the binomial system. The two-word method of naming species, with a generic name and a specific epithet, was first adopted by him in the *Species Plantarum* of 1753 and is still in use today. He had already embarked on a mammoth classification of plants, animals and natural objects in his *Systema Naturae* of 1735 and, such was the authority of his work and the amount of information he assembled, that contemporaries were forced to recognise his new system. Linnaeus also instituted the 'sexual system' of grouping plants according to the number of stamens and pistils and was the target of some derision for his study of 'floral nuptials'. This was to be the basis of future classification, although it has been replaced by a less artificial system. He was a genius but a modest one. *Linnaea*, which was named for him at his request, he described as 'a plant of Lapland, lowly, insignificant, disregarded, flowering but for a brief space – from Linnaeus who resembles it.'

John Claudius Loudon (1783–1843) was one of the most influential figures in the development of Victorian gardening. A prolific writer, his major works include *An Encyclopaedia of Gardening*, 1822, *An Encyclopaedia of Plants*, 1829, *The Manual of Cottage Gardening and Husbandry*, 1830, *The Suburban Gardener and Villa Companion*, 1838, and the monumental eight-volume *Arboretum et Fruticetum Brittanicum* 1838, abridged as *An Encyclopaedia of Trees and Shrubs* in 1842. He founded the *Gardener's Magazine* in 1826, the first popular gardening publication, as well as the *Magazine of Natural History* in 1829 and the *Architectural Magazine* in 1833. He and his devoted wife Jane, herself the author of several books, lived at 3 Porchester Terrace in Bayswater, London, in a house designed by himself. The garden was said to contain some 2,000 species and was notable for its arboretum and its rose and peony collections. Loudon was a tireless campaigner for many causes, such as the proper planting of public parks and squares, the bettering of labourers' gardens and the improvement of cemeteries.

Philip Miller (1691–1771) was appointed gardener at the Apothecaries' Garden in Chelsea (the Chelsea Physic Garden as it is now known) in 1722 and stayed there until 1770. During his long reign stove houses and hot beds were installed, an innovation at the time, and cotton seeds were sent out from the garden to Georgia, to become the staple crop of the colony. By 1764, according to one observer, Miller had 'raised the reputation of the Chelsea Garden so much that it excels all the gardens of Europe for its amazing variety of plants'. He was the leading horticulturist of his day, renowned for his work at Chelsea and even more for his *Gardener's Dictionary*. First published in 1731, this ran to eight editions in his lifetime and was to remain the standard reference book for generations of gardeners. In the final edition Miller bowed to Linnaeus's binomial system and changed his naming and classification of plants accordingly. As a result, it stands as the first modern encyclopaedia of horticulture, a fascinating insight into the plants grown in the eighteenth century still relevant and useful in the twentieth.

John Parkinson (1567–1650) was perhaps the first writer of note to appreciate garden plants for their beauty rather than their supposed medicinal or other attributes. His delightful *Paradisi in sole Paradisus terrestris*, or 'A Garden of all sorts of pleasant flowers which our English ayre will permitt to be noursed up', was published in 1629 and describes with illustrations nearly a thousand plants then in cultivation in Britain. The title is a pun on his own name and may be translated as 'Park in sun's earthly paradise'. Although the book is essentially about pleasure gardening, its author is observant, accurate and much less credulous than Gerard and his predecessors. Ironically in view of his modern approach to flowers, Parkinson also wrote the last great English herbal, the *Theatricum Botanicum* of 1640, which covers almost 4,000 plants. He was an apothecary with a garden in Long Acre, near Covent Garden, and in an official capacity herbarist to James I and botanist to Charles I.

William Robinson (1838–1935) was born in Ireland and served apprentice-ship as a gardener before he launched into the career which was to bring him such fame and fortune. The year 1870 saw the publication of two pioneering books, *Alpine Flowers for the Garden* and *The Wild Garden*. In 1871 he founded *The Garden* magazine, which attracted some of the finest contributors of the time, and followed this with *Gardening* (later *Gardening Illustrated*) in 1879 and the short-lived *Flora and Sylva* in 1903. His most important work, *The English Flower Garden*, was published in 1883 and went through 15 editions in his lifetime (a reprint with revisions by Graham Stuart Thomas came out in 1985). In it he dictated his precepts for the 'natural' style of gardening, although he later found it difficult to put these into practice in his own grounds at Gravetye Manor in Sussex. In theory Robinson hated all signs of formality in a garden, such as terraces and topiary, and he was vehemently opposed to the system of bedding-out with half-hardy and tender plants. He was a persuasive advocate of the rock garden and in particular of the herbaceous border, both of which were enthusiastically adopted by gardeners in the early twentieth century. He was controversial, obsessive and intolerant, insisting for instance that every plant should have an English name and taking this to ludicrous lengths in *The English Flower Garden*. But here and in his prodigious outflow of writings he performed a most valuable service by making known the wealth of plants available to gardeners. He rallied to the defence of the old-fashioned flowers, like his friend Gertrude Jekyll, and also promoted the new introductions then flowing in from Asia. It is sad to see how many of the plants he mentioned have since disappeared.

Ernest Henry ('Chinese') Wilson (1876–1930) transformed the appearance of Western gardens and towers above his fellow plant collectors for the sheer magnitude of his achievement. It is estimated that he introduced some 1,200 new plants, at least half of which are still in cultivation and many of them extremely familiar to gardeners. To him we owe countless species of berberis, cotoneaster, honeysuckle, magnolia, maple, rhododendron, sorbus and viburnum. He also collected some of the first Japanese cherries, *Clematis armandii*, *Rosa moyesii* and, despite nearly losing a leg in an avalanche, *Lilium regale*. This was just one of innumerable dangers he survived, only to be killed in a car accident in the USA. Wilson was born in Gloucestershire and trained at Kew, and was recruited from there by the enterprising firm of James Veitch & Sons of Chelsea, the leading nursery of the day. He was sent out to China in 1899 with general instructions to obtain species likely to prove hardy in Great Britain and living representatives of plants known only from dried specimens, and with the specific task of securing the handkerchief tree *Davidia involucrata*. All three commissions he amply fulfilled on his first and second trips for Messrs Veitch and on his later visits between 1907 and 1911 on behalf of the Arnold Arboretum and other sponsors. From 1914 to 1918 he travelled in Japan and Korea and was then appointed assistant director of the Arnold Arboretum at Harvard University. He became keeper in 1927 on the death of Professor C. S. Sargent, its first director. He wrote several books about his experiences and his plant introductions.

National Collections

Of the 80 genera included in this book, the following 37 are now represented in national collections. These have been set up by mutual agreement between the National Council for the Conservation of Garden Plants and the organisations or individuals concerned. Further details, addresses and information about other national collections and about the scheme in general are available from the NCCPG, Wisley Garden, Woking, Surrey GU23 6QB.

Abutilon
spp and cvs: Somerset College of Agriculture and Horticulture, Cannington
bell-flowered spp
   and cvs: Mr N. Sayers, West Sussex

Acanthus   Mr L. Butler, Wilts

Acer
japonicum and   Forestry Commission, Westonbirt Arboretum, Tetbury,
   palmatum cvs: Gloucs
other than these: Hergest Croft Gardens, Kington, Hereford and Worcs

Aconitum   Cruickshank Botanic Garden, University of Aberdeen

Allium   Mrs P. K. Davies, Berks

Anemone
Japanese: Hadlow College of Agriculture and Horticulture, Kent
nemorosa cvs: National Trust, Cliveden, Maidenhead, Bucks

Aquilegia   Valleyhead Nursery, Dihewyd, Lampeter, Dyfed

Camellia   City of Plymouth Parks Department, Mount Edgcumbe
      Country Park, Devon

Campanula   Mr P. Lewis, Cambs

Clematis   Treasures of Tenbury Ltd, Tenbury Wells, Hereford and
      Worcs

Colchicum   National Trust, Felbrigg Hall, Cromer, Norfolk
      Royal Horticultural Society, Wisley Garden, Woking, Surrey

Convallaria   National Trust, Cliveden, Maidenhead, Berks

Crocus   Royal Horticultural Society, Wisley Garden, Woking, Surrey
      Mr R. Cobb, Notts

Cyclamen   Cyclamen Society

Daphne   Royal Horticultural Society, Wisley Garden, Woking, Surrey

Dianthus
border pinks: Ramparts Nurseries, Colchester, Essex
      Mr and Mrs M. Farquhar, Oxon

Dicentra   Mr R. Brook, North Yorks

Fritillaria
spp: University Botanic Garden, Cambridge
imperialis cvs: City of Cambridge Amenities and Recreation Department

Galanthus	Royal Horticultural Society, Wisley Garden, Woking, Surrey
Gentiana	Cruickshank Botanic Garden, University of Aberdeen
Geranium	
spp and primary hybrids:	University Botanic Garden, Cambridge
cvs:	City of Cambridge Amenities and Recreation Department
Helleborus	Suntrap Horticultural and Gardening Advice Centre (Oatridge Agricultural College), Edinburgh
	Hants NCCPG group
Hemerocallis	Epsom and Ewell Parks Department, Surrey
	Leeds City Council, The Hollies Park, West Yorks
Hesperis	University Botanic Garden, Leicester
Iris	Department of Botany, Reading University, Berks
unguicularis:	Mr R. D. Nutt, Bucks
Muscari	Miss J. Robinson, Suffolk
Paeonia	
spp and primary hybrids:	National Trust, Hidcote Manor Garden, Chipping Campden, Gloucs
pre-1900 cvs:	Gloucs NCCPG group
Papaver	
orientale cvs:	West of Scotland Agricultural College, Auchincruive, Ayr
Polygonatum	Hardy Plant Society northwest group
	Mr and Mrs K. Beckett, Norfolk
Potentilla	Barnsley Metropolitan Borough Council, Cannon Hall Country Park, South Yorks
Primula	
allionii cvs:	Mr J. Main, Wisley Garden, Woking, Surrey
alpine auriculas:	Wigan College Horticulture Centre, Greater Manchester
Asiatic spp:	Mr R. S. Masterton, Cluny House, Aberfeldy, Tayside
European spp:	Mr and Mrs C. Quest-Ritson, Wilts
vulgaris cvs:	Mrs P. Gossage, Somerset
	Mr J. W. Martin, Salop
Rosa	
pre-1900 shrub:	National Trust, Mottisfont Abbey, Romsey, Hants
Scabiosa	Mrs S. Parrett, North Yorks
caucasica:	National Trust, Hardwick Hall, Worksop, Notts
Stuartia	High Beeches Garden, Handcross, West Sussex
Tulipa	
spp and primary hybrids:	University Botanic Garden, Cambridge
Vinca	Mr J. Sharman, Cambs
Viola	
bedding violas and violettas:	University Botanic Garden, Leicester
odorata cvs:	Mrs Y. S. Matthews

A Note on Nurseries

There is an ever increasing number of small or specialist firms which stock unusual plants. Many of them exhibit at the Royal Horticultural Society shows in Vincent Square and advertise in the Society's journal. Further information may be obtained from the RHS, Wisley Garden, Woking, Surrey, and from the National Council for the Conservation of Plants and Gardens, at the same address.

Other good sources are private gardens open to visitors under the National Gardens Scheme, which often sell uncommon plants, and the plant sales outlets of National Trust and similar great gardens.

Lists of nurseries and suppliers are also available from:

National Trust, Spitalgate Lane, Cirencester, Gloucs GL7 2DE;
Hardy Plant Society, 10 St Barnabas Rd, Emmer Green, Caversham, Berks RG4 8RA;
Alpine Garden Society, Lye End Link, St Johns, Woking, Surrey GU21 1SW;
Scottish Rock Garden Club, 21 Merchiston Park, Edinburgh EH10 4PW.

Helpful publications include:

Horticultural Trades Association Reference Book and Buyers' Guide, annual;
The Good Gardener's Guide, Consumers' Association, 1985;
The Gardener's Directory, Lorraine Johnson, 1984;
Trehane's Plantfinder, 1986.

Bibliography

This is a selection of the books and journals consulted, which is also recommended for further reading. (Place of publication is London unless otherwise stated. Latest editions are given in brackets where possible.)

General
· Anderson, E. B., *Seven Gardens*, 1973.
Baytop, T., and Mathew, Brian, *The Bulbous Plants of Turkey*, 1984.
Bean, W. J., *Trees and Shrubs Hardy in the British Isles*, 1914, revised edn by Desmond Clarke, 4 vols, 1970–80.
Bloom, Alan, *Hardy Plants of Distinction*, 1965.
Bowles, E. A., *My Garden in Spring*, 1914 (1972).
– *My Garden in Summer*, 1914.
– *My Garden in Autumn and Winter*, 1915 (1972).
Coats, Alice M., *Flowers and their Histories*, 1956.
– *Garden Shrubs and their Histories*, 1963.
· – *The Quest for Plants*, 1969.
Davis, P. H., ed., *Flora of Turkey and the Eastern Aegean Islands*, 9 vols, Edinburgh, 1965–85.
Ellacombe, Canon H. N., *In a Gloucestershire Garden*, 1895 (1982).
– *In My Vicarage Garden and Elsewhere*, 1902.
Elliott, Clarence, *Rock Garden Plants*, 1935.
Elwes, H. J., and Henry, A., *The Trees of Great Britain and Ireland*, 7 vols, Edinburgh, 1906–13.
Farrer, Reginald, *My Rock Garden*, 1907.
– *In a Yorkshire Garden*, 1909.
– *The English Rock Garden*, 2 vols, 1919 (1938).
Fish, M., *Cottage Garden Flowers*, 1961.
Fisher, John, *The Origins of Garden Plants*, 1982.
Fletcher, H. R., *A Quest of Flowers: the Plant Explorations of F. Ludlow and G. Sherriff*, Edinburgh, 1973.
Gerard, John, *Herbal*, 1597, revised by Thomas Johnson, 1633.
Gilbert, Samuel, *The Florist's Vade Mecum*, 1683.
Glenny, George, *Handbook of Practical Gardening*, 1851.
Gorer, Richard, *The Development of Garden Flowers*, 1970.
Grey-Wilson, C., and Matthews, V., *Gardening on Walls*, 1983.
Hadfield, Miles, *A History of British Gardening*, 1960, revised edn 1979.
Hanbury, Revd William, *A Complete Body of Planting and Gardening*, 1770.
Hanmer, Sir Thomas, *The Garden Book*, 1659, published 1933.
· Hay, Thomas, *Plants for the Connoisseur*, 1938.
Hibberd, Shirley, *Familiar Garden Flowers*, 1898.
Hilliers' Manual of Trees and Shrubs, 1972 (1981).
Hogg, Thomas, *A Treatise on the Carnation, Pink, Auricula* etc., 1823.
Ingwersen, Will, *Classic Garden Plants*, 1975.
– *Manual of Alpine Plants*, 1978.

Jekyll, Gertrude, *Wood and Garden*, 1899 (1981).
  - *Home and Garden*, 1900 (1982).
  - *Colour Schemes for the Flower Garden*, 1908 (1982).
Johnson, A. T., *The Mill Garden*, 1950.
Kingdon Ward, Frank, *The Land of the Blue Poppy*, Cambridge, 1913.
Loudon, J. C., *An Encyclopaedia of Gardening*, 1822 (1871).
  - *An Encyclopaedia of Plants*, 1829.
  - *Arboretum et Fruticetum Brittanicum*, 8 vols, 1838.
Mackintosh, C., *The Flower Garden*, 1838.
Maddock, J., *The Florist's Directory*, 1792.
Mansfield, T. C., *Alpines in Colour and Cultivation*, 1942.
Miller, Philip, *Gardener's Dictionary*, 1731 (1807).
· Nelson, E. Charles, *An Irish Flower Garden*, Dublin, 1984.
Nicholson, G., ed., *Illustrated Dictionary of Gardening*, 4 vols, 1884 (1901).
Parkinson, John, *Paradisi in sole Paradisus terrestris*, 1629 (1976).
Rea, John, *Flora, Ceres and Pomona*, 1665.
Rehder, Alfred, *Manual of Cultivated Trees and Shrubs*, 2nd edn, New York, 1940.
· Rix, Martyn, and Phillips, Roger, *The Bulb Book*, 1981.
Robinson, William, *The Wild Garden*, 1870 (1929).
  - *Alpine Flowers for the Garden*, 1870.
  - *The English Flower Garden*, 1883, revised edn by Graham Stuart Thomas 1985.
Royal Horticultural Society, *Dictionary of Gardening*, 2nd edn, Oxford, 1956, with
  revised supplement by Patrick Synge, 1969.
  - *Some Good Garden Plants*, 1938 (1962).
Scott-James, Anne, *The Cottage Garden*, 1981.
Sitwell, Sacheverell, *Old-Fashioned Flowers*, 1939.
Stearn, W. T., *A Gardener's Dictionary of Plant Names*, 1972.
Stern, F. C., *A Chalk Garden*, 1960 (1974).
Step, E., and Watson, W., *Favourite Flowers of Garden and Greenhouse*, 1897.
Sweet, Robert, *The British Flower Garden*, 3 vols, 1823–9, 2nd series, 4 vols, 1831–8.
Synge, Patrick, *Plants with Personality*, 1939.
Taylor, Geoffrey, *The Victorian Flower Garden*, 1952.
Taylor, George M., *Old-Fashioned Flowers*, 1946.
Thomas, Graham Stuart, *Plants for Ground Cover*, 1970 (1978).
  Perennial Garden Plants, 1976 (1982).
Tutin, T. G., *et al*, eds, *Flora Europaea*, 5 vols, Cambridge, 1964–83.
Veitch, James, *Hortus Veitchii*, 1906.
· Walsh, Wendy, *An Irish Florilegium*, Dublin, 1983.
Walters, S. M. *et al*., eds, *European Garden Flora*, II, Cambridge, 1984; I, 1986.
Wilson, E. H. *A Naturalist in Western China*, 1913.

Journals, periodicals and occasional papers
Addisonia, New York Botanic Garden, 1916–55.
Alpine Garden Society *Bulletin*, 1930–.
Annals of Botany, 1887–1936, new series 1937–.
Baileya, New York, 1953–.
La Belgique Horticole, Liège, 1851–85.
The Botanical Magazine (Curtis's), 1787–1947, new series 1948–84, now continued as
  The Kew Magazine.
The Botanical Cabinet (Loddiges's), 1817–33.

The Botanical Register (ed. Sydenham Edwards, then John Lindley), 1815–47.
Edinburgh Royal Botanic Garden *Notes*, Edinburgh and Glasgow, 1900–.
Flore des Serres et des Jardins de l' Europe, Ghent, 1845–83.
Gentes Herbarum (ed. L. H. Bailey), New York, 1920.
The Garden (ed. William Robinson etc.), 1871–1927.
The Gardeners' Chronicle, 1841–.
Garden and Forest, New York, 1888–97.
Hardy Plant Society *Bulletin*, 1957–.
Icones Plantarum (Sir W. J. Hooker), 1836–53, continued as *Hooker's Icones Plantarum*, 1853–.
Kew Bulletin, 1887–.
Moorea, journal of the Irish Garden Plant Society, Dublin, 1981–.
National Council for the Conservation of Plants and Gardens *Newsletter*, 1982–.
New Flora and Sylva, 1928–40.
Paxton's Flower Garden (ed. John Lindley and Joseph Paxton), 1850–53, 2nd series 1882–4.
Paxton's Magazine of Botany, 1834–49.
La Revue Horticole, Paris, 1842–.
Royal Horticultural Society *Journal*, 1866–1975, now continued as *The Garden*.
Scottish Rock Garden Club *Journal*, Edinburgh, 1937–.

By genus
Sealy, J. R., *A Revision of the Genus Camellia*, 1958.
International Camellia Journal, 1962–.

Bailey, L. H., and Lawrence, G. H. M., *The Garden of Bellflowers*, New York, 1953.
Crook, H. C., *Campanulas: their Cultivation and Classification*, 1951.
 – *Campanulas and Bellflowers in Cultivation*, 1959.

(*Cardiocrinum* see *Lilium*)

· Lloyd, Christopher, *Clematis*, 1965 (1978).

(*Colchicum* see *Crocus*)

Bowles, E. A., *A Handbook of Crocus and Colchicum*, 1924, revised edn 1952.
Mathew, Brian, *The Crocus: a Revision of the Genus Crocus*, 1982.
Maw, George, *A Monograph of the Genus Crocus*, 1886.

Saunders, D. E., *Cyclamen: the Genus in the Wild and in Cultivation*, 1975.
Cyclamen Society *Journal*.

Brickell, C. D., and Mathew, Brian, *Daphne: the Genus in the Wild and in Cultivation*, 1975.

Allwood, M., *Carnations and All Dianthus*, 1935.
Bailey, L. H., *The Garden of Pinks*, New York, 1938.
Brotherston, R. P., *The Book of the Carnation*, 1904.
Moreton, C. Oscar, *Old Carnations and Pinks*, 1955.

⁃ Beck, Christabel, *Fritillaries: a Gardener's Introduction to the Genus Fritillaria*, 1953.

, Stern, F. C., *Snowdrops and Snowflakes*, 1956.

Bartlett, Mary, *Gentians*, 1975.
Berry, G. H., *Gentians in the Garden*, 1951.
Wilkie, David, *Gentians*, 1936 (1950).

Yeo, Peter, *Hardy Geraniums*, 1985.

Dallimore, W., and Jackson, A. B., *A Handbook of Coniferae and Ginkgoaceae*, revised edn 1966.

Li, Hui Lin, *The Origin and Cultivation of Shade and Ornamental Trees*, Pennsylvania, 1963.

Stout, A. B., *Daylilies*, New York, 1934.

· Dykes, W. R., *Irises*, 1912.
   – *The Genus Iris*, Cambridge, 1913.
   – *A Handbook of Garden Irises*, 1924.
· Mathew, Brian, *The Iris*, 1981.
Iris Yearbook.

Elwes, H. J., *A Monograph of the Genus Lilium*, 1877–80.
Grove, A. S., and Cotton, A. D., *A Supplement to Elwes' Monograph*, 1934–40.
Jekyll, Gertrude, *Lilies for English Gardens*, 1901 (1983).
· Synge, Patrick, *Lilies: A Revision of Elwes' Monograph and its Supplements*, 1980.
· Woodcock, H. B. D., and Stearn, W. T., *Lilies of the World*, 1950.
Lily Year Book, 1932–79.

Taylor, G., *An Account of the Genus Meconopsis*, 1934.

(*Metasequoia* see *Ginkgo*)

Harding, A., *The Book of the Peony*, 1917.
Stern, F. C., *A Study of the Genus Paeonia*, 1946.
Stearn, W. T., and Davis, P. H., *The Peonies of Greece*, 1984.
Wister, J. C., ed., *The Peonies*, 1962.

The Genus Pleione, in *Botanical Magazine*, 1983.

Genders, Roy, *Primrose*, 1959
   – *The Polyanthus*, 1963.
Green, R., *Asiatic Primulas*, 1976.
Hecker, W. R., *Auriculas and Primulas*, 1971.
Smith, G. F., Burrow, B., and Lowe, D. B., *Primulas of Europe and North America*, 1984.

Bunyard, E. A., *Old Garden Roses*, 1936.
Jckyll, Getrude, *Roses for English Gardens*, 1902 (1982).
Redouté, J. P., *Les Roses*, 3 vols, Paris, 1817–21.
Thomas, Graham Stuart, *The Old Shrub Roses*, 1955 (1961).
   – *Shrub Roses of Today*, 1962 (1974).
   – *Climbing Roses Old and New*, 1965 (1978).
Willmott, Ellen, *The Genus Rosa*, 2 vols, 1910–14.
Young, Norman, *The Complete Rosarian*, 1971.

Blunt, Wilfrid, *Tulipomania*, 1950.
Botschantzeva, Z. P., *Tulips*, Rotterdam, 1982.
Hall, A. Daniel, *The Book of the Tulip*, 1929.
   – *The Genus Tulipa*, 1940.
Jacob, J., *Tulips*, 1912.

Stearn, W. T., in *The Vinca Alkaloids*, edited by Taylor, W. I., and Farnsworth, N. R., 1973.

· Coombs, Roy, *Violets: the History and Cultivation of Scented Violets*, 1981.
Crane, H. H., *The Book of the Pansy, Viola and Violet*, 1908.
· Genders, Roy, *Pansies, Violas and Violets*, 1958.
Zambra, Grace, *Violets for Garden and Market*, 1938.

Index